Man in the Living Environment

Report of the Workshop on
Global Ecological Problems
1971

ROBERT F. INGER, Chairman of the Board, The Institute of Ecology
ARTHUR D. HASLER, President, International Association for Ecology
F. HERBERT BORMANN, President, Ecological Society of America
W. FRANK BLAIR, Director, U.S. International Biological Program

Co-Principal Investigators

Man in the Living Environment

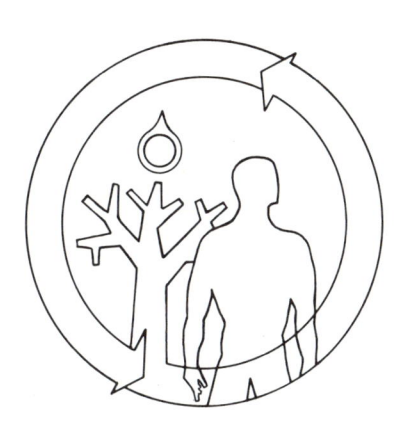

Published for
THE INSTITUTE OF ECOLOGY
by
THE UNIVERSITY OF WISCONSIN PRESS

Published 1972
The University of Wisconsin Press
Box 1379, Madison, Wisconsin 53701
The University of Wisconsin Press Ltd.
70 Great Russell Street, London

Copyright © 1972
The Regents of the University of Wisconsin System
All rights reserved

Printings 1972, 1973, 1974

Printed in the United States of America
ISBN 0-299-06050-0 cloth, 0-299-06054-3 paper
LC 77-187506

Foreword

The Institute of Ecology was incorporated in February, 1971. It was founded as, and remains, an international organization committed to the support of ecological research, the design and development of ecological research programs to meet human needs, the incorporation of ecological analyses in policy formation, and public education on ecological principles. Its Board of Trustees is elected by Founding Institutions, universities and other organizations that formally endorse the Institute, and an Assembly, individuals and organizations having strong interests in ecology.

The workshop on Global Ecological Problems is our first effort. We find its report worthy of our profession, and are pleased to have been able to sponsor such a study. We are grateful to the National Science Foundation, U.S., for their rapid and generous support. A grant was made to four co-principal investigators representing large groups o ecologists: Robert F. Inger, Chairman of the Board, The Institute of Ecology; Arthur D. Hasler, President, International Association for Ecology (INTECOL); F. Herbert Bormann, President, Ecological Society of America; W. Frank Blair, Director, U.S. International Biological Program. They were able to assemble the talent needed in the task groups of the Workshop.

For the Institute, and for the Co-Principal Investigators, I wish to thank those who participated in the Workshop.

Arthur D. Hasler, Trustee
The Institute of Ecology

Contents

1. INTRODUCTION 3

2. ECOLOGY OF THE HUMAN POPULATION - WORKSHOP SUMMARY 11

    Summarizes major findings in Chapters 3-6, and contains recommendations approved by the Workshop as a whole.

    A. Introduction 13
    B. Population and Resources 14
    C. Wise Management of Resources 19
    D. The Challenge to Produce More Food 24
        Intensively Managed Systems 25
        Moderately Managed Systems 27
        Lightly Managed Systems 31
    E. Possible New Forms of Intensive Management 33
        On the Land 33
        In the Water 34
    F. The Coastal Zone--An Endangered Resource 35
    G. Pollution, a Major Threat to Productivity 37

3. CYCLES OF ELEMENTS - TASK GROUP I REPORT 41
    A. Major Findings 42
    B. Introduction 45
    C. Human Activity 46
    D. Cycles of Phosphorus, Sulfur, and Nitrogen 48
    E. Phosphorus Cycle 48
    F. Sulfur Cycle 59
    G. Nitrogen Cycle 63
        Nitrogen Fixation 65
        Nitrates 66
        Nitrogen Dioxide 67

H.	Interrelations of Biogeochemical Cycles	69
	Organic Synthesis	69
	Alternative Sources of Oxygen	70
	Atmospheric Interactions	72
	Eutrophication of Water	73
	Eutrophication of Land	74
I.	Quantitative Estimates	75
	Sulfur	77
Appendix		84

4. ECOSYSTEMS FOR HUMAN BENEFIT - TASK GROUP III REPORT 91

A.	Major Findings	92
B.	Introduction	98
C.	Prospects and Problems in the Management of Ecological Systems	101
	Self-Maintaining Natural Systems	101
	Natural Ecosystems with High Nutrient Flow	104
	Strongly Driven Systems of Modern Agriculture	107
D.	Diversity and Stability	112
	Evidence for the Relation Between Diversity and Stability	112
E.	Diversity, Stability and Pest Control	117
	Problems with Chemical Pest Control	118
	Integrated Pest Control	123
	Biological Control	124
	Crop and Habitat Management	125
	Crop Breeding	126
	Pesticide Use with Field Monitoring of Pests	127
	Pest Control in Developing Nations	128
F.	Intensity of Demands on Ecosystems	131
	Diversity, Stability and Maintenance Costs	131
	Benefits from Natural Species Diversity	136

Figures

2.1	Effect of different levels of fertilizer use on yield-value index and increase in yield-value for each 10 kg/ha increase in fertilizer use	16
2.2	Rate of growth of world manufacturing and world trade with respect to population growth	16
2.3	Population growth over the past 300 years and the range of future projections	18
2.4	Relationships between the human population, resources, industry, agriculture, and the sea	21
2.5	A natural, balanced ecosystem	23
3.1	The phosphorus cycle	49
3.2	The sulfur cycle	60
3.3	The nitrogen cycle	63
3.4	Nitrate levels in surface waters of Illinois rivers	66
4.1	Inorganic nutrient cycling in a forest in Belgium	102
4.2	Food web (trophic structure) of the biological community in a Georgia salt marsh	106
4.3	Complex energy transfer pattern in part of a rain forest ecosystem	110
4.4	Energy transfer in a simple tribal grazing system in Uganda	111
4.5	Energy transfer under monsoon agriculture in India	111
4.6	Energy transfer in fuel-subsidized industrial agriculture such as that in the United States	111
4.7	Patterns of species diversity on vegetation and in the air across three different patches of vegetation	116
4.8	The rise in number of species of insects and mites resistant to one or more pesticides	120
4.9	Trends in gross yield, maintenance costs, and net yield with increasing intensity of use	133
4.10	Changes in production per animal and production per hectare with increasing grazing intensity	133

4.11	Interrelations of major deep-water species of Lake Michigan at various periods	135
5.1	Distribution of tropical lowland forest	175
5.2	Land use practices in the tropical forests of Latin America	178
5.3	Distribution of tropical savanna	184
5.4	Distribution of temperate grasslands	184
5.5	The effects of man's interference on the savanna ecosystem	188
5.6	Distribution of arid and semi-arid lands	196
5.7	Regions within which severe pollution may develop by the year 2000	200
6.1	World fish catch, 1938-1968	224
6.2	Overfishing of North Atlantic fish stocks	227
6.3	Trend in total world marine fish catch	238
6.4	Number of whales caught, by species	238
6.5	Two-layered system of circulation found in many coastal plain estuaries	246
6.6	Life history of an estuarine shrimp	246
6.7	Life history of fish using estuary as nursery	246
6.8	Comparative production rates among terrestrial and aquatic systems	250

Tables

1.1	Relationship of Workshop output to the proposed organization and structure of the Stockholm conference	6
3.1	Annual production and consumption of phosphates, sulfuric acid, and nitrogenous fertilizers	47
3.2	Atmospheric release in 1968 of oxides of sulfur and nitrogen due to human activities	47
3.3	Movement of phosphorus in the biosphere	52
3.4	Sources of phosphorus entering Lake Mendota	52
3.5	Concentration in ppm of P in natural material	54
3.6	Estimated use of phosphorus fertilizer to feed world populations of various sizes at the present average nutritional level combining data from the UN and the phosphorus-to-yield function of PSAC	54
3.7	Examples showing trends of sulfur in the environment	71
3.8	Preliminary estimates of rates of production of organic nitrogen (protein) in the biosphere	71
3.9	Budget for the nitrogen cycle	76
3.10	Sulfur reservoirs	78
3.11	Annual rates of sulfur exchange	81
3.12	Trace gases in the atmosphere, PPB	82
4.1	Annual transfer of N, P, K, and Ca between components of the Douglas-fir ecosystem	103
4.2	Comparative net gains or losses of dissolved solids in runoff following clear cutting in the Hubbard Brook Experimental Forest	103
4.3	Summary of salt marsh energetics	105
4.4	Fish meal production from annual Peruvian anchoveta catch	105
4.5	Identified inputs of agriculture	108
4.6	Cross-resistance of citrus red mites to various organophosphorous pesticides	122
4.7	Changes in malaria morbidity in countries before and after mosquito control	141

4.8	Primary uses of lead in the U.S.A., 1968	145
4.9	U.S. production of mercury	148
5.1	Land settlement trends in tropical lowlands in some Latin American countries	175
5.2	Relative ozone sensitivity of two-week-old seedlings of selected desert plants and Black Valentine bean	200
5.3	Comparison of planned level financing for the National Forest System and the actual expenditures for the period fiscal years 1963-1970	205
5.4	Actual and allowable cut on Montana portion of the Bitterroot National Forest, fiscal years 1966-1969	206
6.1	Steps used by Ryther to calculate the potential fish production of the three major zones of the ocean	229
6.2	PCB residues in fish, birds, and mammals	255
6.3	Concentrations of mercury in sea water, sediment, and aquatic organisms	258

Index of Recommendations

1) INTERNATIONAL COOPERATION----------------19, 29, 39, 42, 44, 92, 93(2), 95, 109, 131(1), 147, 154, 166, 167(2), 220, 221(1), 221(3), 222, 236, 244, 251, 260.

2) PUBLIC EDUCATION-------------------------19, 94, 131(2).

3) DATA COLLECTION AND ANALYSIS--------------19, 44, 83, 97, 147, 167.

4) TECHNICAL AND FINANCIAL ASSISTANCE-------39, 94, 97, 109, 131(2), 154, 221(3), 244.

5) RESEARCH, DEVELOPMENT AND DESIGN---------93(1), 93(2), 131(1), 166, 167(1).

6) ESTABLISHING STANDARDS-------------------39, 83, 96(1), 147, 154, 222, 260.

7) REGULATION AND CONTROL-------------------29, 39, 95, 96(1), 96(2), 97, 144, 147, 154, 167(2), 222, 251, 260.

8) ESTABLISHING INTERNATIONAL AGENCIES------19, 29, 42, 59, 97, 131(1), 154, 221(2), 221(4), 236, 240.

9) PRESERVATION OF SPECIES------------------167(2), 221(4), 240, 241, 251.

Numbers indicate pages on which recommendations can be found.

Participants

John Kadlec, Workshop Coordinator
The University of Michigan
School of Natural Resources
Ann Arbor, Michigan 48104

Linda Weimer, Workshop Editor
Assistant Science Editor
University of Wisconsin
Madison, Wisconsin 53706

Paul Fuchs, Workshop Illustrator
News and Publications
University of Wisconsin
Madison, Wisconsin 53706

Ronald Atlas
Department of Biochemistry and Microbiology
Rutgers University
New Brunswick, New Jersey 08903

W. Frank Blair
Department of Zoology
University of Texas
Austin, Texas 78712

Wallace Bowman
Environmental Policy Division
Congressional Reference Service
Library of Congress
Washington, D.C.

Reid Bryson
Environmental Studies Institute
University of Wisconsin
Madison, Wisconsin

George Bunn
Professor of Law
University of Wisconsin
Madison, Wisconsin

Myron Coler
New York University
New York City, New York

Charles Cooper
The National Science Foundation
Washington, D.C.

William Cooper
Department of Zoology
Michigan State University
East Lansing, Michigan 48823

Grant Cottam
Department of Botany
University of Wisconsin
Madison, Wisconsin

Rezneat M. Darnell
Department of Oceanography
Texas A & M University
College Station, Texas 77843

Edward Deevey, Jr.
Florida State Museum
University of Florida
Gainesville, Florida

C. C. Delwiche
Department of Soils and Plant Nutrition
University of California
Davis, California

Josephine Doherty
The National Science Foundation
Washington, D.C.

Jacqueline Easby
Department of English
McMaster University
Hamilton, Ontario

Robert L. Edmonds
Botany Department
University of Michigan
Ann Arbor, Michigan 48104

Deborah Fairbanks
Department of Biology
San Diego State College
San Diego, California 92115

Harold E. Goeller
P. O. Box X
Oak Ridge National Laboratory
Oak Ridge, Tennessee 37880

Arturo Gómez-Pompa
Instituto de Biologia, UNAM
Ciudad Universitoria
Apartado Postal 70-233
Mexico 20, D.F.

Douglas Gordon
Idaho Water Resources Research Center
University of Idaho
Moscow, Idaho 83843

Larry D. Harris
Natural Resource Ecology Laboratory
Colorado State University
Fort Collins, Colorado 80521

Arthur D. Hasler
Laboratory of Limnology
University of Wisconsin
Madison, Wisconsin 53706

William Hazen
Department of Biology
San Diego State College
San Diego, California 92115

Joseph J. Hickey
Department of Wildlife Ecology
University of Wisconsin
Madison, Wisconsin 53706

Dian Hitchcock
Norton Lane
Farmington, Connecticut 06032

S. Blair Hutchison
U.S. Forest Service
P. O. Box 6123
Washington, D.C. 20044

Conrad Istock
Department of Biology
University of Rochester
River Campus Station
Rochester, New York 14627

Dale Jenkins
Smithsonian Institution
Washington, D.C.

Harold Jorgenson
Bureau of Land Management
U.S. Department of the Interior
Washington, D.C.

Calvin Kaya
Laboratory of Limnology
University of Wisconsin
Madison, Wisconsin 53706

Jean Lang
Science Writing Division
University Industry Research Program
University of Wisconsin
Madison, Wisconsin 53706

Royce LaNier
The International Youth Conference on the Human Environment
McMaster University
Hamilton, Ontario

Joseph H. Leach
Ontario Department of Lands and Forests
Lake Erie Fisheries Research Station
R. R. #1
Wheatley, Ontario

Monte Lloyd
Department of Biology
The University of Chicago
1103 East 57th Street
Chicago, Illinois 60637

John Magnuson
Laboratory of Limnology
University of Wisconsin
Madison, Wisconsin 53706

Kenneth H. Mann
Fisheries Research Board of Canada
Marine Ecology Laboratory
Bedford Institute
Dartmouth, Nova Scotia

William H. Matthews
Massachusetts Institute of Technology
Cambridge, Massachusetts
Consultant to the Secretary General
U.N. Conference on the Environment

Robert M. May
School of Physics
University of Sydney
Sydney, Australia

Gordon Mott
Northeast Forest Experiment Station
151 Sanford Street
Hamden, Connecticut 06514

William W. Murdoch
Department of Biological Sciences
University of California
Santa Barbara, California 93106

Braulio R. Orejas-Miranda
Department of Scientific Affairs
Organization of American States
Constitution Ave. & 17th St.
Washington, D.C. 20006

David Pramer
Director of Biological Sciences
Rutgers University
9 Huntington Street
New Brunswick, New Jersey 08903

Robert A. Ragotzkie
Director, Marine Studies Center
University of Wisconsin
1225 W. Dayton Street
Madison, Wisconsin 53706

Felix J. Rimberg
Peat, Marwick, Mitchell, & Co.
1025 Connecticut Avenue
Washington, D.C. 20036

Carl Runge
Professor of Law
University of Wisconsin
Madison, Wisconsin 53706

John Skujins
Professor of Bacteriology and Public Health
Utah State University
Logan, Utah 84321

Frederick Smith
Graduate School of Design
Harvard University
Cambridge, Massachusetts 02138

Stephen Stephenson
Department of Botany
Michigan State University
East Lansing, Michigan 48823

Boyd R. Strain
Department of Botany
Duke University
Durham, North Carolina 27706

Minze Stuiver
Department of Geology
University of Washington
Seattle, Washington 98105

John Teal
Woods Hole Oceanographic Institute
916 Woods Hole Drive
Woods Hole, Massachusetts 02543

Fred H. Tschirley
U.S. Department of Agriculture
Room 331E
Washington, D.C.

Robert I. Van Hook
Ecological Sciences Division
Oak Ridge National Laboratory
Oak Ridge, Tennessee

Carol G. Wells
Southeast Forest Experiment Station
P. O. Box 12254
Research Triangle Park, North Carolina 27709

Mark Westoby
Ecology Center
Utah State University
Logan, Utah 84321

Thomas Yuill
Department of Wildlife Ecology
University of Wisconsin
Madison, Wisconsin 53706

Man in the Living Environment

Chapter

1

Introduction

This report is the result of a Workshop on Global Ecological Problems. It presents the collective analysis of important problems of environmental quality and management by a group of ecologists. The Workshop grew from a desire to transmit the ecologist's view of such problems to the 1972 U.N. Conference on the Human Environment in particular and to concerned citizens in general. It was patterned after the Study of Critical Environmental Problems (SCEP), sponsored by the Massachusetts Institute of Technology and published in the report "Man's Impact on the Global Environment." The ecological section of that report was the starting point for this workshop.

With respect to the U.N. Conference, the output of the Workshop falls generally within the purview of Committee 2 (main subjects II and V of the proposed Conference Agenda). Because of the comprehensive nature of the ecological approach, however, it was necessary to pursue points which are to be considered by Committees 1 and 3. Table 1.1 is provided to assist the reader in locating material relative to the proposed organization and structure of the Stockholm Conference (Committee Report A/CONF. 48/ PC/9). In addition, some of the topics considered in our report provide input into other subjects proposed for 3rd level action. These cases are also indicated in Table 1.1.

Planning for the Workshop began with a meeting of a small group of ecologists on May 10, 1971. Attending were Edward Deevey (Dalhousie University), Frederick Smith (Harvard), Stanley Cain (University of Michigan), Paul Zinke (University of California, Berkeley), Craig Nelson (Indiana University), Frank Golley (University of Georgia), Steve Preston (University of Michigan), Charles Cooper (National Science Foundation), and John Kadlec (University of Michigan, Workshop Coordinator). The group discussed an extensive list of suggested problems to be considered by the Workshop. In

Table 1.1. Relationship of Workshop output to the proposed organization and structure of the Stockholm Conference.

Section of report	Committee 1 I	Committee 1 IV	Committee 2 II	Committee 2 V	Committee 3 III	Committee 3 VI	Other 3rd level Subjects
2A			x				
2B	x	x	x	x		x	
2C			x	x			Soils
2D			x	x		x	Conservation, genetic pools
2E			x	x	x		Soils
2F			x	x			Conservation
2G			x	x	x	x	
3B			x				
3C			x		x		
3D			x				Soils
3E			x	x		x	Soils
3F			x		x		Soils
3G			x		x	x	Soils
3H			x				Marine pollution, soils
3I			x			x	Monitoring
4B			x		x		
4C		x	x	x		x	
4D			x				
4E		x	x	x		x	
4F			x	x			
4G			x	x	x	x	
5B			x	x		x	
5C			x	x		x	
5D	x	x	x	x	x	x	Soils, conservation, monitoring
5E			x	x			
5F		x	x				
6B			x				Marine pollution
6C			x	x			
6D	x	x	x	x	x	x	
6E			x	x	x		Marine pollution, monitoring & pollution release
6F			x			x	Conservation, gene pools
6G	x	x	x			x	
6H			x		x		Marine pollution, monitoring, pollution release

Conference Agenda Main Subjects:
I. The Planning and Management of Human Settlements for Environmental Quality
II. The Environmental Aspects of Natural Resources Management
III. Identification and Control of Pollutants and Nuisances of Broad International Significance
IV. Educational, Informational, Social and Cultural Aspects of Environmental Issues
V. Development and Environment
VI. The International Organizational Implications of Action Proposals

assessing potential topics, they looked for those that conformed with
the proposed agenda for the U.N. Conference, and yet were essentially
ecological in character. The planning group finally organized the
Workshop around four major topics, each to be considered by a Task
Group. They were:

  Task Group I. Biogeochemical cycles of elements essential to protein production.

  Task Group II. Ecological constraints on man's use of land, particularly as a result of vegetation-soil interactions.

  Task Group III. Terrestrial food webs, diversity, and stability.

  Task Group IV. Man's impact on aquatic systems, particularly the coastal zone.

The topics were broadly defined purposely to give Workshop participants the opportunity to redefine and refine them as needed.

A number of obviously important ecological problems were not considered in depth by the Workshop. The planning group and later the Task Groups chose those problems, among the many possibilities, that could be studied adequately within the time constraints of the schedule.

The subject of pollution, for instance, is treated not as a separate topic, but only as one of the factors influencing the living environment of man. This was intentional. Many environmental scientists are applying themselves effectively to the questions of the origins, amounts and toxicities to man of the numerous pollutants in the environment.

Our expertise qualifies us to speak particularly about the interactions among living organisms and about the properties of whole ecosystems. These are large and complex problems, to which insufficient attention has hitherto been given.

Between May 10 and June 13, the Task Groups were formed and began communicating to refine topics and accumulate background materials. On June 14 about 50 scientists assembled on the University of Wisconsin campus in Madison for two weeks of intensive work. In general, the Task Group subject areas remained as originally suggested, but there were some substantial shifts of emphasis as deliberations continued. These are reflected in the Task Group Reports.

The content of each of the four Task Group reports was completed during the Workshop. A week of intensive editing, with some rewriting, followed. During that week Chapter 2, Ecology of the Human Population, was constructed. It was based primarily on the Task Group results and total Workshop discussions that had taken place during the second week.

Because one of our goals was an input to the 1972 U.N. Conference on the Human Environment, the editorial process was severely abridged. This meant each Workshop participant was not consulted in detail about editorial changes. These were the responsibility of the Task Group Chairmen and Workshop Coordinator. Every effort was made to protect original meaning, and insofar as possible, all substantial editorial changes were cleared with the appropriate Task Group member.

A few recommendations were agreed to by the entire Workshop. These appear in Chapter 2. Other recommendations and conclusions appear in the Task Group Reports. These were examined in rough draft form by all the participants. They are, however, basically Task Group statements, and it should not be assumed that all participants concur completely with them.

In addition to the support of the National Science Foundation, a number of institutions contributed greatly to our workshop. We are indebted to:

A.D. Little, Inc.
Agricultural Research Service, U.S. Department of Agriculture
Bureau of Land Management, U.S. Department of Interior
Field Museum of Natural History, Chicago

Forest Service, U.S. Department of Agriculture
Harvard University
Idaho Water Resources Research Center
Library of Congress
Massachusetts Institute of Technology
Oak Ridge National Laboratory
Ontario Department of Lands and Forests
Organization of American States
Peat, Marwick, Mitchell, and Co.
Secretariat of the U.N. Conference on the Human Environment
Smithsonian Institution
Texaco, Inc.
University of Michigan
University of Wisconsin
Utah State University

Without their support and the efforts of all the participants listed on pages xvii-xxiii, this study would not have been possible.

We are particularly indebted to Dr. Robert McCabe, Chairman of the Department of Wildlife Ecology at the University of Wisconsin, who arranged working space for the group. The Departments of Forestry and Entomology and the University-Industry Research Program were particularly generous in giving space to the Workshop. We are grateful also to Dr. Arthur Hasler and the Laboratory of Limnology who assisted in many ways to make our stay in Madison pleasant and productive.

We deeply appreciate the efforts and enthusiasm of Mr. Felix Rimberg of Peat, Marwick, Mitchell, and Co., who helped to arrange the Workshop and later facilitated its operation.

Chapter 2

Ecology of the Human Population

2.A. INTRODUCTION

Ecology has become a catchword of the seventies representing the movement to clean up our environment. In the process, the meaning of the word ecology has become broadened and confused to a point where the study of ecology is often considered synonymous with environmental science. But there is a distinction. Ecology is concerned not only with the environment, but also with the organisms in that environment and their relationships to each other and to their surroundings.

One such organism is man. Many of the techniques which ecologists have developed for the study of plant and animal populations are applicable to the human population as well. It is true that human society is more complex than any animal society and that social and cultural aspects of human behavior make the study of the human population far more complex than that of animal populations. Nevertheless, man has to live in a viable relationship with the other organisms in his environment or perish. What follows is an analysis of that relationship.

Civilization ideally protects the individual from many of the vagaries of nature, offering security and the opportunity for self-development. Civilization commonly finds its expression in the city, a complex of people, buildings, industries and communications, coupled with an energy source usually derived from fossil fuel. The city, however, cannot exist in isolation. People must be fed, and the city is part of a much larger system which uses the sun's energy, the minerals of earth and water, and an intricate web of living organisms to produce food. The interaction of that system with nature continues unabated, though civilization's shield can lure people into forgetting the importance of our planet's life-support system.

2.B. POPULATION AND RESOURCES

Technological advances have made possible a tremendous increase in our ability to combat disease, to control our immediate environment and to produce food and other natural materials. Such gains may be used either to increase the welfare of existing individuals or to provide for the subsistence of an added number of people. Insofar as population growth has lagged behind technological growth, at least in some areas of the world, the well-being of individuals has improved. However, in the world as a whole, population growth has consumed the majority of gains from technological growth. The relationship has been expressed by the simple equation (1):

$$\text{well-being} = \frac{\text{resources}}{\text{population}}$$

Well-being refers here to such things as living space, food supply, health and education, and not directly to the more intangible aspects of well-being like mental health or cultural achievements.

The relationship expressed in the equation above is approximately true at medium levels of population density. For a given level of resources, depending upon the size of the country and the technology available, the well-being of an individual decreases as the size of population sharing those resources increases. There are exceptions at very low levels of population. In North America 200 years ago, there was probably some advantage in having more people available to bring the land under cultivation and to exploit the mineral resources. At the other end of the scale, however, there is a point at which individual well-being begins to decrease faster than the population is increasing. This is because in very dense populations, the resource needs of each individual tend to increase with population density. Communication, transportation and job specialization all become so much more complex that it becomes difficult to satisfy the basic needs of the individual. As a result, the whole range of these relationships can be defined more accurately as:

$$\text{well-being} = \frac{\text{resources}}{(\text{population})^n}$$

where n is less than 1 in very low population densities, equal to 1 at moderate population densities and greater than 1 at high population densities.

Examples of the effect of increasing complexity can be found in the SCEP report (2):

(a) While food industries grow 6% per year, global food production grows only 3% per year. The other 3% growth goes to offset the increasing complexity of getting produced food to the people.

(b) Mining grows 5% per year while industries based on mining grow 9% per year. Four percent of their growth is swallowed up by the increasing complexity of products.

There is an ecological concept of environmental resistance which says that for an animal population exploiting a finite resource, the larger that population grows the more difficult it is for each individual to grow and reproduce. This is akin to the economic law of diminishing returns; the more intensively an enterprise exploits a market, the more difficult it is for that enterprise to maintain its rate of returns. In different ways, both principles say that a process becomes more difficult and less rewarding when it is intensified beyond some optimum level.

In the business of food production, the same principle operates. Figure 2.1, taken from FAO data, shows different levels of farm technology (indicated by fertilizer use) in 41 developed and developing countries (3). The yield increases less and less as more and more fertilizers are used. The principle is reemphasized in Figure 2.2, which shows that world manufacturing and trade are growing two to three times faster than the population. In part this reflects rising standards of living, at least in some nations, and in part it reflects

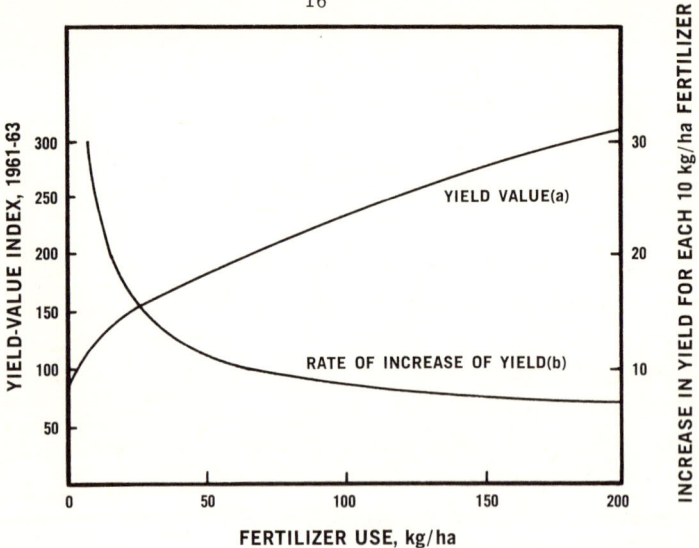

Figure 2.1. (a) The effect of different levels of fertilizer use on the yield-value index and (b) the increase in yield value for each 10 kg/ha increase in fertilizer use. Note that the use of more fertilizer is always accompanied by the use of better seed and more pesticides.

Source: Panel on the World Food Supply, 1967.

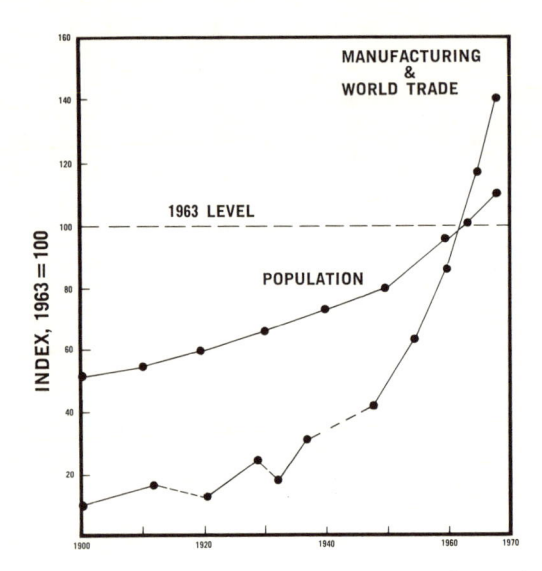

Figure 2.2. Rate of growth of world manufacturing and world trade with respect to population growth.

Source: United Nations Statistical Yearbook, 1969. © United Nations 1969. Reproduced by permission.

the increasing complexity of supporting larger populations.

Analysis of world data shows that at the present level of technological expertise, to provide twice the present amount of food and support twice the present level of population, we would need 6.5 times as much fertilizer, 6 times as much pesticide and 2.8 times more power than we have now (3).

Although conditions vary greatly from country to country, we know that the resources of the globe are limited. The six elements of key importance for the maintenance of life are carbon, hydrogen, oxygen, nitrogen, sulfur and phosphorus. Of these, it will be shown in Chapter 3 that phosphorus is the most nearly limiting. Its known potential supplies could be exhausted before the end of the 21st century. Beyond limits of mineral resources, agricultural production is limited in many areas by lack of water. In others, excessive rainfall can wash away soil, leaving infertile ground. We are therefore confronted with a situation in which the human population is growing rapidly (Figure 2.3) in the face of limited world resources. The number added in each decade of the present century is shown below:

	People added (millions)
1900-1909	120
1910-1919	132
1920-1929	208
1930-1939	225
1940-1949	222
1950-1959	488
1960-1969	604
1970-1979 (projected)	848

In a finite world it is the numbers of individuals added, and not the percentage increase, that best describes the added burden to

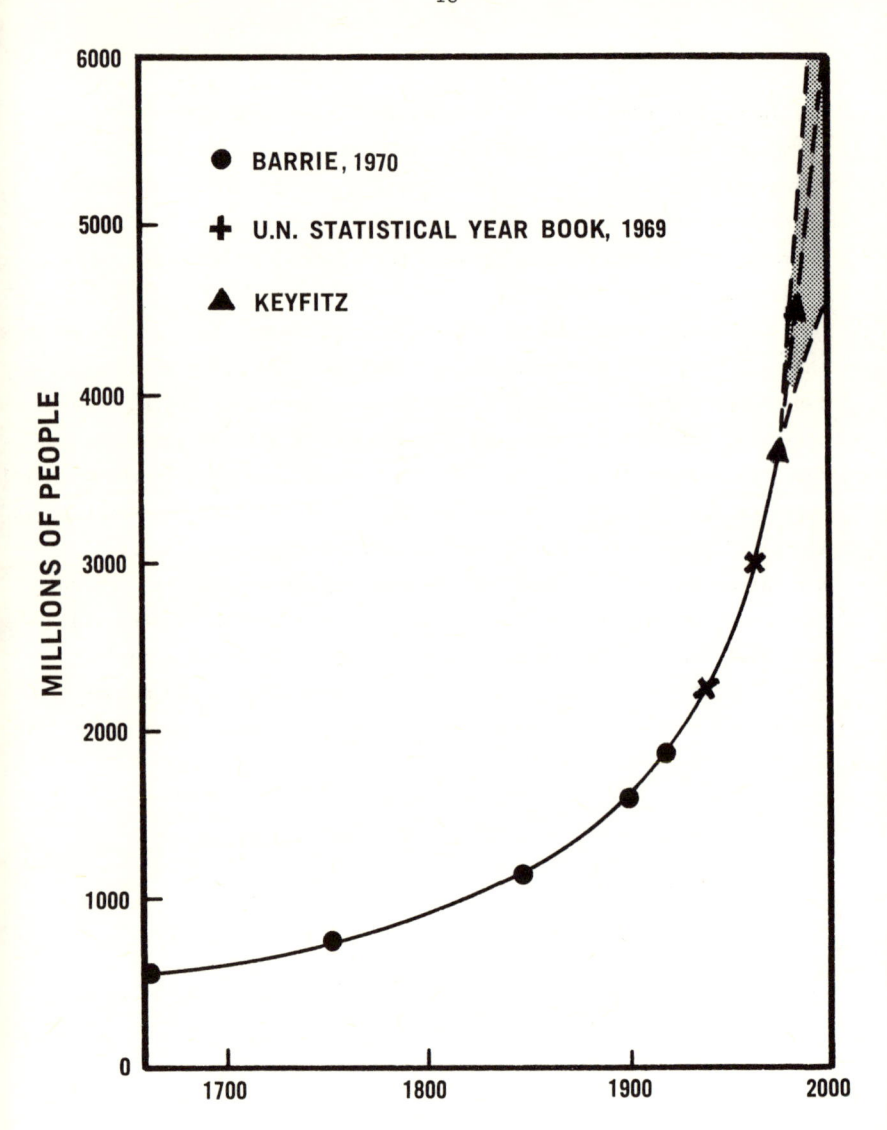

Figure 2.3. Population growth over the past 300 years and the range of future projections.

the system. It is misleading to point to a 2% annual growth rate that is constant, or slowly decreasing, when the addition of individuals is greater than ever before. A projected population increase of 848 million people in the 1970's, compared with 604 in the 60's and 488 in the 50's, describes a rapidly worsening situation.

It is clear that we are in a period of population crisis, the outcome of which cannot be forseen. It is also clear that gains in personal well-being, which technology has brought to most of the world's population in some degree, are in the process of being nullified by population growth. In short, mankind is on a collision course with nature.

RECOMMENDATIONS

We recommend that every effort be devoted to ensuring that the world population stop growing at the earliest possible date.

We recommend that an international agency be established to conduct a study of the effect of changes in population size on changes in the quality of life. The work of this agency will be to: (1) analyze in depth the relations between population, resources and individual welfare, as they have developed historically and continue to develop today among the nations; (2) accumulate information on the effectiveness with which various programs and practices tend to bring population size into balance with resources; and (3) inform and advise the nations and their peoples of the most effective ways to improve human welfare through population planning.

In the absence of a world population policy supported by a consensus of nations and based on sound knowledge, it is impossible to formulate effective policies for the utilization of the world's resources.

2.C. WISE MANAGEMENT OF RESOURCES

The current population explosion is no excuse for being profligate with the earth's resources. In fact, it is the best possible reason for making the most economical use of them. The general relationships between mineral resources, the human population, industry, agriculture and the sea are shown in Figure 2.4. The high levels of agricultural output which sustain our urban populations are made possible by the output of fertilizers, pesticides, machinery and the fuel to operate it which come from our industrial system.

One end result of supplying food and water to a city is a voluminous output of sewage which is traditionally passed into the nearest river estuary, often without prior treatment. This material passes eventually to the sea. The scale of this operation is far greater than anything previously known on the face of the earth. It is a gigantic one-way flow of elements, essential to life, from the earth and the air into the sea. This human phenomenon is in stark contrast with natural communities of plants and animals which have been living in balance with their surroundings for thousands of years (see Figure 2.5). There, substances essential for life are taken from the air and from the soil and are used with the sun's energy by plants to manufacture organic materials which, in turn, provide food for herbivores and carnivores in a food chain. At each stage of the process materials are returned to the soil, where they decay and liberate nutrients for the plants to reuse. Ecologists call this a balanced ecosystem. Some nutrient material may be washed out of the soil by rain, but it is replaced by natural weathering of the rocks. The only input of energy is from the sun. This kind of system is viable for thousands of years, and the key to its success is the recycling of elements within the system.

Long ago when man was a hunter, he operated within such a system without upsetting it. But, at the dawn of civilization, when he began to settle in large groups, he began altering the system to meet his needs. Domestication of animals and selection of crop plants began the progressively intensive management of ecosystems which culminated in modern industrialized agriculture whose levels of production were undreamed of by our ancestors. To maintain this system, however, requires

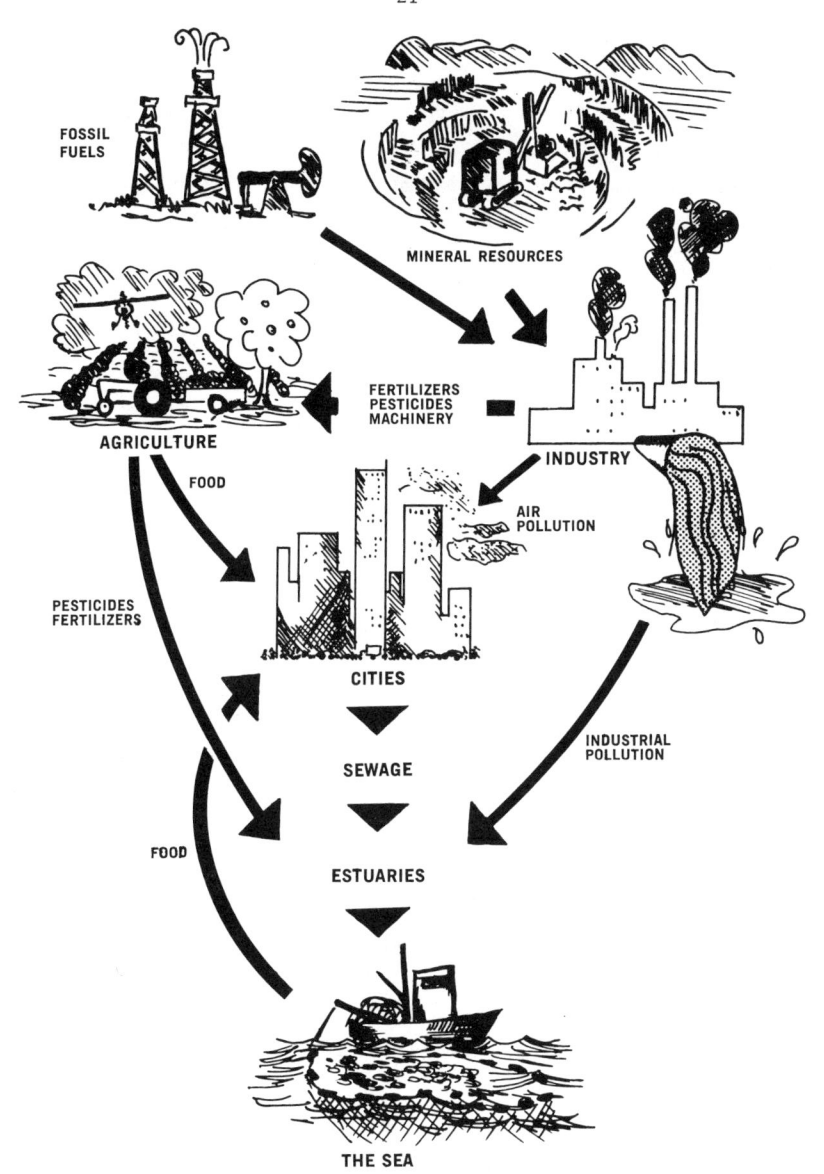

Figure 2.4. Relationships between the human population, resources, industry, agriculture and the sea.

an enormous flow of fertilizers to replace the plant nutrients taken up by the crops or otherwise lost from the soil. It requires a heavy application of pesticides to eliminate unwanted weeds and plant-eating insects and a tremendous input of fossil fuel energy for the mechanized operations. There is little recycling within this system. Man adds phosphorus to the land at a rate of over seven million metric tons per year, and all of it is soon lost, diluted beyond recovery in soils and sediments (Chapter 3).

The discharge of sewage into lakes, rivers and the sea is another waste of substances in limited supply. In addition, it causes health hazards, creates a lack of oxygen in the water and leads, generally, to the water's aesthetic deterioration. It is essential for several reasons, then, that society devise methods for returning these nutrients to the terrestrial cycle of biological production.

Most of the processes which lead to recycling occur in the soil. A wealth of microscopic organisms work to decompose the organic matter in fallen leaves, animal droppings and dead organisms and to release plant nutrients. So, one of the most important aspects of wise use of land resources is optimum management of the soil. The problems in this area vary greatly according to the climate, latitude and geology.

For example, studies of natural north temperate forests have shown that of the total nutrients cycled only about 10% comes from outside the system (Chapter 4). And yet, when a forested hillside is denuded of trees, loss of soil and nutrients is vastly accelerated by rain rushing down the hillside. In one study, nitrate loss of cleared ground was 30 to 50 times greater than that of uncleared ground (Chapter 4). In Japan intensive removal of forests during and after World War II caused repeated flood disasters and great loss of fertility.

A special problem in tropical rain forests is that when a forest area is cleared, the layer of plant litter on the forest floor decomposes rapidly under high temperature and moisture and releases

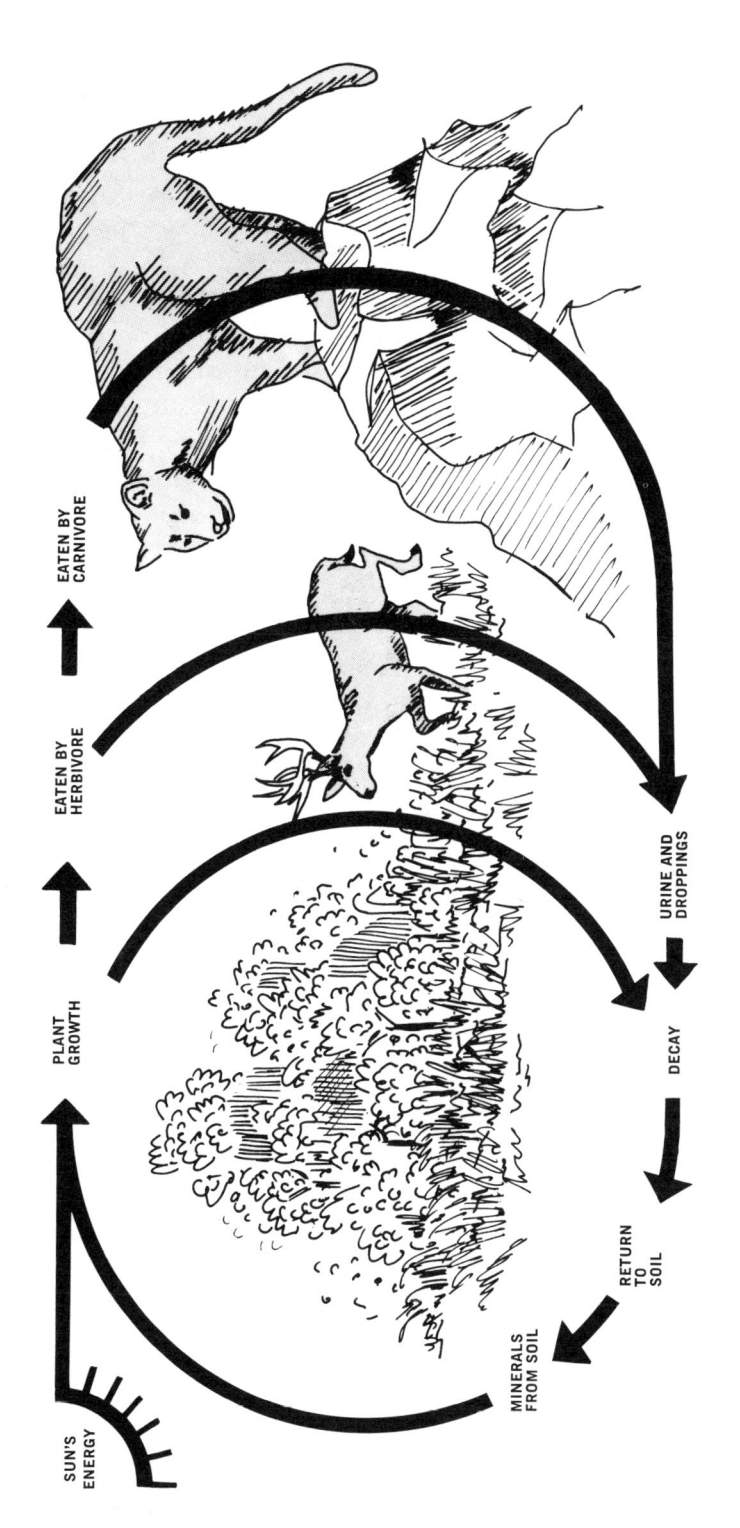

Figure 2.5. A natural, balanced ecosystem.

nutrients which are immediately washed out of the soil and lost from the system.

Tropical areas with low rainfall are savannas, expansive grasslands with widely spaced trees. In man's attempt to graze large herds of livestock there, he has often opened up new waterholes to increase the carrying capacity of the land. Overgrazing follows and, because the grasses cannot grow properly and soil texture is impaired by livestock trampling, the soil becomes incapable of holding moisture during the dry season (see Chapter 5). Overgrazing also causes soil problems in really arid areas. There, the accumulation of pebbles cemented by lime often leads to the formation of a delicate surface crust known as desert pavement. Within the constraints of the climate, the soil has a limited fertility; but when the crust is broken by overgrazing, the soil becomes very susceptible to wind and water erosion.

There is a tendency for those in search of food for the expanding population to go into these various ecological areas and attempt to cultivate the soil without a clear understanding of the subtle vulnerabilities of the system. Chapter 5 makes a strong case for developing a rational policy of land management on a global scale, with particular attention to the careful preservation of the soil's ability to recycle essential nutrients.

2.D. THE CHALLENGE TO PRODUCE MORE FOOD

In surveying the extent to which man has altered the face of the globe to suit his needs, it is estimated that 11% of the land surface is intensely managed, 30% moderately managed and 59% subject to little management. The challenges, posed by the widespread occurrence of malnutrition and by the expectation that more than 800 million people will be added to the world's population in the next decade, have stimulated us to look hard at proposed strategies for producing more food.

Intensively Managed Systems

There is fairly general agreement that the best hope for increasing the world's food supply is to continue intensifying modern industrial agriculture and perhaps to develop a comparable expertise in aquaculture. However, examining modern agriculture from an ecological point of view reveals several practices which are cause for concern: the profligate waste of essential plant nutrients, which cannot continue much longer; the need to control the system by the use of selective poisons which are threatening the productivity of large areas of the globe; and the reliance of the whole agro-industrial complex on lightly managed parts of the biosphere to absorb its wastes.

The main features of the agricultural system have been referred to in Figure 2.4. Its enormous productivity depends in part on the careful selection of animal and plant breeds which are able to grow rapidly if well fed. Equally important is the liberal use of fertilizers, especially compounds of nitrogen and phosphorus. Nitrogen is obtained primarily by industrial fixation from the air; phosphorus is produced primarily from the mining of phosphatic rock (Chapter 3). Between 1954 and 1968 the world consumption of nitrogenous fertilizer increased by a factor of four and phosphate fertilizer by a factor of two to three.

After being taken into plants, eaten, digested and excreted, most of these substances travel with sewage down the rivers and estuaries to the sea. As they travel, they stimulate great increases in the growth of aquatic plants, many of which cannot be used by animals in the aquatic food chains leading to fish. The result is an accumulation of rotting plant material which is aesthetically unpleasant and leads to loss in the amenity of lakes, rivers and estuaries.

Since nitrogen can be replaced from the atmosphere, its loss from the land may not be a serious problem. But, at present rates of population growth and phosphorus consumption, known phosphorus reserves will be used up in 90 years, by which time there will be 20,000 million people on this planet. Without commercial phosphate fertilizers, however, the planet will be able to support only 2,000 million people (Chapter 3).

Conclusion

With respect to phosphorus cycling in agriculture, we must use the world's supply of the raw material wisely, develop economic methods to recover phosphorus released to the environment in sewage effluents and foster research into even more intensively managed systems of agriculture where the cycling of nutrients can be completely controlled.

* * *

The second feature of current agricultural systems which concerns us is the maintenance of stability. In lightly managed systems ecologists recognize that when a particular organism increases its numbers rapidly (i.e., an insect species which becomes a pest), there is a tendency for the outbreak to be controlled by that species' natural enemies. This kind of checks and balances system is constantly being demonstrated in natural, balanced ecosystems which contain a large variety of species. It appears that this stability is a function of diversity. In agricultural systems, however, species diversity is deliberately reduced in the interests of efficiency. "Weed" plants are kept to a minimum, often by using chemical herbicides. Pests are controlled by insecticides and fungicides. Further, the use of these substances increases steeply with more intensive use of the land. As a result of the reduction in species diversity, when a species begins to reach pest proportions, its natural enemies are not present to check it; and the only alternative is to use still more chemicals to control it.

There is evidence that chemical control is getting out of hand. A rapidly increasing number of insects are developing resistance to a broad spectrum of insecticides (Chapter 4). Perhaps even more important, pesticides have been harming biological systems far removed from the point of pesticide application. For instance, DDT is now widespread in the oceans and can be found as far away as Antarctica.

Conclusion

We strongly urge that a great deal of effort be put into seeking alternatives to purely chemical methods of pest control. Possibilities which should be explored are changes in crop management practices (e.g., crop rotation), the controlled introduction of predators (biological control) and the deliberate planning of agricultural practices to give the greatest possible amount of species diversity over a broad area.

Moderately Managed Systems

A useful distinction may be made between those ecological systems which are stable because they are coupled to a stable source of nutrient materials and those systems which recycle their materials and can provide a stable food supply only if they are carefully managed. Agriculture falls into the first category. If there are constant, liberal supplies of fertilizer and chemical control agents, the output of food from this system is reasonably assured, subject only to local variations in climatic conditions.

An example of this type of system in nature is the anchoveta fishery off the Peruvian coast. The current patterns of the ocean cause water rich in nutrients to well up along a 300 km length of the Peruvian coast. This water stimulates intensive phytoplankton production which, in turn, supports an enormous population of anchoveta. At the present time over 11 million tons of fish are removed from this system annually by man (Chapter 4). So long as the current patterns in the South Pacific remain stable, which seems likely, the production of anchoveta will continue at a high level. There is no threat to the system from pollution since it is well-isolated from local sources of pollution as the waters well up from a great depth and spread away from the center of production. The only threat to its continuation would be over-exploitation of the grossest kind.

Anchoveta are small fish which are almost entirely converted to fish meal and used to feed poultry, pigs and cattle. Most of those fish which are eaten directly by man, however, are caught on the continental shelves and are part of much more complex assemblages of species which require careful management to provide a steady supply of food. The potential of the oceans to supply protein is very great indeed. In Chapter 3, approximate comparisons are made between the productivity of the land and that of the oceans. Land plants are relatively rich in carbon and poor in nitrogen, mainly because of their high cellulose content. Aquatic plants, on the other hand, are rich in protein. In fact, the ocean appears to be a more important source of protein than the land. Ocean food chains could be larger producers of meat than terrestrial systems if herbivorous fish were harvested.

A recent calculation (7) has shown that almost all the fish production important to man occurs in the coastal zone rather than in the open sea. At present, about one-fifth of the world's protein comes from the oceans. The fish catch has been rising steadily in recent decades (Chapter 6), and there are projections which suggest that man could double, treble or quadruple present landings. However, it is doubtful whether this is a wise course of action. All over the world examples may be found of fish stocks which have been fished almost to extinction. A recent tragedy was the failure of nations fishing the Antarctic whales to reach an effective agreement in time to prevent the collapse of the blue and humpback whale stocks. To take three or four times more protein from the sea would require the removal of small fish, young fish and plankton. Man would then be competing with the large fish, birds, whales and seals for their food supply, and it is almost certain that this competition would mean the elimination of many of their stocks. Further, because a diverse assemblage of species is probably necessary for stability in natural or moderately managed systems, it is extremely likely that marine systems would become unstable and suffer from frequent and unpredictable outbreaks of pest species.

The story of the whale stocks illustrates a problem which Garret Hardin has called "The Tragedy of the Commons" (8). Resources which are held in common, like the oceanic fisheries, are almost never managed wisely by a loosely organized group in which each component is seeking to maximize its own benefit. Rather, a strong central authority is needed to work out and implement wise management policies. The world resources of phosphorus are in similar need of careful management, but that problem is somewhat different. Although there is a worldwide need for phosphorous, the deposits are owned by the countries in which they are located.

RECOMMENDATION

As the supplies of finite resources continue to be exploited, the need for international or worldwide regulation is increasing. It is imperative that means be established, either through institutional structures or international agreement, by which this can be done.

* * *

With respect to terrestrial areas, Chapter 5 documents the fact that a great deal of the earth's surface is unsuitable for intensive management along the lines that have evolved in many industrialized countries. Yet, the pressure to produce food is enormous. We have emphasized the dangers of converting areas of diverse ecological type to agriculture with too little regard for the consequences, but what are the alternatives? There is no simple statement that we, as ecologists can make; rather, we can draw attention to a whole range of techniques that might be employed to produce more food while avoiding environmental deterioration.

For example, in Colombia, Ecuador, Peru, Bolivia and Costa Rica, it is estimated that about one million people have moved from the higher ground down into the wetter and less populated tropical rain forest regions; and population pressures are creating a need for several million more to follow them. In these areas a system of shifting agriculture known as "slash-burn" has been evolved by trial and error. Near the end of the dry season, trees and shrubs are cut down and burned, liberating large quantities of plant nutrients in the ash. Crops like corn, beans and cassava are planted in the newly enriched soil and are grown for three or four subsequent years. During this period, the accumulated mat of roots and humus in the forest is broken down at a rate of about six tons per hectare per month. After about four years, when the organic matter left behind by the forest has decomposed and the soil rapidly deteriorates, the farmer moves on to slash and burn another area. Regeneration of forest trees occurs fairly rapidly, and the process of rebuilding the organic content of the soil begins again.

Clearly, the way of life associated with this shifting agriculture is very different from that associated with the permanent settlement of an area. Nevertheless, it is probably the best system that could have been devised under these ecological conditions. The search for ways of marrying the ecological advantages of such techniques to the economic requirements of large settled populations should be given a high priority.

The natural, tropical forest is one of the most productive systems on earth. Unfortunately, forest trees produce enormous quantities of woody material, like cellulose, which are completely indigestible to man and most animals. But recent research has shown that microorganisms (such as yeasts) can be used to convert cellulose to proteins and sugars, which could then be used to feed livestock, and possibly man, if these processes were developed on a large scale.

In settled tropical areas in which intensive agriculture is being developed, there is a tendency to take weapons of chemical pest and weed control from the arsenal developed in the north temperate latitudes. Certain difficulties arise from this practice. Chemical sprays are rapidly diluted and washed away in areas of high rainfall. The high rate of reproduction of insect pests in hot climates makes the development of more toxic and persistent pesticides tempting, even though the ecological consequences of liberating them in the biosphere could be disastrous.

We propose that a great deal of research and resources be put into developing alternatives to the "agro-industrial complex" of developed nations. We should strive to: preserve species diversity in the landscape by mixing small areas of different crops or one crop in different stages of growth; control insect pests biologically; and defeat pest species with crop rotation programs. An integrated program of such techniques is likely to serve the needs of developing countries far better than the techniques of intensive agriculture used in the temperate climates.

Lightly Managed Systems

The urgent need to produce more food leads many people to feel that we should undertake extensive exploitation of large areas of the globe which are now relatively undisturbed. With the explosive growth of the human population, this pressure will mount. As ecologists, we foresee the possibility of such large scale environmental degradation that the quality of human life on this planet will decline irreversibly. Unless substantial areas of the earth's surface are preserved from exploitation and pollution, we foresee the disappearance of large numbers of species and a loss of the opportunities they might offer future generations.

In the past, man has benefited greatly from the earth's vast array of species. He has been able to select wild plants and animals and develop them into useful and productive domesticated varieties. Many of our valuable drugs, antibiotics and industrial products are derived from natural, wild species. Further, the abundance of wildlife in nature is a source of profound aesthetic satisfaction to many people. To reduce this abundance of species in man's environment is to invite instability, to reduce man's freedom to choose new species for exploitation, and to impoverish the quality of his life.

Man's record in past times is not encouraging, and population pressure then was much less than it is now. There are well-documented examples of human pressure leading to the total disappearance of large animals like the Arizona elk, the great auk, the labrador duck, the passenger pigeon, the Carolina parakeet, the Eskimo curlew, and the Heath hen. When Europeans first moved into North America there were 5,000 million passenger pigeons and 50 million bison. The former are gone, and only 6,000 of the latter remain.

In the past 50 years, the Indian tiger population has been decimated; the Great Indian rhinoceros in India and Nepal has been reduced to about 700 specimens; and the Asiatic cheetah is extinct in India, and only a few hundred of them remain in other parts of Asia (9). The International Union for the Conservation of Nature (10) lists about 200 species of mammals that are endangered in the contemporary world. Blue whales are the largest animals ever to have lived on earth; yet in the past 40 years, man has reduced their estimated population size from over 30,000 to perhaps 300. It is doubtful whether the species can now survive.

In addition, there are six major world fish stocks which have declined markedly in the past 25 years and shown no sign of recovery. These are listed on the following page with the date when their decline began:

East Asian sardine	1945
California sardine	1946
Northwest Pacific salmon	1950
Atlanto-Scandinavian herring	1961
Barents Sea cod	1962
Antarctic fin whales	1962

For every country of the world, a list of rare and endangered species could be produced. Some have been deliberately hunted to extinction, but the major reason for their decline has been the alteration of the ecosystems to which the species are adapted (9).

Conclusion

During this period of unprecedented population growth, we owe it to future generations to preserve, in as natural a state as possible, large areas of each kind of ecological system as reservoirs of species for the future use and enjoyment of mankind.

2.E. POSSIBLE NEW FORMS OF INTENSIVE MANAGEMENT

On the Land

The prospect of a world shortage of phosphorus before the human population halts its present explosive growth suggests that careful attention should be given to the possibility of developing even more intensive kinds of agriculture than those currently practiced. Now, nutrients are added to the soil in large quantities, making unprecedented rates of plant production possible. However, when too much fertilizer is applied (over 100 kg/ha), the yield obtained represents only a 10 to 20% return of nutrients; and this yield becomes even lower as rates of use increase. The remaining fertilizer either becomes immobilized in the soil or washes out of the system

One possible way of conserving nutrients would be to greatly increase the use of closed agricultural systems. In a closed system all excess water, including the nutrients in solution, is collected and returned to the system. Thus, it does not escape to groundwater or run off into surface streams.

In irrigated areas, the nutrient content of the solution can be readjusted by adding either water or the required elements. This fertilizer solution can then be used to irrigate another closed field. In areas with an excess of precipitation, the solution can be concentrated to recover the nutrients.

In principle, at least, this method should make a much greater use of valuable nutrients possible. The capital costs involved would, of course, be high; but the ecological advantages would be great. The grave problems involved in feeding an exploding human population may require expensive solutions.

<u>In the Water</u>

Though the potential for protein production is greater in the water than on land, the evidence of over-fishing and the disappearance of valuable species suggests that it would be unwise to encourage very heavy increases in the current exploitation of fish stocks. It has been estimated that three times the present investment in ships and gear will be needed to increase the present harvest from the sea by 50%. This is because the additional stocks fished will be more distant and dispersed.

For a 150% increase there would have to be five or six times the present equipment, if such an increase were feasible at all. From an ecological point of view, it would be much better strategy instead to invest that money in aquaculture--"farming the sea."

During the last decade about three million tons of fish have been produced yearly in intensively managed ponds. In essence, this process involves keeping fish or shellfish under controlled conditions so that they can be produced in desired quantities and qualities. The technique is valuable for providing protein in areas in which there is a dietary deficiency. It is also a valuable method of using

sewage which would otherwise run off into the ocean. An important
aspect of controlling the cultures is to protect them from pests and
enemies. There are obvious ways this can be done, like keeping the
fish in enclosures; but quite often more subtle techniques are used,
like hanging shellfish on ropes, clear of the bottom, so that their
predators cannot reach them. Recently fish have been trained to
congregate in areas for food in response to an underwater sound.
This technique allows the fish to graze freely over a wide area but
makes it possible to collect them in one place for supplementary
feeding, disease control, selective breeding or harvesting.

There are many examples where sewage and other fertilizers are
being used to enhance fish production. Naturally, care must be
taken to avoid transmitting disease-causing organisms, but, in general, this presents little difficulty. Mussel cultures in sewage-enriched seawater produced 300 tons of meat per hectare per year off
the coast of Spain. Schemes now being developed use sewage effluents
to grow algae, which are, in turn, being fed to oysters. Worms
then feed on the droppings of oysters and fish feed on the worms.
Such a system, if kept in balance, could reuse most of the sewage
wastes of a large city.

Other possibilities include speeding up the growth of fish and
shellfish by keeping them in the heated effluents of power stations
and pumping nutrient-rich water from the ocean depths to oyster ponds
in warm climates.

2.F. THE COASTAL ZONE--AN ENDANGERED RESOURCE

The coastal zone of the oceans, excluding the areas of upwelling, produce the greatest amount of the fish food which is consumed directly by man. Furthermore, an important resource potential
for the future is large scale aquaculture, which will necessarily
occur in inland waters and in the coastal zone.

Unfortunately, the production potential of this zone is under
serious pressure from human population in many parts of the world.

The effects may be considered under two headings—pollution and other man-made changes produced by physical operations such as dredging. The coast, continental shelf, estuaries and river basins make up the coastal zone, which owes its high fish productivity to a number of factors: the special features of estuaries, where rivers meet the sea; the high biological productivity of vegetation along the edge of the sea, particularly in salt marshes and seaweed zones; and the runoff of organic matter and nutrients from the land.

Estuaries (see Chapter 6) have special properties stemming from their structures. The combination of an inflow of fresh water on the landward side and rhythmical tidal movements of salt water on the seaward side, often supplemented by wind-generated currents, produces a mixing of surface waters and deeper, nutrient rich waters, resulting in very high biological productivity. Organisms in the estuary are profoundly influenced by seasonal patterns of river flow. For example, the spring thaw in northern latitudes coincides with a time of high biological productivity in the estuaries. The volume of river water flowing into the estuary also affects the gradients of salinity from fresh water to the sea. Over thousands of years, organisms have adapted their lives in the estuaries to the patterns of circulation and salinity. When man throws a dam across a river or uses river water for power generation or irrigation, he disrupts the patterns of life in the estuaries and productivity declines.

Among the world's most productive areas are salt marshes which form where the silt, carried by the rivers, is deposited. Most of the organic matter they produce is used in the estuaries or in adjacent coastal waters. Seaweed zones are also highly productive. Their organic production is likewise fed into the coastal waters when seawater, bringing them nutrients, washes over them and carries away their waste materials. Nevertheless, the tendency in industrialized countries is to encroach on marshes and seaweed zones by filling, draining or building walls around bays and marshes. It is estimated that in the U.S.A. between one-quarter and one-half of the coastal marshes have already been destroyed or greatly modified (Chapter 6). Even aquaculture development, if sited carelessly, could be detrimental to the overall productivity of the coastal zone.

Conclusion

We conclude that the coastal zones of the ocean are of inestimable value as a source of high quality protein food and have great recreational and aesthetic value as well. We see the need for detailed study of estuaries and coastal ecosystems and of the effects of man's impact on them. We believe that every effort should be made to protect the coastal zone on a worldwide scale.

2.G. POLLUTION: A THREAT TO PRODUCTIVITY

There is a major difficulty in the rational development of inland and coastal waters as a source of dietary protein. Evidence is appearing from many directions that pollutants are contaminating aquatic production systems to the point that consumption of their products may constitute a hazard to human health. On the land high levels of atmospheric pollutants are known to damage or kill the vegetation, often reducing the value of agricultural crops. Nitrate poisoning of livestock and insecticide accumulations in dairy products are examples of damage to terrestrial food chains.

A clear distinction should be made between the effects of natural organic and inorganic nutrients like sewage and phosphate fertilizers, which have always been part of the normal ecological cycle, and industrial pollutants like pesticides and heavy metals, which occur as a direct result of industrialization. Fecal matter, urine and plant nutrients have always been a part of the natural recycling process. But one aspect of their distribution is new. Man, with his unprecedented population growth and aggregation in cities, is pouring out huge concentrations of sewage into lakes, rivers and estuaries. The effect of this is eutrophication, a stimulation of biological productivity to such a point that more plant material is being produced than the system can decompose. Oxygen in the water is used up, fish are killed or replaced by more resistant species and unpleasant accumulations of rotting plant material ruin the water's amenity value. The cure for this is to recycle the organic matter and nutrients within the ecological system: man must find economic ways of returning sewage to the land or of using it productively in aquatic systems. As a last resort, dissipation of domestic waste in the ocean, though wasteful of nutrients, is not in the short run a harmful practice. On the land, this enrichment can be beneficial to the vegetation.

Contamination with industrial products is an altogether different and more serious problem. As well as having direct effects, many substances, both organic and inorganic, concentrate in food chains. As material passes from plants to herbivores to carnivores, it may increase in concentration in the tissues of each organism. The danger is twofold: organisms, such as fish or livestock, which concentrate these materials may succumb to the toxic substances or behave abnormally under sublethal accumulations. Alternatively, man, in consuming these products, may endanger his health.

The effects of some toxic substances on man and other organisms are, as yet, little understood, but there is ample cause for alarm. Many of the substances polluting our food chains have been shown to have tumor-inducing, genetic and deformation-producing effects in other organisms. There is added evidence that the effect of one contaminant may reinforce another. It is therefore essential that mankind make every possible effort to keep these substances out of the living environment by containing them within the industrial process.

Workshop members looked in some detail at the sources, toxicities and human health hazards of lead, mercury, cadmium, DDT and PCB's (polychlorinated biphenyls), and in less detail at arsenic, beryllium, nickel, polyvinyl chloride by-products, oil, nitrogen and sulfur oxides, ozone, nitrates and nitrites. We concur in all cases with the conclusions and recommendations of the SCEP report (2) and offer the following more general recommendations.

RECOMMENDATIONS

We recommend that an International Pollution Control Commission be established. It should set and enforce safe standards for toxic materials in the environment and in human food. Particular attention should be given to pesticides, heavy metals and organic materials with known or suspected genetic, carcinogenic or teratogenic effects. The Commission should maintain a program of emission inspection for all global pollutants. Subsidies and loans should be made available to allow newly established industries in developing nations to operate from the outset under the same pollution emission standards applied in the industrialized nations.

We recommend that all nations adopt comprehensive regulations to control the production and the release of toxic materials within their boundaries.

REFERENCES

1. Agency for International Development (AID). 1970. Population program assistance. AID, Washington, D.C.
2. Study of Critical Environmental Problems (SCEP). 1970. Man's impact on the global environment. The MIT Press, Cambridge. 319 p.
3. Panel on the World Food Supply. 1967. The world food problem. Vol. III. U.S. Government Printing Office, Washington, D.C. 332 p.
4. United Nations. 1969. United Nations statistical yearbook. Statistical Office of the United Nations, New York. 770 p.
5. Keyfitz, N. 1971. The numbers and distribution of mankind, p. 31-52. In W. W. Murdoch (ed.), Environment. Sinauer, Stamford, Conn.

6. Borrie, W. D. 1970. The growth and control of the world population. London. 340 p.
7. Ryther, J. H. 1969. Photosynthesis and fish production in the sea. Science 166:72-76.
8. Hardin, G. 1968. The tragedy of the commons. Science 162:1243-1248.
9. Ehrenfeld, D. W. 1970. Biological conservation. Holt, Rinehart and Winston, New York. 226 p.
10. Simon, N. 1968. International union for the conservation of nature. Red Data Books, Morges, Switzerland.
11. Ricker, W. E. 1969. Food from the sea, p. 87-108. *In* Preston Cloud (Chairman), Resources and man. W. H. Freeman, San Francisco.

Chapter

3

Cycles of Elements

TASK GROUP:

Frederick Smith, Chairman
Deborah Fairbanks, Reporter
Ronald Atlas
C. C. Delwiche
Douglas Gordon
William Hazen
Dian Hitchcock
David Pramer
John Skujins
Minze Stuiver

3.A. MAJOR FINDINGS

1) Man has increased and, in some cases, doubled the global flow of elements essential to life. As a result, biological production on the earth as a whole has probably increased. While this increased production on land may improve the capacity of land systems to support the human population, overgrowth in aquatic systems is often a problem. Further, when the increase in the flow of elements in any of these environments becomes too great, it may have toxic effects which will suppress biological productivity.

2) Known potential supplies of phosphorus, a non-renewable resource essential to life, will be exhausted before the end of the 21st century. Without phosphate fertilizers, the planet can support between one and two billion people.

RECOMMENDATION

We recommend the establishment of an international agency to advise on the prudent production, distribution and use of the phosphate resources of the world.

3) Phosphorus, the key element in the overgrowth of plants in lakes and estuaries, is the only major nutrient that has no atmospheric circulation and cannot be replenished by interaction between the air, water and living systems. The removal of phosphorus from enriched effluents will prevent algae overgrowth and will also permit recycling, extending the lifetime of phosphorous reserves.

4) The rapidly increasing use of nitrogenous fertilizers (now 11% per year) has doubled the world rate of nitrogen fixation. This increase has been so rapid that the effect on nitrate levels in groundwater remains to be assessed, but elevated nitrate levels are

known to be a health hazard to animals and to man, especially infants.

Conclusion

Monitoring data of nitrate in groundwater should be collected systematically from the same wells over periods of years and analyzed regionally for trends. Health standards for nitrates in drinking water should be examined, and world levels established (this supports the recommendation in Chapter 2 on global standards).

5) The "natural" emissions of several nitrogenous gases into the atmosphere are not known. But knowledge of microbiology, soil science and ocean chemistry indicates that these are only trivial sources of the nitrogen oxides compared to those produced in combustion chambers. The flow of ammonia from the land and the sea to the air is indicated by levels observed in the atmosphere, but it has not yet been measured.

Conclusion

The global significance of air pollution with nitrogen oxides cannot be assessed until microbiologists, meteorologists and oceanographers work together to elucidate the system that is affected.

6) Altogether, man may have doubled the atmospheric cycle of sulfur, which could have a significant effect on the abundance of particulates in the atmosphere. Sulfur oxides produced in the combustion of fossil fuel appear to be the largest single source of sulfur in the atmosphere. The amount of biological production of sulfur as hydrogen sulfide, which oxidizes rapidly to sulfate, is not known; but it may also be increasing due to man's pollution of water and tidal areas.

Conclusion

Intense local problems caused by air pollution with sulfur oxides are well known. But, an additional global effect on atmospheric particulates should be reexamined, since natural biological sources appear to have been overestimated.

7) The analysis of geochemical cycles depends heavily on worldwide chemical analyses of rain and river waters, collected systematically over a long period of time. Present estimates are fragmentary and inadequate, often including values measured over a century ago. Inadequate data on the analyses of air, vegetation, soil and organic matter is an outstanding example.

RECOMMENDATION

We recommend that global monitoring programs, like those being considered by the Monitoring Commission, be organized so as to provide greatly improved global estimates of the rates of flow and pool sizes in the biogeochemical cycles of elements essential to life.

3.B. INTRODUCTION

Of the many elements necessary for life, six rank as the most important: carbon, hydrogen, oxygen, nitrogen, sulfur, and phosphorus. The first three are combined in energy-rich materials such as carbohydrates and oils. These, together with nitrogen and sulfur, are essential ingredients in all proteins. The sixth, phosphorus, is needed for the transfer of chemical energy within protoplasm, whether this energy is used for activity (respiration) or growth.

Life flourishes only where all of these necessary elements are available. For example, a lack of water (the major source of hydrogen) prevents the development of life in deserts, and a lack of minerals (especially phosphates and nitrates) similarly depresses biological activity in vast areas of the open oceans. On the other hand, these essential materials are relatively abundant in the coastal oceans and vegetated land areas of the planet. Only in these regions can the energy in sunlight and carbon dioxide in air or water become significant factors limiting biological productivity.

Each of these six elements circulates through air, land, sea and living systems in a vast biogeochemical cycle. The circulation of water (hydrologic cycle), the very slow erosion and uplift of continents (geologic cycle) and the opposing processes of photosynthesis and respiration (ecologic cycle) are all involved. Human activities and demands have become measurable on the scale of these global cycles, and, locally, they are sometimes overwhelming. Man's substantive effect on carbon dioxide and his trivial influence on global supplies of oxygen, for example, are documented in the SCEP report (1). In this report, therefore, our attention is restricted to the cycles of phosphorus, sulfur and nitrogen, except where they interact with the cycles of carbon and oxygen.

This focus on phosphorus, sulfur and nitrogen emphasizes the dependence of life on more than the flows of energy and carbon, two aspects of biological cycles most often studied. It emphasizes the roles of protein and protoplasm in the nutritional needs of man and affirms that human activities have a much more profound influence on the cycles of these materials than they do on those of carbon dioxide, oxygen or water.

3.C. HUMAN ACTIVITY

Three kinds of human activities may affect the cycles of phosphorus, sulfur and nitrogen:

1) Production for industrial or agricultural use
2) Inadvertent release from other activities
3) Secondary concentration following man's use of these elements.

Phosphorus is produced primarily from the mining of phosphatic rock, and most of it is marketed as phosphate fertilizers.

Sulfur is also produced primarily from mining elemental sulfur or pyrites which contain elemental sulfur. Increasingly, sulfur is being recovered as a by-product in the fossil fuel industries. Most sulfur is converted to sulfuric acid for use--the largest of which is in the extraction of phosphates from phosphatic rock. This, together with its use in sulfate fertilizers, accounts for half of the production. The rest is used in a variety of industrial processes.

Nitrogen is produced primarily by industrial fixation from nitrogen gas in the atmosphere, yielding ammonia and various nitrate compounds. Its primary use is in fertilizers. Table 3.1 shows the commercial production and consumption of these materials for the last 15 years (an annual production of 3.6 million metric tons is equivalent in 1970 to a world average of one kilogram per person).

Such production represents a mobilization of these elements from inactive to active forms in the biosphere. Additional sources arise from other activities, associated primarily with the combustion of fossil fuel. The amounts of phosphorus mobilized in this fashion are negligible. Sulfur oxides, however, are released to the atmosphere from the oxidation of sulfur present in the fuel, and nitrogen oxides are released from the high-temperature fixation of gaseous

		1953	1963	1968
Production:	Phosphate Rock (estimated 12% P)	3.1	5.9	10.2
	Sulfuric Acid	10.3	18.8	26.3
	Nitrogenous Fertilizer	6.6 (1954)	14.9	26.6
		1954	1963	1968
Consumption:	Phosphate Fertilizer	3.3	5.4	7.6
	Nitrogenous Fertilizer	6.3	14.0	24.5

Table 3.1. Annual production and consumption of phosphates, sulfuric acid, and nitrogenous fertilizers. Units are millions of metric tons of the elements P, S, N (2).

	SO_x		NO_x	
Source	U.S.	World	U.S.	World
Coal	10.1	50.0	1.2	5.9
Oil	2.6	7.3	2.7	7.6
Gas	–	–	1.5	2.3
Other	3.9	11.2	0.9	2.6
Total	16.6	68.5	6.3	18.4

Table 3.2. Atmospheric release in 1968 of oxides of sulfur and nitrogen due to human activities. Units are millions of metric tons of the elements S and N. U.S. estimates from SCEP (1), extrapolated to world estimates using Table 7.3 of SCEP (1).

nitrogen as the air passes through the combustion chamber. The amounts of both that are produced over time have tended to follow the increase in consumption of fossil fuel (about 5% per year). Estimates of release from various sources in 1968 are shown on Table 3.2.

These materials mobilized by man are directly or ultimately dispersed to the environment. Along the way, however, they may be reconcentrated to a significant degree, effectively resulting in secondary sources of release. Both primary and secondary sources offer opportunities for pollution control and recycling.

Phosphorus and nitrogen, and organic matter in general, are increasingly reconcentrated by three kinds of activities: 1) sewerage systems and treatment plants, 2) food-processing industries and 3) feedlots. All three are growing considerably faster than the population and apparently as fast as the general rate of industrial growth.

3.D. CYCLES OF PHOSPHORUS, SULFUR AND NITROGEN

The effect of man upon global cycles of these elements can be evaluated only by considering the workings of these cycles, our understanding of which is qualitatively fair and quantitatively poor. Only the major components will be considered here, and quantitative analysis is restricted to those areas in which human activity intervenes. More detailed quantitative analyses are given at the end of the chapter.

The cycles differ in both major and minor respects. The phosphorus cycle is the simplest and that of nitrogen the most complex. The major pool of phosphorus is found in rocks (lithosphere), while the major pool of sulfur is in the oceans (hydrosphere) and nitrogen is pooled in the atmosphere. The effects of these differences on the dynamics of the cycles will become evident.

3.E. PHOSPHORUS CYCLE

Phosphorus exists in the biosphere almost exclusively as phosphate. Due to the abundance of calcium, aluminum and iron, all of

Figure 3.1. The phosphorus cycle

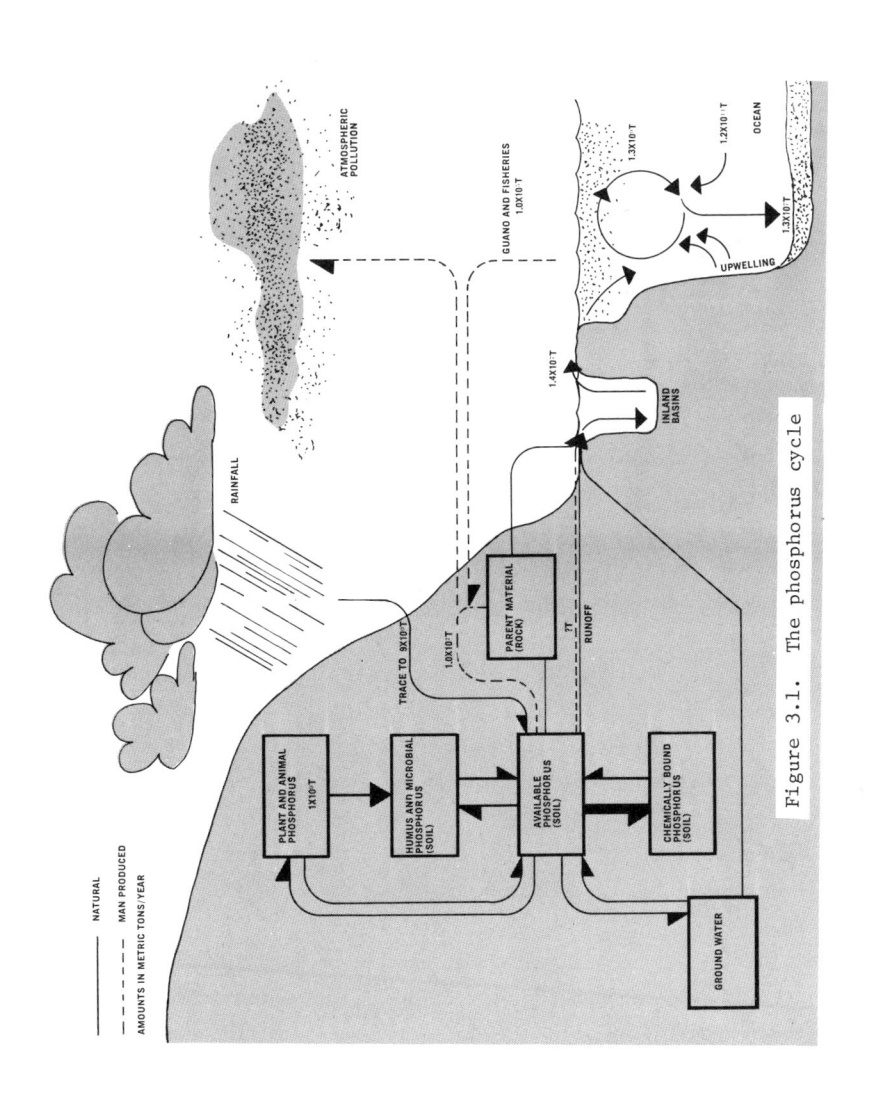

which form phosphate salts with very low solubilities in water, most of the earth's phosphorus is immobilized in rock, soil or sediment.

The natural movement of phosphorus is slow. Phosphates which are leached (in dissolved form) or eroded (in particulate form) from the land find their way to streams and lakes (see Figure 3.1 and Table 3.3). Some of them are precipitated in lake sediments, but the rest enter the ocean where they, too, are precipitated.

As the bodies of animals and plants that have accumulated phosphorus fall to lower levels, surface waters of the oceans become depleted of phosphate supplies. But, deep water tends to be nearly saturated (calcium is abundant), so that the additions from above are precipitated to the sediment. Upwelling of deep water returns some phosphorus to the surface, but this amount is always limited by the relative insolubility of calcium phosphate.

Return of phosphorus to the land depends then almost entirely upon the geological uplift of sediments. It is the formation of new land, and not a return to old land, that closes the cycle; and the rate at which this takes place is so low that, on the human scale, it is virtually zero. For man's purposes, phosphorus is essentially a "non-renewable" resource.

The only significant exceptions to geological rates of return to land are the land deposits of manure from fish-eating birds (guano) and man's fish harvests. Although these are small amounts on a global scale, they are important to man as sources of fertilizer and food.

The amounts of phosphorus that move through the atmosphere as dust or are emitted as phosphene gas from swamps are exceedingly small.

On a local scale, ecological systems on land and in water accumulate and cycle phosphorus (see Figure 3.1). These systems are adapted to environments low in available phosphorus and respond strongly to enrichment.

Subsequent cropping of the vegetation depletes this ecological pool of phosphorus, most rapidly where soil organic matter is low (wet tropics) and least rapidly where it is high (temperate grasslands). Thereafter, unless phosphate fertilizers are used, yields are limited to the rate at which phosphorus is released from its insoluble salts. It is estimated that these natural rates of mobilization would support a world population of between one and two billion people (4).

Man has significantly increased the natural rate of phosphate mobilization by mining phosphatic rock and extracting phosphate fertilizers. In 1968, fertilizer applications exceeded 50% of the estimate of total global phosphorus runoff to the oceans (compare Tables 3.1 and 3.3). The major part of phosphorus added as fertilizer is immobilized in the soil because of abundant supplies of calcium, aluminum and iron which bind with it in the presence of oxygen.

A second part of phosphate fertilizer is removed in crops. This is released later as waste when the crops are processed or consumed. Urbanization and sewerage systems concentrate wastes so that they can be treated, but even with secondary treatment about 70% of the phosphorus passes through into the effluent (5). Other concentrations of phosphorus occur at food processing factories and at feedlots, often contributing to the enrichment of waterways. Although only a minor part of phosphate fertilizer is leached or eroded from the land, drainage systems collect from large areas; and the total downstream effect can be considerable. Table 3.4 shows an analysis of the sources of phosphorus to a lake. At least three-fourths of this phosphorus input is due to human activities, even though they cannot be separated one from another.

Phosphorus in waterways may cycle rapidly through aquatic systems, greatly increasing their biomass, but it is soon lost to the sediment and must be replaced continuously by new additions.

Thus, all phosphorus mobilized by man is eventually immobilized in soil or sediment; and once in the soil, it is slowly transferred by leaching and erosion to sediment. The loop is not closed in less

Millions of Metric Tons

Annual land to sea	14
Loss to sediments	13
Phytoplankton cycling	1,300
Ocean reserve	120,000
Return to land	0.1

Table 3.3. Movement of Phosphorus in the Biosphere (3).

Source	% of Total P
Precipitation	2
Ground Water	2

Runoff
    un-manured rural
    manured rural
    urban
	
	12
	30
	17

Waste	36

Table 3.4. Sources of Phosphorus Entering Lake Mendota (6).

than geologic time. Phosphatic rock containing 12% phosphorus is mined, processed, used and lost in materials which contain less than 0.1% phosphorus (Table 3.5). Maximum recycling from secondary sources of concentration (i.e., sewage) could not reclaim more than 20% of the phosphorus used on the fields (8).

The rapid immobilization of phosphorus in soil precludes an efficient use of added amounts. An empirical study of the relation between fertilizer input and agricultural yield shows that fertilizer use must increase 2.7 times more rapidly than the increase in yield (9). Assuming that the present level of food per person is a minimal goal for the future, we can conclude from this that the use of fertilizers must increase at least 2.7 times faster than the population.

Phosphatic rock reserves and potential supplies are variously estimated to contain between 11,000 and 22,000 million tons of phosphorus (8, 10). This includes rock with a phosphorus content as low as 8%, which, though not now economically useful, is expected to become so in the future (10). The U.S. Bureau of Mines estimates the potential yield to be 19,800 million tons of phosphorus (10).

The total production of phosphate in 1968 is estimated at 11.3 million tons of phosphorus (2). Thus, at present rates of use, known reserves and supplies will last 1750 years. It is expected, however, that rates will increase as world populations increase and higher standards of living are achieved.

At present, 39% of the world's population (in the more developed countries) uses 86% of the world's fertilizers (9). Bringing all people to this level of consumption would increase the use of fertilizers by a factor of 2.6. If this were done immediately, the lifetime of known supplies would be only 675 years.

The effect of population growth is much more severe. If present average nutritional levels are maintained, the fertilizer requirements for a population of any size can be estimated by using the 2.7 growth ratio of fertilizers/yield described above. Such estimates are

Igneous rock	1,050
Shales	700
Sandstone	170
Limestone	400
Phosphate rock	120,000 (est. ave. 12%)
Soil	650
Fresh water	0.005
Ocean	0.07
Oven-dry plant material	2,000
Dry invertebrate tissue	4,000 - 9,000
Dry mammal tissue	43,000
Lake sediments	150

Table 3.5. Concentration in ppm of P in Natural Material (7).

Population (thousand millions)	Phosphorus Use/Year (millions metric tons)	Lifetime of known reserves (years)
1.8	1.7	11,700
3.6	11.3	1,750
7.2	73	271
12	291	68
20	1170	17

Table 3.6. Estimated use of phosphorus fertilizer to feed world populations of various sizes at the present average nutritional level combining data from the UN (2) and the phosphorus-to-yield function of PSAC (9).

given on Table 3.6, together with the lifetime of known reserves if such populations existed now. A doubling of the present population is expected very early in the 21st century, and levels of 12 to 20 billion people have been suggested as future "steady states" which the world can support (53). This analysis does not support such predictions. By contrast, if phosphorus use is estimated for half the present world population, the lifetime of reserves would be increased many thousands of years.

Another approach is based upon the current rates of increase of phosphorus and of populations and their expected rates in the future. Recently the population has grown at an annual rate of 1.9% (2), and the use of phosphate fertilizers at 5.25% (10). The second is 2.76 times higher than the first, conforming well with the fertilizer/yield analysis given above. If these growth rates are projected into the future, known reserves and supplies will be used up in 90 years--stranding a population of 20 billion. At somewhat lower rates of growth, reserves may last for 130 years.

New reserves will certainly be found. The total phosphorus supply, however, is not limitless. An upper boundary can be set by the accumulated effects of erosion and deposition on this planet over the last half billion years. The total amount of primary (igneous) rock eroded has mobilized an estimated 1,600,000 million tons of phosphorus. Sedimentary rocks account for the loss (at concentrations of less than 0.1% phosphorus) of about 1,000,000 million tons (11). Thus, about 600,000 million tons may exist in materials with higher concentrations. The great bulk of this is not likely to contain more than one or two percent phosphorus (see reference 12 for a discussion of the origin of phosphatic rock). If as much as 5% is sufficiently rich in phosphorus to be potentially usable (8% or more), then no more than 30,000,000 million tons of usable phosphorus exist on the planet. Supplies are limited.

This being so, what must we do to insure a supply of phosphorus for the longest possible time? While none of the following proposals alone will increase the supply by more than a factor of two; if used in unison, they might extend the planet's phosphorus supply by a total factor of 5 to 10:

1) We should increase recovery from phosphate rock presently being lost in washing and flotation operations. We should protect and rework phosphate rock tailing dumps before they are lost by natural erosion and leaching processes.

Losses in washer and flotation operations, which follow removal of phosphate rock from the ground, range from 40% of the phosphorus in the Florida land-pebble fields to more than 50% in some Tennessee areas (10). Similar beneficiation processes (which separate out that portion of ore containing more phosphate) are used in the U.S.S.R. deposits. The higher-grade ores of the Western United States, however, need little or no washing or beneficiation (8). Discarded material from washing and flotation contains 5.5 to 7.5% phosphorus and not only entails the loss of a valuable resource but is expensive to dispose of as well. The U.S. Bureau of Mines is presently conducting research to develop alternate beneficiation methods.

Underground mining of Western U.S. and North African phosphorus deposits (8) is designed to uncover high-grade beds. But, because it is often necessary to strip low-grade phosphate beds (4.5 to 8% P) to recover the underlying high-grade ores, a large amount of phosphate rock is lost to tailing dumps. These dumps are analogous in concentration of phosphorus to the ores which will have to be mined in less than 100 years. Therefore, they should be safeguarded either by being covered over or by other means, so that they will be available in the future. To neglect them will result in a large loss of materials to wind and rain.

2) Contaminants of phosphate rock should be salvaged as by-products. This recovery, in the future, could defray part of the increasing cost of mining poorer grade phosphate rock and will extend

our dwindling resources of uranium and fluoride. Furthermore, the recovery of these elements will prevent additional chemical and radioactive pollution of the land, soil and water.

The uranium content of phosphate rock varies from 45.4 g to 181.4 g of uranium per ton. It can be recovered by the wet process method, although the cost of this process is higher than that of mining and processing uranium ores. In 1968, more than 454 tons of uranium could have been recovered in the United States (10) from phosphate rock. Since contaminant levels will increase as lower-grade ores begin to be used, recovering them could become more profitable.

3) Nations should decrease the amount of phosphorus fertilizers they use to approach the recommended 2/1 ratio. This will conserve phosphorus and still produce desirable, high yields.

Agronomists indicate that a 2/1 ratio of nitrogen to phosphate (N/P_2O_5) fertilizers will best meet the overall requirements of the soils and crops of the developing nations (9). However, the ratio of nitrogenous to phosphatic fertilizers actually used by different nations is highly variable and appears to be dictated more by fertilizer availability and economics.

4) We should curtail uses of phosphates for purposes other than fertilizers.

In the U.S., 80% of the phosphate supplies are used in fertilizer manufacture, 15% in phosphate detergents and 5% in producing phosphorus compounds for industry (12). In the rest of the world, the proportion used for fertilizers is higher (85 to 90%). Thus, eliminating non-fertilizer uses will increase the ultimate amount available for fertilizer by 20 to 25% at the most. Fortunately, detergent manufacturers, because of tightening controls on release of phosphorus to the environment, are endeavoring to develop more suitable substitutes. The use

of phosphorus in industry is proportionately so small that it almost
can be considered inconsequential.

5) We should develop economic methods to recover phosphates
released to the environment in effluents.

The likelihood of reclaiming unused phosphate fertilizer and
detergents from streams and estuaries is relatively poor because of
their great dilution and mixture with other materials. By the time
such material reaches the sea, its concentration is no greater than
0.1%, essentially the same percent as occurs naturally. Likewise,
recovery from seawater will probably forever remain economically infeasible because of the tremendous pumping costs required. But,
recovery from tertiary sewage treatment plants, though costly, may
prove a source of reclaimed phosphorus.

6) We should intensify the search for additional phosphate
raw materials.

At present, apatite or natural phosphate rock (calcium and/or
aluminum hydroxy-fluorophosphate) is the major source of commercial
phosphates. As resources dwindle over the next century, alternative
sources should be sought. Phosphorite deposits (protophosphate rock)
have been fairly well delineated off the Georgia-South Carolina coast of
the U.S.A.; similar deposits on continental shelves should be sought
and mapped in other parts of the world as future resources.

Implementation of all these proposals suggests the need for an
institution of adequate prestige to manage the world use of phosphorus
and to work toward its conservation. Phosphate supplies are in short
supply and may run out in the next century. As a result, phosphate
rocks should be treated as a common resource in order to conserve the
world supply. Most nations must import phosphates from the few that
produce them (2).

RECOMMENDATION

We recommend the establishment of an international agency to advise on the prudent production, distribution and use of the phosphate resources of the world.

3.F. SULFUR CYCLE

Sulfates, the oxidized forms of sulfur, are more soluble than phosphates and move easily from the land to the oceans, where they accumulate (Figure 3.2). Sulfur is 240 times more abundant in seawater than in fresh water, and sulfate deposits occur when shallow seas evaporate and calcium sulfate crystals (gypsum) are formed. This process of removal from the oceans is not taking place in this millennium, but a reduced form of sulfur is deposited continuously in ocean sediments. When sulfate is thrown into the atmosphere in sea spray, the spray evaporates and the particles formed fall back into the sea.

A second source of atmospheric sulfur is in the mud flats bordering seawater. Unlike phosphates, sulfates can be reduced biologically in the absence of oxygen. Various microbes are able to use the oxygen released in this process in respiration, producing hydrogen sulfide. In the deep waters of lakes or seas, this hydrogen sulfide either combines with iron to precipitate as iron pyrites or drifts upward into oxygenated water where it oxidizes spontaneously back to sulfate. When this process occurs in sediments, the hydrogen sulfide tends to precipitate as iron pyrites.

Along the coast where the supply of sulfate from seawater is large, hydrogen sulfide gas escapes to the air when mud, rich in organic matter, is exposed at low tide. The global amount of H_2S produced in this manner is entirely unknown. In the air, it oxidizes rapidly and forms very small particles that ultimately fall as sulfate in rainwater. Pollution with organic matter can increase the rate of sulfate reduction greatly (13).

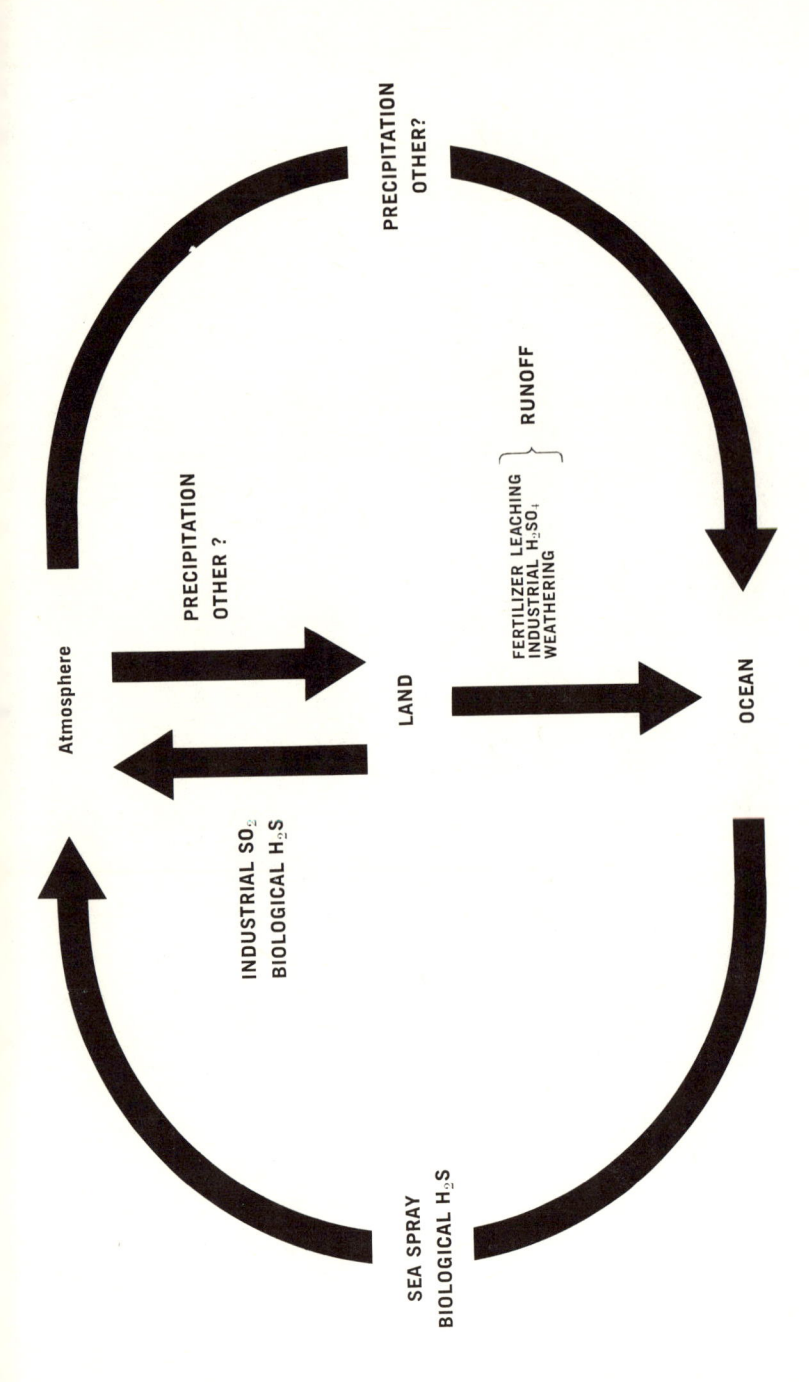

Figure 3.2. The sulfur cycle

Sulfur is essential to living systems. It is used in the folding of amino acid chains to form protein molecules in protoplasm. The sulfur, in a reduced form, is attached to several kinds of amino acids. Unlike plants and microbes, which can reduce sulfate for use in protein synthesis, animals depend upon adequate supplies of sulfur-bearing amino acids in their diet.

Under natural conditions, sulfate is abundant in the environment. It tends to be leached from soils but is replenished slowly in rain, and natural vegetations are usually able to meet their needs. However, continual cropping can deplete sulfate supplies, making it advantageous to add moderate amounts in fertilizer.

Man, himself, has created a third source of atmospheric sulfur. Sulfur exists as an impurity in fossil fuel and is converted to sulfur oxides when man burns these fuels. In the presence of atmospheric water, these sulfur oxides become sulfate and mix to some degree with naturally produced sulfate. It is estimated that in 1968, 68 million metric tons of sulfur were released to the atmosphere in this way (see Table 3.2).

The importance of this source depends upon the magnitude of natural sources, and the natural biological production of hydrogen sulfide has not yet been measured. Sulfate in rainfall is estimated to be 165 million metric tons per year for the entire planet (14). If this figure were used to estimate what went up, pollution emissions would account for 43% of the atmospheric circulation of sulfur. (Reasons for rejecting estimates of large amounts of dry fallout, to be added to the values for rain, are given in the appendix to this chapter.)

If human impact is large, it should be evident in the environment and it is. Rising levels of sulfate in air, rain and lakes, along with the increasing acidity of rain and lake waters, are documented locally and regionally. A few examples in Table 3.7 show the magnitude of these changes.

Another aspect, the role of atmospheric sulfur in the formation of particulates--especially very small particles--is beyond our competence to judge. Since sulfur is a dominant component of particulates in the atmosphere (troposphere and stratosphere), specialists on particulates should reexamine in this light the possible effects of human activity.

Much of the commercially produced sulfur in acid finds its way sooner or later into the rivers. Even if all this production is added to river water, however, the increment is not large.

Sulfur reserves do not present a problem. In fact, if sulfate emission to the atmosphere is controlled and the sulfur is produced as a by-product, the amount (see Table 3.2) would be considerably larger than current sulfur production levels (see Table 3.1).

Conclusions

Sulfur oxide emissions are having an increasingly large impact on the atmospheric cycling of sulfur and currently account for nearly half of the flow. (The deleterious effects of sulfur oxides have not been summarized here.)

Pollution abatement techniques can yield more sulfur than the market demands.

Natural biological sources of atmospheric sulfur are either poorly known or poorly evaluated.

Meteorologists, working together with microbiologists and ecologists, should reevaluate man's influence on the amount of sulfur-containing particulates in the atmosphere.

3.G. NITROGEN CYCLE

The global cycling of nitrogen is biologically and chemically the most complex of the biogeochemical cycles. Its major processes are shown on Figure 3.3, a chemical flow chart for nitrogen.

The largest reservoir of nitrogen is found in the atmosphere, which is 78% nitrogen gas. A portion of atmospheric nitrogen is

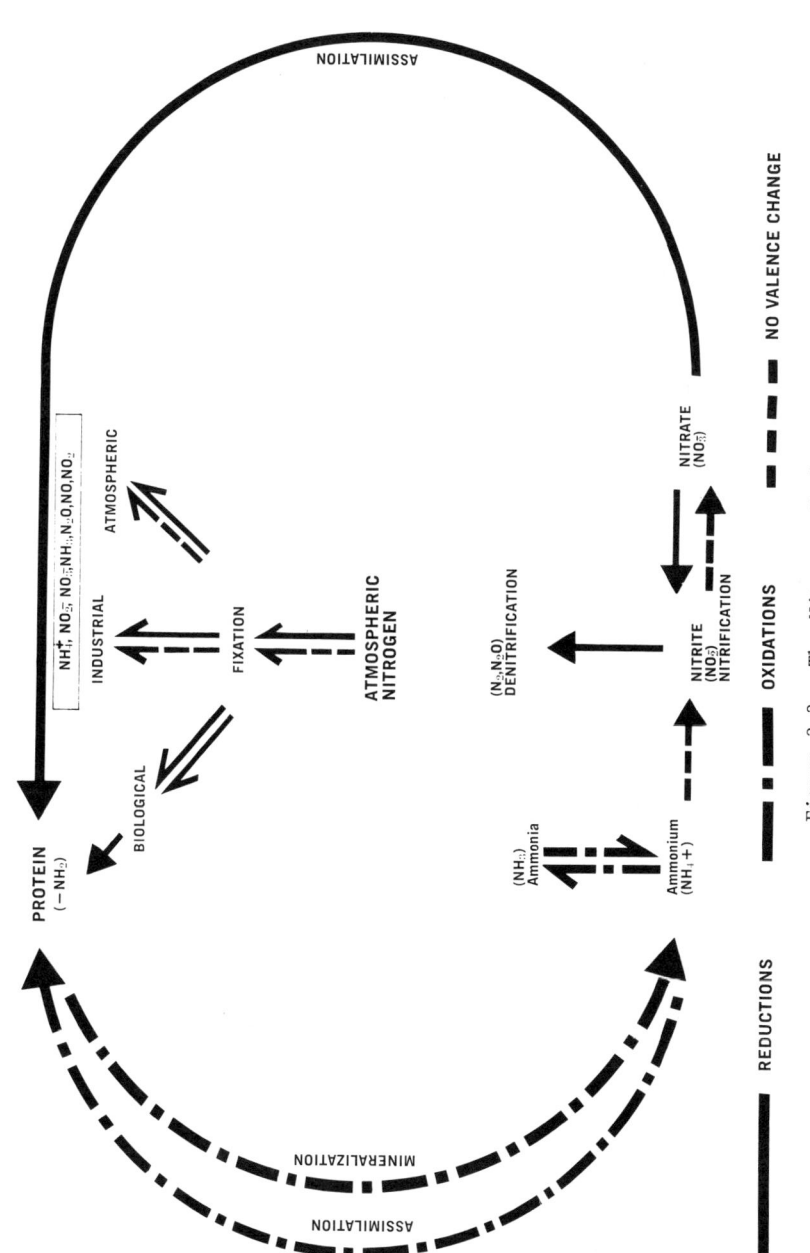

Figure 3.3. The Nitrogen Cycle

removed by microbial action and incorporated into living tissue by a variety of biochemical pathways. Such a process is called nitrogen fixation.

The fixed nitrogen can then be taken up by plants (including microbes) and assimilated, a complex process by which fixed nitrogen is incorporated into protein. Later, this material is either returned directly to the environment or consumed by animals (including man) before it is ultimately released.

When fixed nitrogen is returned to the environment, a process of degradation takes place during which ammonia is released. Ammonia may be reassimilated by plants, evaporated into the air or changed by microorganisms into nitrate.

This latter process, known as nitrification, is an extensive one in nature. It changes the ammonia, which is retained by soils, to nitrate, which leaches into groundwaters. Plants can assimilate only a part of those naturally formed nitrates present in soils.

A natural microbial process, denitrification, removes most of the nitrate by changing it to nitrogen or to nitrous oxide, a gas which requires reasonably large amounts of organic matter as food for the microorganisms and an absence of oxygen. Thus, it has its limitations of effectiveness.

The atmospheric and ecologic cycles of nitrogen are so strong and rapid that its geologic aspects are trivial.

Nitrogen Fixation

Man has roughly doubled the rate at which fixation occurs. In the next 30 years, a further increase to four or five times the "natural" fixation rate is expected (9). Though this will have no effect on the vast amount of atmospheric nitrogen, it may produce changes in other parts of the nitrogen cycle.

Man's fixed nitrogen tends to be transformed to nitrate which, not bound by soils, is leached into groundwater, rivers and estuaries and eventually reaches the ocean. Some of this nitrate is converted to nitrogen gas or nitrous oxide and returned to the atmosphere; but the capacity of this denitrification process and, hence, its capability of coping with increased amounts of nitrates is unknown.

Nitrates

A trend of increased nitrate concentrations in natural waters has followed the increased use of industrially fixed nitrogen fertilizers. Trends over time are shown for four Illinois rivers on Figure 3.4 (18). When very high levels occur, they tend to coincide in time with the spring crest of high water flow. A curve of fertilizer use has been added for comparison (55). Between 1955-61 and 1961-66 fertilizer use increased 179 percent, while the average increase in the four sets of river data was 54%. Although fertilizer use increased seven-fold during the earlier period, levels were apparently low enough to have little effect on natural waters.

A similar increase of nitrate in sewage releases has been noted for the last twenty years. Another possible source of nitrate in natural waters is increased irrigation practices which can leach naturally accumulated nitrates from soils, particularly in arid or semi-arid areas.

The main effect of increased nitrate concentrations in natural waters is eutrophication or over-fertilization. Decay of the excess plant growth requires a lot of oxygen, depleting the water's oxygen supply and resulting in a loss of fish life and damage to the water's economic and recreational value (19).

Increased nitrate concentrations in groundwaters used for drinking are also undesirable. Under anoxic conditions in the digestive tract, this nitrate is reduced to nitrite. When this happens in infants, it produces a "blue baby" condition called methemoglobinemia. Hogs and cattle are also affected adversely by nitrates and grow poorly. Nitrates can also cause gasteroenteritis and diarrhea and in some cases can be lethal. Toxic human doses of nitrate have been reported as

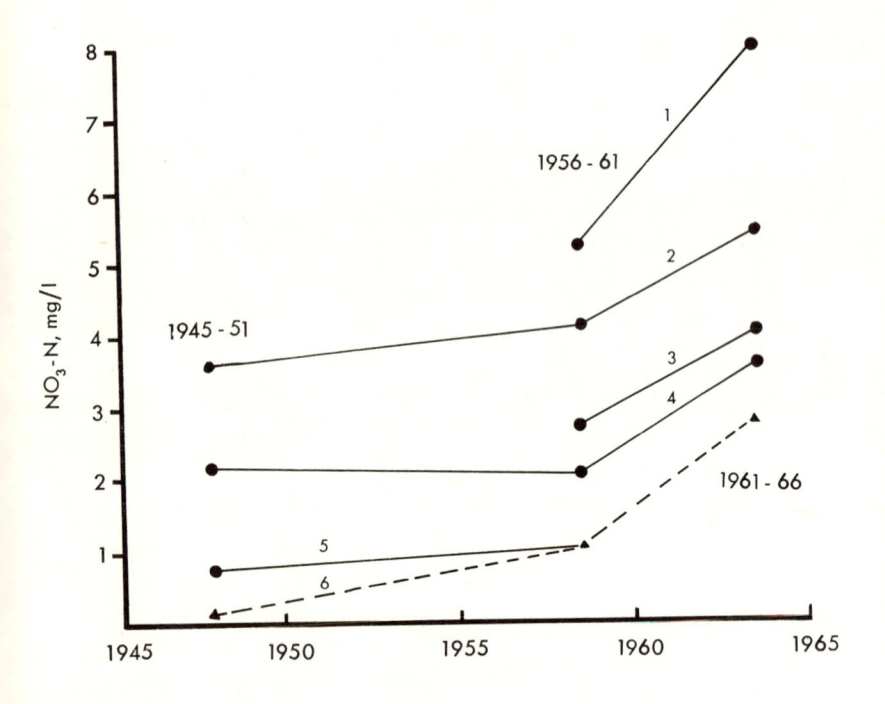

Figure 3.4. Nitrate levels in surface waters of Illinois rivers.
1. Kaskaskia River (Shelbyville). 2. Illinois River (Peoria).
3. Rock River (Como). 4. Kaskaskia River (New Athens). 5. Skillet Fork (Wayne City). 6. Nitrogen fertilizer used in Illinois, 100,000 metric tons of N. (Ordinate scale the same as that used for mg./l. of NO_3-N in river water.) River data are 90th percentiles for the period indicated, fertilizer data are averages. (18, 55).

0.56 g nitrate-nitrogen per day (20) and 1.04 g nitrate-nitrogen/kg body weight (21). The U.S. limit for approved drinking water is 45 mg/l nitrate (2).

A further concern with nitrate buildup is its influence on the sulfur cycle. Nitrate is known to decrease the reduction of sulfate to sulfide (3), and this could result in a lowering in the pH of soils and natural waters.

Methods have been proposed for removing nitrate-rich waters locally by flushing them into economically unimportant areas. But such proposals do not remedy the problem of nitrate in usable drinking water sources; and, generally, these methods do not remove excess fixed nitrogen from the biosphere. Other methods proposed by Wuhrmann (22), Ludzak and Ettinger (23) and Johnson and Schoepfer (24) are based on controlled microbial denitrification processes which would recycle the nitrate into atmospheric nitrogen gas. A final method which might become essential if the nitrate in natural water continues to rise would be instituting desalinization processes to produce suitable nitrate-free drinking water.

Conclusions

Support should be given for increased efforts to develop methods for recycling nitrogenous waste materials and for removing excess nitrates carried in groundwater and in surface water supplies.

Safe limits of nitrates in water and food should be determined more carefully, and international standards should be established. This conclusion supports the recommendation of Chapter 2 for the creation of an international agency to establish worldwide safety limits on toxic materials.

Nitrogen Dioxide

A second focal point of concern with the nitrogen cycle is with levels of nitric oxide (NO) and nitrogen dioxide (NO_2). These two oxides are the products of high temperature combustion. Nitric oxide is rapidly transformed to nitrogen dioxide by atmospheric ozone. Though there are natural sources of nitrogen dioxide in the atmosphere which have not yet been elucidated, man puts about 20 million tons of NO_2 into the atmosphere yearly. The present pool of nitrogen dioxide and nitric oxide in the atmosphere is estimated at about one million metric tons (25). The present yearly input of nitrogen dioxide from man-made sources is about 20 million tons. The amount of nitrogen dioxide that, in turn, precipitates out of the atmosphere has not been clearly established; but by assuming that equal amounts are continuously added and removed from the atmosphere and that other sources are small, the residence time of nitrogen dioxide is less than three weeks. Nevertheless, a continuous increase in the rate of nitrogen dioxide input into the atmosphere will undoubtedly increase its pool size in the atmosphere.

Increased nitrogen dioxide levels in the atmosphere have many unpleasant side effects for man. Nitrogen dioxide can be toxic in high concentrations and forms corrosive acids when hydrated. Beyond that, it is a key compound in the photochemical production of smog. Even though nitrogen dioxide is present in the atmosphere from natural sources, the concentrations necessary for smog production are of man-made origin. This is exemplified by the fact that the nitrogen dioxide concentrations in cities is about ten times that found in rural areas (25). Continued fuel-burning practices will only further increase this pollution of city air. And, as yet, no methods of NO_2 removal appear feasible. It is now removed naturally from the air by rainwater and is dissipated in soil as nitrate and nitrite ions.

Because nitrogen dioxide can be found in well-isolated areas, seemingly beyond the range of contamination from polluted city air, several possible explanations have been proposed in the literature for the origin of natural nitric oxide and hence natural nitrogen dioxide emissions. These range from biological means (26) to the oxidation of ammonia (27) to the transformation of N_2O_2 (27). None of these proposed origins seems satisfactory. There is no convincing evidence that these oxides can be generated biologically. In certain acid soils, which also contain high nitrate concentrations, nitric oxide will evolve; but such soils are not common. We are left with an enigma and are unable to determine whether any human practices other than fuel combustion add to atmospheric nitrogen dioxide.

Conclusions

A monitoring system for levels and sources of nitrogen dioxide in the atmosphere is needed. It should have enough precision to detect trends, especially in rural areas.

Scientists of several disciplines should work together to solve the mystery of "natural" sources of nitrogen dioxide.

3.H. INTERRELATIONS OF BIOGEOCHEMICAL CYCLES

The diverse cycles of hydrogen, oxygen, carbon, nitrogen, sulfur and phosphorus ultimately intersect in living material, where they show fairly constant ratios of abundance to each other. The cycles also interact in other places, with the result that human influence on one cycle can affect another. Although many of these interactions have not been well studied, enough is known about some of them to permit discussion.

Organic Synthesis

Organisms require various forms of carbon, nitrogen, sulfur and phosphorus and are not always able to make them. Generally, organic carbon (carbohydrate) is produced by green plants through photosynthesis and then distributed to animals and decomposers. The organic nitrogen and sulfur in proteins are produced by green plants and decomposers and must be supplied to animals in their food. Phosphates can be acquired from inorganic sources by all organisms.

Organic carbon and organic nitrogen production need not proceed at the same rate in the biosphere. Land plants are relatively rich in carbon and poor in nitrogen, due primarily to the extensive production of cellulose. Aquatic algae are relatively rich in protein and, hence, have relatively more nitrogen than land plants have. Since the global rates of organic carbon production are reasonably well known (1, 28) and the carbon to nitrogen ratios are known for a variety of materials (11, 28), the global rates of organic nitrogen production by green plants can be estimated. Nitrogen production by decomposers can then be estimated by considering bacterial and fungal growth in relation to plant and animal litter (29). The results are shown on Table 3.8. Even though they are only approximate, they suggest that the ocean is the most important source of protein and that ocean food chains could be larger producers of meat than terrestrial systems. A major problem is the length of the food chain, which is about twice as long in fisheries as in agriculture. The table also suggests that a large potential source of protein exists in the soil.

Conclusions

The oceans are the largest source of protein synthesis. Since marine plant production is more edible (less cellulose) as well as more nutritious (more protein), the oceans contain the greatest source of protein for man.

Since large quantities of protein are produced in the soil, the use and harvest of this material (e.g., mushrooms) for human use should be intensified.

Alternative Sources of Oxygen

Living in a world rich in oxygen, we are accustomed to the use of molecular oxygen for respiration. In soil, mud, sediments and in the deep waters of many lakes and seas, however, oxygen is depleted; and organic matter accumulates there faster than oxygen can enter by diffusion.

Microbes therefore utilize several other sources of oxygen, two of which are described here. In the absence of oxygen, some organisms are able to use the oxygen in nitrates, releasing nitrogen to the

1. Sulfate in surface waters of Linsdley Pond, Connecticut, increased from 0.25 mg/liter in 1937 to 7.0 mg/liter in 1963 (15).

2. Sulfate reduction and precipitation rates in bottom muds are 10 to 30 times post-glacial rates (15).

3. Sulfate in Japanese rain increased from 1.13 mg/liter in 1946 to 4.5 mg/liter in 1959 (a 4-fold increase) while industrial output of sulfur oxides increased from 0.26 to 1.2 million metric tons (a 4.6 fold increase) (16).

4. Maps of average non-marine sulfate in rainfall for the U.S. show higher concentrations over industrial regions than over rural regions (17).

5. Aitken nuclei concentrations increased in Wyoming and Colorado by a factor of ten within five years in the middle 1960's (1).

6. Sulfur levels in the air doubled between 1952 and 1962 in three rural areas of Sweden (54).

Table 3.7. Examples showing trends of sulfur in the environment.

Source	Green Plants N	Green Plants C	Bacteria & Fungi N	Bacteria & Fungi C	Total N	Total C
Land	1.6	56	1.7	–	3.3	56
Oceans	3.7	22	0.2	–	3.9	22
Total	5.3	78	1.9	–	7.2	78

Table 3.8. Preliminary estimates of rates of production of organic nitrogen (protein) in the biosphere (1, 11, 28). Units are thousand millions of metric tons per year. Production rates of carbon (1) are shown for comparison.

atmosphere in the process. In the absence of both oxygen and nitrates, microbes use the oxygen in sulfates, producing hydrogen sulfide in the process. Whether first the oxygen, then the nitrate and finally the sulfate are depleted depends upon the amount of organic matter (carbohydrate) present. Thus, all four cycles interact in this portion of the biosphere.

Man affects this system in several ways, two of which may be important. The flow of nitrates to groundwater and then to drinking water is prevented primarily by denitrification. This in turn depends on the presence of organic material and an absence of oxygen, both of which are affected by intensive agricultural practices. In general, then, agricultural practices tend to increase oxygen content and deplete organic matter which could depress denitrification and lead to an increase in the amount of nitrates in drinking water. However, the magnitude of this effect is not known.

A second area of man's influence is on the coastal tidal flats. In these muds, the rate of sulfate reduction depends upon the amount of organic matter present. Non-polluted mud produces relatively little hydrogen sulfide, most of which is precipitated with iron. Polluted muds, however, can produce 10 to 20 times as much hydrogen sulfide, a large part of which may escape to the atmosphere (13).

Conclusions

The interaction between agricultural practices (fertilization, mulching, plowing) and denitrification, and the resultant flow of nitrates to groundwater, deserves intensive study.

Polluted mud flats can produce as much or more atmospheric sulfur as is currently produced from the combustion of fossil fuels.

Atmospheric Interactions

Atmospheric sulfur is most rapidly removed from the air as a complex salt of ammonia and sulfate. In polluted urban air, however, removal of man's added sulfur oxides tends to be slowed by a relative scarcity of ammonium.

Nitrogen oxides added to urban air tend to hasten the formation of particulates from hydrocarbons that have also been emitted, but it is scant comfort that the processes leading to photochemical smog production also hasten the rate of removal of hydrocarbons from the air.

Eutrophication of Water

Runoff from agricultural lands is relatively rich in nitrates, since these are more soluble than phosphates. By contrast, effluent from sewage treatment plants is relatively poor in nitrates and rich in phosphates. Not only is much of the original nitrate denitrified under the anoxic conditions of sewage treatment, but the amount of phosphate is increased by its use in laundry and dishwater detergents.

The ratio of phosphate to nitrate influences the kinds of algae that flourish in lakes. Green algae, which are more edible and rapidly enter the food chain, require nitrate or ammonia in the water; whereas many blue-green algae, which are often inedible and, so, tend to accumulate, are able to fix their own nitrogen. Thus, pollution with sewage effluents favors the growth of undesirable algae and large aquatic plants.

Algal overgrowth can occur only if all of the essential elements are abundant. Some lakes, in basins lacking limestone, are deficient in carbonate. Others are acid, making the biological fixation of nitrogen difficult or slow. Most water bodies are relatively deficient in phosphorus, for the reasons described in the preceding sections. Furthermore, phosphorus is the least renewable resource, and its absence precludes any possibility of algae overgrowth.

Conclusion

The management of phosphate is the key to the management of eutrophication in most bodies of water. The maintenance of optimal levels for water quality and fish production would require its removal from many sources, especially sewage effluents. The recycling of this essential and non-renewable resource is an additional argument for its removal.

Eutrophication of Land

Human activity is "stirring up" the biogeochemical cycles of many materials. To the degree that atmospheric levels of nutrient materials are increased, the possibility exists that man is also enriching the land.

Carbon dioxide levels in the atmosphere are rising (1). Since laboratory studies show a linear relation betwen photosynthetic rates and carbon dioxide levels (1), enhancement of photosynthesis by man-made increases in CO_2 is expected in terrestrial vegetation.

The same processes that produce carbon dioxide also add oxides of sulfur and nitrogen in the atmosphere. In addition, man's pollution of mud flats may increase atmospheric sulfates; and where he uses ammonium fertilizers there may be increases in atmospheric ammonia (30). Phosphatic dust from phosphate industries and additional traces of phosphate from other industries also find their way into the atmosphere, although the total amount is small.

Once the acid effect of oxides is neutralized, all of these materials become nutrients and many of them come down in rain. As a result, the possibility of a small but worldwide fertilization of vegetation should not be overlooked.

Since land systems have problems in retaining nutrient material, as opposed to aquatic systems in which these materials accumulate, this kind of eutrophication of land should be generally useful and may in general increase land productivity.

Conclusion

The total effect of man on the global circulation of elements leads to many problems in aquatic environments (see Chapter 6) but may be beneficial to terrestrial systems.

3.I. QUANTITATIVE ESTIMATES

Although this section may seem to be of interest primarily to the scientific community, it provides an objective means of evaluating the accuracy of the foregoing analyses and concludes with a major recommendation regarding world monitoring programs.

Some quantitative problems are common to all these cycles: estimates of river runoff, precipitation values, rates of biological activities, etc. These are discussed here at length for the sulfur cycle but are meant to apply as well to the cycles of phosphorus and nitrogen.

The phosphorus cycle is relatively simple, and major rates of transfer have already been presented (Table 3.3). These are considered to be accurate enough for the use that is made of them, even though they have probable errors of $\pm 40\%$ (if the estimate is 20, the odds are one-half that the true value lies between 12 and 28). But, if changes in the phosphorus cycle are to be detected, better estimates will be necessary.

The nitrogen cycle is so complex and has so many exchange rates, that time did not allow a critical evaluation of their accuracy or of the widely different values used by different authors. Table 3.9 lists the rates that were used for the analysis of the nitrogen cycle in Section 3.G. Also given is the group's best guess on the probable errors of these estimates. These ranges do not include published estimates that have been rejected, which in some cases differ by factors of 10 to 100.

Conclusions

Many of the quantitative rates for element cycles lack direct estimation or are poorly known. A major problem lies in discrepancies between inferences from atmospheric studies and knowledge of biological systems. For instance, the flows of NH_3, NO, NO_2 and N_2O from the so-called "natural" or "biological" processes--between the

	Land		Sea		Atmosphere	
	rate/yr	% error	rate/yr	% error	rate/yr	% error

Input

Biological nitrogen fixation	--	--	10	50	--	--
Symbiotic (31)	14	25	--	--	--	--
Non-symbiotic (31)	30	50	--	--	--	--
Atmospheric nitrogen fixation (31)	4	100	4	100	--	--
Industrially fixed nitrogen fertilizer (31)	30	5	--	--	--	--
N-oxides from combustion*	14	25	6	25	20	25
Return of volatile nitrogen compounds in rain	?	--	?	--	--	--
River influx (31)	--	--	30	50	--	--
N_2 from biological denitrification (31)	--	--	--	--	83	100
Natural NO_2	--	--	--	--	?	--
Volatilization (HN_3)	--	--	--	--	?	--
Total Input	92+		50		103+	

Storage

Plants (31)	12,000	30	800	50	--	--
Animals (31)	200	30	170	50	--	--
Dead organic matter (31)	760,000	50	900,000	100	--	--
Inorganic nitrogen (31)	140,000	50	100,000	50	--	--
Dissolved nitrogen (31)	--	--	20,000,000	10	--	--
Nitrogen gas (31)	--	--	--	--	3,800,000,000	3
$NO + NH_4$ (25)	--	--	--	--	Less than 1	50
$NH_3 + NH_4$ (17)	--	--	--	--	12	50
N_2O (33)	--	--	--	--	1,000	50
Total Storage	912,200		21,000,970		3,800,001,013	

Loss

Denitrification (31)	43	--	40	100	--	--
Volatilization	?	--	?	--	--	--
River runoff (31, 32) (includes enrichment from fertilizers)	30	50	--	--	--	--
Sedimentation (31)	--	--	0.2	50	--	--
N_2 in all fixation processes	--	--	--	--	92	50
NH_3 in rain	--	--	--	--	Less than 40	50
NO_2 in rain	--	--	--	--	?	--
N_2O in rain	--	--	--	--	?	--
Total Loss	73		40.2		132+	

*See Table 3.2.

Table 3.9. Budget for the nitrogen cycle. All numbers are in millions of metric tons. The error columns list plus-or-minus probable errors as a percentage of the estimate.

land and the air and also between the ocean and the air--will not be clarified until scientists from the different disciplines work together to find a solution.

Sulfur

The distribution of sulfur on our planet is shown in Table 3.10. Most of the sulfur is involved in a very slow geologic cycle between the land and the oceans, while a much smaller amount is involved in the much more rapid atmospheric and ecologic cycles. Only the latter are of interest on the human time scale.

On the land, the sulfur reservoir is comprised of igneous rock, which contains 260 ppm of sulfur, and sedimentary rocks, in which it is present primarily as iron sulfides and calcium sulfate. Most weathered sulfur is derived from sedimentary rocks which represent a sulfur reservoir of 3.6 billion metric tons (11, 13, 34).

Sulfur is also abundant in the ocean as sulfate ions and is present in much smaller quantities as organic sulfur in the biomass.

Atmospheric sulfur occurs in gaseous form as H_2S and SO_2, both of which are short lived, and as sulfate or "ammoniated sulfate" in aerosol or particulate form. In addition, some sulfur is present in sea salt particles formed by evaporation of sea spray. The concentrations, lifetimes, sources and fates of these atmospheric forms of sulfur have been the subject of extensive experimental and theoretical investigation, but the phenomena are so complex that no clear picture has yet emerged. (See References 14, 17, 26, 35-95.)

Most of the sulfur acquired by plants is taken up by the roots from sulfate in soil water, but they may also take in gaseous SO_2 directly (26). Some sulfur, in turn, is liberated to the air when vegetable matter decomposes.

The most significant biological role in the sulfur cycle is the reduction of sulfate to hydrogen sulfide in aquatic or mud environments rich in organic matter and depleted of oxygen and

		Metric Tons
Land	Inorganic S in igneous rock (11)	5,700,000,000
	Inorganic S in sedimentary rock (11)	3,600,000,000
	Organic and inorganic S in soils (11)	28,000
	Land biomass (46)	510
Ocean	S as SO_4^{--}	1,215,000,000
	Organic S in ocean biomass (11,47)	23
Atmosphere (Troposphere)	H_2S (40)	10 to 48
	SO_2 (40)	5 to 50
	Aerosol and particulate SO_4^{--}	variable
	Sea salt particles	variable

Table 3.10. Sulfur reservoirs.

nitrate. Under these anoxic conditions, bacteria (generally of the Desulphovibrio type) utilize dissolved sulfate ions as hydrogen acceptors and oxidize organic matter according to the following overall reactions:

$$2CH_2O + SO_4^{--} \rightarrow H_2S + 2HCO_3^-$$

$$4CH_2NH_2COOH + 4H_2O + 3SO_4^{--} \rightarrow H_2S + 2HS^- + 8HCO_3^- + 4NH_4+$$

There are two important sulfur cycles which must be considered in the construction of a sulfur budget: the transfer of weathered sulfur from the land to the ocean by means of continental runoff and the exchange of sulfur between the atmosphere and the surface. Estimates of exchange rates for these cycles are given in Table 3.11. These two cycles interact in that some of the sulfur in river runoff is derived from the atmosphere-surface cycle.

The surface sources of atmospheric sulfur are: volcanic emissions of SO_2 and H_2S, industrial emissions of SO_2 (mostly from fossil fuel combustion), sulfate in sea salt derived from the evaporation of ocean spray, and biogenic hydrogen sulfide produced in anoxic marine or freshwater environments.

Atmospheric sulfur returns to the surface in precipitation and by means of "dry deposition," the sedimentation of atmospheric particles or their scavenging by vegetation, and the direct gaseous absorption of SO_2 by water and land surfaces.

The agricultural use of sulfate fertilizer and sulfur-containing industrial effluents added to streams also contribute to the continental river runoff.

Human influences can be estimated from production and consumption statistics. The sulfur in river runoff and precipitation can be monitored. Most of the remaining exchanges of sulfur between air, land, water and living systems are difficult to measure.

Global estimates of river runoff for various elements have been compiled by Livingstone (48). When his estimates are used, it is worthwhile to examine his sources. In the case of sulfur, many of the data for European rivers were recorded in 1848 and most of it before 1900. Most of the values for the United States were recorded in the 1940's and early 1950's. Beyond that, differences in techniques for chemical analysis and the lack of multiple sampling or sampling in all seasons make them unreliable for present use, as it has been shown that ion concentrations vary during the year with varying precipitation (48). Finally, the distribution of samples does not represent the different land areas of the globe equally.

Precipitation data appear to be scanty and difficult to interpret because the ion content of the rain depends upon the rain's intensity, duration and frequency and also upon the gaseous and particulate contents of the atmosphere, which may vary widely with locality, season and meteorological conditions. Except for very isolated locations, we have found few useful sources of bulk precipitation data from which mean annual atmosphere-to-surface transport rates may be calculated (49, 50), even though such data are easy to collect. Most atmospheric composition and precipitation chemistry studies have been concentrated in a few regions of relatively industrialized temperate zone countries and should not be extrapolated to the globe as a whole.

Recent studies of remote, non-urban areas (Panama, Antarctica and the Amazon rain forest) suggest that their atmospheric chemistry may differ appreciably from that of temperate continental zones (40, 42, 43). The introduction of new measurement techniques and their use in remote areas have resulted in revisions of estimates of probable global mean concentrations of trace elements in the atmosphere. Table 3.12 reflects the magnitude of the revisions, contrasting widely used estimates of global tropospheric trace element composition, compiled in 1963, with more recent estimates. The more recent estimates, themselves, should be considered tentative (Cadle, personal communication).

Tables 3.10 and 3.11 indicate the possible sulfur reservoir sizes and exchange rates. For the most part, they are based on figures

	Sulfur (millions metric tons)
Land surface to ocean (river runoff) (48)	123
Rock weathering (13,14)	15-43
Atmosphere to surface 　Sulfate in precipitation over land*(14) 　Sulfate in precipitation over ocean*(14) 　Dry deposition over land and ocean***	60 60 0.5-100
Surface to atmosphere 　Volcanic emissions (SO_4^{--} and H_2S) (16) 　Industrial emissions (SO_2)	7-12 68
Industrial effluents on land**(2)	27
Ocean to atmosphere 　Sea salt (precipitated over land) (14,51) 　Sea salt (precipitated over ocean) (14,51) 　H_2S	5-25 39-195 unknown
Ocean to ocean sediments (iron pyrites) (34)	7

* Excludes S originating from sea salt.
** Industrial sulfuric acid including fertilizers.
*** Calculated from dry deposition rates given in (26) and (14).

Table 3.11. Annual Rates of Sulfur Exchange.

	Background		Polluted
	Published Means	Recent	
Oxygen	209,000,000		
Carbon Dioxide	300,000	320,000	
Methane	1,400	1,250	
Hydrogen	700	500	
Nitrous Oxide	420	240	2,000
Hydrogen Sulfide	10	2	500
Sulfur Dioxide	10	1	2,000
Ammonia	10	15	2,000
Formaldehyde	5	4	1,000
Nitrogen Dioxide	2	0.5	2,000
Nitric Oxide		0.5	

Table 3.12. Trace Gases in the Atmosphere, PPB (40).

frequently quoted in the literature. Where possible, we have attempted to indicate the uncertainty in these data by showing a range of estimates presented by different authors. With few exceptions, the figures may be seriously questioned (see Appendix). Taken together, they do not provide an adequate basis for an evaluation of the impact of human activities on the sulfur cycle; and, since this impact may be large, we urge action to improve this information base.

These problems are common to analyses of many biogeochemical cycles. At the present time, efforts are being made to design global monitoring networks which will include measures of various rates of flow in element cycles. For those elements essential to life, this may give rise to several compatible and consistent sources of information. This will provide not only a check on the validity of existing data but will also add insight into man's influence on the environment.

RECOMMENDATION

We recommend that global monitoring programs, such as those being considered by the Monitoring Commission, be organized so as to provide greatly improved global estimates of the various rates of flow and pool sizes in the biogeochemical cycles of elements essential to life.

APPENDIX   (D. Hitchcock and F. Smith)

Within the last decade the phenomenon of leaching has been studied extensively by plant physiologists and ecologists. This is a process by which minerals taken from the soil pass through the plant and are washed from the leaves by rain. Rain which passes through the vegetation (throughfall) then carries to the surface not only its original minerals and those that have fallen onto the leaves in dry fallout but also those leached from the leaves. The contributions from leaching, in fact, dominate the composition of throughfall water. A good reference for the role of these processes in a forest is a study by Duvigneaud and Denaeyer-De Smet (52).

In at least two cases we have studied (16, 17), meteorologists have used rain collected from beneath vegetation, in comparison with rain collected in the open, as a means of estimating dry fallout. In the first example (16), the estimated dry fallout was three times the amount in rain (for calcium it was eight times greater). Unfortunately, none of these estimates is valid because none takes leaching into account.

Likens et al. (49) attempted to measure dry fallout by comparing fallout in permanently open collectors with that in collectors that opened only when it rained. They found virtually no dry fallout. Using the same technique, Swank (personal communication) at the Coweeta site in the southern Appalachians has been finding dry fallout amounts for various elements that range from 0.12 to 0.35 of their concentration in rain water. Both studies suggest a relatively small contribution of elements from dry fallout in humid areas. (Airborne dust in arid regions may contain sulfur and contribute significant amounts locally, 17.)

However, if a large sulfur dry fallout is presumed and is added to the amount of fallout in rainwater, a similarly large flow from the surface back to the atmosphere is needed to balance the atmospheric cycle. This has led to the presumption that there are large naturally occurring sources of sulfur like the hydrogen sulfide (which oxidizes rapidly to sulfate) from exposed mud flats (14, 17, 26). If this emission is large in comparison with industrial sources it should show up in regional analysis of precipitation, such as those given for the United States in Junge (17, p.334). But although the effect of megalopolitan areas is evident in those data, no trace of coastal enrichment appears--not even along the Gulf coast where air movement is often shoreward across large mud flats. Some evolution of hydrogen sulfide undoubtedly does occur, especially in polluted areas, but the amount remains unknown.

Exchanges of hydrogen sulfide and sulfur oxide between the soil and its immediate atmosphere may be large on a global scale, but the extent to which the overlying atmosphere is involved and the amount of air affected by this process are not known (26, 39). It is difficult to imagine that if this exchange were as large as some have supposed, the influence of man could have such strong effects in so many places.

For all these reasons, we feel that the burden of proof rests with those claiming that the quantity of sulfur returned to the surface is appreciably larger than the amount measured in precipitation.

REFERENCES

1. Study of Critical Environmental Problems (SCEP). 1970. Man's impact on the global environment. The MIT Press, Cambridge. 319 p.

2. United Nations. 1969. United Nations statistical yearbook. Statistical Office of the United Nations, New York. 770 p.

3. Alexander, M. 1971. Microbial ecology. John Wiley and Sons, New York. 511 p.

4. Goeller, H. E. 1971. The ultimate mineral resource situations. ORNL DWG 71-3865 (Oak Ridge National Laboratory, Tenn.).

5. American Chemical Society, Committee on Chemistry and Public Affairs. 1969. Cleaning our environment; the chemical basis for action. American Chemical Society, Washington, D.C. 249 p.

6. Biggar, J. W., and R. B. Corey. 1967. Agricultural drainage and eutrophication. In National Academy of Sciences, Eutrophication: causes, consequences, correctives. NAS, Proc. of Symposium. Washington, D.C. 661 p.

7. Fortescue, J. A. C., and G. G. Marten. 1970. Micronutrients: forest ecology and systems analysis, p. 173-198. In D. E. Reichle (ed.), Analysis of temperate forest ecosystems. Springer-Verlag, New York. 304 p.

8. Sauchelli, V. 1965. Phosphate in agriculture. Reinhold Publ. Co., New York. 277 p.

9. President's Science Advisory Committee, Panel on the World Food Supply. 1967. The world food problem. Vol. III. U.S. Govt. Printing Office, Washington, D.C. 332 p.

10. U.S. Bureau of Mines. 1970. Mineral facts and problems. U.S. Dept. Int., Bull. 650. Washington, D.C. 1291 p.

11. Bowen, H. J. M. 1966. Trace elements in biochemistry. Academic Press, New York. 241 p.

12. Chemical Economics Handbook. 1969. Stanford Research Institute, Menlo Park, Calif.

13. Berner, R. A. 1971a. Sulfate reduction, pyrite formation, and the oceanic sulfur budget. Paper presented at Nobel Symposium, Stockholm, 1971.

14. Eriksson, E. 1963. The yearly circulation of sulfur in nature. J. Geophys. Res. 60:4001-4008.

15. Stuiver, M. 1967. The sulfur cycle in lake waters during thermal stratification. Geochimica st. Cosmochimica Acta 31:2151-2167.

16. Koyama, T., N. Nakai, and E. Kamata. 1965. Possible discharge rate of hydrogen sulfide from polluted coastal belts in Japan. J. of Earth Science (Nagoya Univ.) 13:1-11.

17. Junge, C. E. 1963. Air chemistry and radioactivity. Academic Press, New York and London. 382 p.

18. Harmeson, R. H., and T. E. Larson. 1969. Interim report on the presence of nitrates in Illinois surface waters. Proceedings, 1969 Illinois Fertilizer Conference. Agronomy Department, College of Agriculture, University of Illinois.

19. Hasler, A. D. 1970. Man-induced eutrophication of lakes, p. 110-125. In S. F. Singer (ed.), Global effects of environmental pollution. Springer-Verlag, New York. 218 p.

20. Gilbert, C. S., H. F. Eppson, W. B. Bradley, and O. A. Beath. 1946. Nitrate accumulation in cultivated plants and weeds. Wyoming Agr. Sta. Bull. p. 227.

21. Whitehead, E. I., and A. L. Moxon. 1952. Nitrate poisoning. S. Dakota Agr. Exp. Sta. Bull. 424 p.

22. Wuhrman, K. 1964. Nitrogen removal in sewage treatment processes. Verh. Int. Ver. Limnol. 15:580-596.

23. Ludzak, F. J., and M. C. Ettinger. 1961. Controlling operation to minimize activated sludge effluent nitrogen. J. Water Pollut. Control Fed. 34:920-931.

24. Johnson, W. K., and G. J. Schroepfer. 1964. Nitrogen removal by nitrification and denitrification. J. Water Pollut. Control Fed. 36:1015-1036.

25. Ripperton, L. A., L. Kornreich, and J. J. B. Worth. 1970. Nitrogen dioxide and nitric oxide in non-urban air. J. Air Pollut. Center Assoc. 20:589-592.

26. Robinson, E., and R. C. Robbins. 1970. Gaseous atmospheric pollutants from urban and natural sources, p. 51-64. In S. F. Singer (ed.), Global effects of environmental pollution. Springer-Verlag New York. 218 p.

27. Georgii, R. W. 1963. Oxides of nitrogen and ammonia in the atmosphere. J. Geophys. Res. 68:3933-3970.

28. Olson, J. S. 1970. Models of the hydrologic cycles, p. 268-285. In D. E. Reichle (ed.), Analysis of temperate forest ecosystems. Springer-Verlag, New York. 304 p.

29. McLaren, A. D., and J. Skujins (ed.). 1971. Soil biochemistry. Vol. 2. Marcel Dekker, Inc., New York. 527 p.

30. Loewenstein, H., L. E. Engelbert, O. J. Attoe, and O. N. Allen. 1957. Nitrogen loss in gaseous form from soils as influenced by fertilizers and management. Soil Science Society, Proc. 21:397-400.

31. Delwiche, C. C. 1970. The nitrogen cycle. Sci. American 223:137-158.

32. Clarke, F. W. 1924. The data of geochemistry. 5th ed. U.S. Geo. Survey Bull. 770. 841 p.

33. Schutz, K., C. E. Junge, R. Beck, and B. Albrecht. 1970. Studies of atmospheric N_2O. J. of Geophys. Res. 75:2230-2246.

34. Berner, R. A. 1971b. Worldwide sulfur pollution of rivers. J. Geophys. Res. (Under review).

35. Eriksson, E. 1959. The yearly circulation of chloride and sulfur in nature; meteorological, geochemical, and pedological implications, 1. Tellus 11:375-403.

36. Martell, E. A. 1966. The size distribution and interaction of radioactive and natural aerosols in the atmosphere. Tellus 18:486-498.

37. Friend, J. P. 1966. Properties of the stratospheric aerosol. Tellus 18:465-473.

38. Junge, C. E., E. Robinson, and F. L. Ludwig. 1969. A study of aerosols in Pacific air masses. J. Applied Meteorology 8:340-347.

39. Georgii, H. W. 1970. Contribution to the atmospheric sulfur budget. J. Geophys. Res. 75:2365-2371.

40. Pate, J. B., J. P. Lodge, Jr., D. C. Sheesley, and A. F. Wartburg. 1970. Atmospheric chemistry of the tropics. In Symp. proc. on Environment in Amazonia; 24 April 1970. Part I. Instit. Nacio. Pesq. Amazon, Manaus, Brazil. p. 43.

41. Beilke, S., and H. W. Georgii. 1968. Investigation on the incorporation of sulfur-dioxide into fog and rain droplets. Tellus 20:435-442.

42. Lodge, J. P., Jr., and J. B. Pate. 1966. Atmospheric gases and particulates in Panama. Science 153:408-410.

43. Fischer, W. H., J. P. Lodge, Jr., J. B. Pate, and R. D. Cadle. 1969. Antarctic atmospheric chemistry: preliminary exploration. Science 167:66-67.

44. Cadle, R. D., and E. R. Allen. 1970. Atmospheric photochemistry. Science 167:243-249.

45. Cadle, R. D. 1971. Formation and chemical reactions of atmospheric particles. J. of Colloid and Interface Science. (In press).

46. Deevey, E. S., Jr. 1970. Mineral cycles. Sci. Amer. 223:148-159.

47. Whittaker, R. H., and G. E. Likens. 1961. Woodland Forest Working Group of International Biological Program. (Unpublished).

48. Livingstone, D. A. 1963. Chemical composition of rivers and lakes, Chapt. G. In M. Fleischer (ed.), Data of geochemistry. 6th ed. Geolog. Survey Prof. Paper 440-G. U.S. Govt. Printing Office, Washington, D.C. 64 p.

49. Likens, G. F., F. H. Bormann, N. M. Johnson, D. W. Fisher, and R. S. Pierce. 1970. Effects of forest cutting and herbicidal treatment on nutrient budgets in the Hubbard Brook Watershed-Ecosystem. Ecol. Monogr. 40:23-47.

50. Feth, J. H. 1967. Chemical characteristics of bulk precipitation in the Mojave Desert region, California. U.S. Geol. Survey Prof. Paper 575-C:222-227.

51. Blanchard, D. C. 1963. The electrification of the atmosphere by particles from bubbles in the sea, p. 71-202. In M. Sears (ed.), Progress in oceanography. Vol. 1. Pergamon Press, New York.

52. Duvigneaud, P., and S. Denaeyer-DeSmet. 1970. Biological cycling of minerals in temperate deciduous forests, p. 199-225. In D. E. Reichle (ed.), Analysis of temperate forest ecosystems. Springer-Verlag, New York. 304 p.

53. Keyfitz, N. 1971. On the momentum of population growth. Demography 8:71-81.

54. Royal Commission on Natural Resources. 1968. Environmental research. Report of the Royal Comm. on Nat. Resour., Stockholm.

55. United States Department of Agriculture Statistical Reporting Service. 1971. Commercial Fertilizers: Consumption of commercial fertilizers, primary plant nutrients, and micronutrients. Statistical Bulletin No. 472 (1971).

Chapter 4

Ecosystems for Human Benefit

TASK GROUP:

Conrad Istock, Chairman
Jacqueline Easby, Reporter
William Cooper
Harold E. Goeller
John A. Kadlec
Monte Lloyd
Gordon Mott
William W. Murdoch
Fred H. Tschirley
Robert I. Van Hook
Mark Westoby

4.A. MAJOR FINDINGS

1) When the practice of industrial agriculture is interpreted in the light of current knowledge of ecosystems, a picture emerges which suggests that the future dependability of such agriculture is in grave doubt.

2) The simple ecosystems of industrial agriculture are absolutely dependent on a reliable industrial base. As developing countries become more committed to modern agricultural practices, in order to feed their peoples, they will also acquire dependence on the industrial complexes of other nations. Eventually all the components of industrial agriculture may be transferred to the developing nations. But during the transitional period it must be accepted as a general principle that the coupling of industry in one country with the agriculture of another involves a direct sharing of responsibility for the welfare of the people dependent on that agricultural system.

RECOMMENDATION

We recommend that carefully worked out international accords be concluded for situations where the industrial base of one nation is used to promote and sustain modern agricultural practices in another nation.

3) It is now essential that the one-way coupling of nutrient flow from agricultural land to urban areas and to fresh and salt waters be altered by returning these nutrients to croplands or by diverting such nutrients to other productive uses such as aquaculture. All future designs for intensely managed ecosystems must involve such recycling of nutrients and wastes.

4) Insecticide cross-resistance should be subjected to

extensive study using both current and potential pest insects. A
diagnosis of the present state of cross-resistance is required in
order to predict the effectiveness and subsidiary consequences of
chemical insect pest control programs.

5) Dependence on chemical pest control endangers the long-term
dependability of our agricultural ecosystems, causes serious environmental degradation and sometimes poses a health hazard. Every effort
should be made to replace chemical pest control with other methods
and in particular with an integrated approach that will develop and
use ecological diversity.

RECOMMENDATIONS

We recommend that agricultural research agencies in all countries initiate experiments on the effects of increasing the spatial
heterogeneity within agricultural landscapes. The first problem will
be to determine feasible scales and geometrical patterns applicable
to modern agriculture.

We recommend the creation, with continuing international support,
of several centers in the tropics for the development of integrated
pest control and crop management techniques. Support for such work
should also be given to existing tropical research or agricultural
centers.

6) With the emerging concerns over complex environmental problems, considerable emphasis will be placed on the development of planning for large heterogeneous landscapes. Management techniques required to control such complex systems must also be developed. Tradeoffs between technical feasibility, economic viability, social acceptability and ecological stability will require decision processes other
than those we now use.

RECOMMENDATION

We recommend that the United Nations initiate and fund a program to encourage institutions of higher learning to provide training in the planning and managing of environmental systems. These programs should impart understanding of the ecological constraints, life styles, social institutions and political and economic interrelations of the major geographical areas of the world.

7) There are strong reasons for preserving local and global species diversity:

a) Many pest species can be brought under biological control only if their original parasites and predators or a large number of potential (though not coadapted) parasites and predators remain in existence.

b) Genetic variation in wild populations of crop species and related species serves as a long-run resource for future development of desirable properties in crop species. Disease and pest resistance, adaptation to various physical and chemical conditions of husbandry and higher yields are examples of properties for which such genetic resources serve as raw material.

c) Locally diverse ecological assemblages harbor the controlling species whose interspecies relations check the growth of many potential pest species. The problems of pest control will be increased in most areas of the world if local species diversity is reduced.

d) Present wild species may in the future be used by man as crop species or for other uses. The loss of wild species would thus reduce future opportunities for the development of human societies. Even if a species does not become completely extinct, a substantial reduction of its global population may serve to eliminate much of its genetic variation and, thus, much of its value as a natural resource.

e) Partially managed ecosystems require much of the structure of a preexisting natural ecosystem to sustain populations of exploited species. Thus it is necessary that some natural ecosystems be preserved. It is not only the biological species which are irreplaceable, but also the quantitative framework of exchanges, interactions and organization which must be preserved and which underlie the stability of ecosystems.

f) Aesthetic aspects of diversity remain essential to man. Many pleasures of life and opportunities for individual human enrichment cannot exist without a varied and lovely landscape.

8) Increasing use of pesticides and rising pesticide residue levels in the environment offer cause for concern. The various pesticides, however, differ in toxicity to man; toxicity to non-target species; and the length of time which they persist in organisms, soils and water. Therefore, considering the current dependency of high agricultural yields and disease control on the use of pesticides, it becomes essential to differentiate among the characteristics and safe uses of the various pesticides.

RECOMMENDATION

We recommend that all pesticides suspected of causing environmental damage or hazards to human health be subject to international restrictions and that the use of such pesticides be banned by international agreement when alternatives are available.

9) Research should be done immediately to determine the effects in man of chronic low-level lead poisoning. At the same time research on the passage of lead through food chains and the chronic effects of lead on ecosystems should be expanded.

RECOMMENDATIONS

We recommend that all use of tetraethyl lead in gasoline be eliminated and that international regulations be established which guarantee that only gasolines free of heavy metals will be marketed in all countries. Where substitution of cyclic organic compounds and other additives are envisaged, we recommend sufficient screening to ensure that one form of air pollution is not replaced by another.

We recommend that, where possible, lead-containing products be recycled in order to extend natural lead resources and to curtail the release of lead, particularly lead oxide, to the environment.

10) We agree with SCEP's recommendations that: 1) all use of pesticides containing mercury be curtailed; 2) much more extensive data on mercury concentrations in food organisms and on its effects within ecosystems be obtained; 3) industrial wastes and emissions containing mercury be controlled by recovery of the mercury to the greatest extent possible; and 4) that world production and consumption figures for mercury be obtained. It matters little whether or not global environmental levels of mercury have risen greatly during the recent past. Actual experience with hazardous levels of mercury in the environment is sufficient to justify efforts to prevent further addition of mercury to soils and waters.

11) A worldwide monitoring of cadmium should be initiated. In order to establish maximum allowable concentrations of cadmium, further study should be given to: 1) the fate of cadmium within ecosystems; 2) the toxicology of cadmium; and 3) the specific effects of chronic low-level intake of cadmium. The present maximum permissible levels of cadmium in air, water and food should be reduced.

12) The use of polychlorinated biphenyl compounds (PCB's) should be limited to those applications for which there is no

substitute. Methods of incineration or stack gas cleanup should be
developed which effectively decompose or remove PCB's before release
to the atmosphere. There is also danger of release to groundwaters
by leaching from solid-waste landfills. Data on the world production
of PCB's should be made public by manufacturers.

13) Industrial pollution originating in one country now frequently transcends the boundaries of separate nations. Future programs for the protection or improvement of environments thus require international action.

RECOMMENDATION

We recommend that an international pollution control commission
be established by the United Nations. Subsidies and loans should be
made available to allow newly established industries in developing
nations to operate from the outset under the same pollution emission
standards applied in the extensively industrialized nations. The
commission should maintain a program of emission inspection for all
global, industrial pollutants.

4.B. INTRODUCTION

Humans have engaged in the management of ecological systems for, at least, the past 8,000 years. The intensity of such management and also the area of the planet covered by managed ecosystems have increased dramatically over the past few hundred years. At present, the ecosystems on earth range from intensely managed situations in cities, agriculture and pond-fish culture through the moderately or lightly managed systems of grazing, forestry, fishing and mariculture to the nearly untouched wilderness areas.

Approximately 11% of the land surface is intensely managed, 30% is moderately managed and 59% is subject to little management; and of the latter, about one-half is currently not usable by man (1). Most of the marine and fresh waters of the planet are not intensely managed.

Behind every attempt to manage ecological systems lies some idea about the human benefits to be derived by intentionally altering an ecosystem. In the management process, attention is often focused upon one or a few animal, plant or microbial populations within the ecosystem, and the desired outcome is the exploitation (agriculture, fisheries) or reduction (pest control, disease eradication) of some populations. Often both kinds of population change are required or desired simultaneously.

Benefit from a managed ecosystem is always dependent on interactions (linkages) between the manipulated or exploited populations and their physical and biological environments. When human intervention into ecosystem processes is small, management may proceed successfully in ignorance of these complex interactions. But, intense management of ecosystems as we know it today can never be dependable without a remarkably comprehensive understanding of the workings of the whole ecosystem. This is particularly true for the croplands under modern agricultural cultivation and the stone and concrete islands of the world's great urban centers. Furthermore, urban and agricultural systems are absolutely dependent on coupling with each other and with large auxiliary resources and industrial power. The focus of our report is, to a large degree, on such intensely managed ecosystems and on the extent to which ecological knowledge will help to better design and manage them for human benefit.

When the practice of industrial agriculture is interpreted using current knowledge of ecosystems, a picture emerges which suggests that the future dependability of one of our most essential biological systems is in grave doubt. It is important, therefore, to evaluate the risks associated with industrial agriculture and the degree to which ecological knowledge may help to reduce such risks.

The most impressive feature of industrial agriculture is its high biological productivity. However, the concentration of fertilizer, pesticides and fossil-fuel energy for mechanization to sustain these high yields is equally impressive. These critical, external supports for agriculture actually increase faster than yield itself as productivity is pushed higher and higher. Projected world requirements (2, 3) for these critical inputs call into question any assertion that agricultural systems of the present industrial form will be maintainable and stable over the long run. We have, therefore, ventured a number of recommendations concerning agriculture based on our general understanding of ecosystems and on the diversity-stability studies made by ecologists during the last two decades.

Less intensely managed ecosystems such as those which support forestry, grazing or fishing depend for their perpetuation on the interactions of many unexploited species. As in agriculture, the purpose is still a sustained yield from one or more of the species populations. However, compared to agriculture, little fossil-fuel is invested in the management of such ecosystems; and their perpetuation is left to nature.

In the unmanaged ecosystems diverse assemblages of biological species perpetuate themselves almost without human influence. From studies of natural and exploited ecosystems, ecologists have developed generalizations about the conditions and processes which lead to the regulation and perpetuation of ecosystems. We are thus able to draw some tentative conclusions about the stability of ecological systems. Our general conclusions are that the successful maintenance of man's productive systems will depend on an effective accounting and controlling of the major exchanges of energy and nutrients in ecosystems (see Section 4.C) and on the maintaining or creating of spatial, temporal and species diversity within such systems (see Sections 4.D and 4.E).

Increasing concentrations of toxic substances in the food chains of ecosystems are generating a new set of management problems. In the past all waste materials were degraded and recycled by natural processes. This is no longer true. Now man must manage ecosystems in ways which avoid the accumulation of materials inimical to human welfare either directly through toxic effects or indirectly through damage to the structure and supporting functions of ecosystems (see Section 4.F).

Human dependence on natural ecological processes imposes constraints on the degree to which ecosystems may be altered. Managed ecosystems tend toward a reduction of species diversity. As man-altered ecosystems are simplified, further human intervention is usually required to maintain stability. Biological evolution has imposed some of the strongest of these constraints. The species in natural communities fit together in complex ways that cannot easily be reconstructed when species are radically reassorted in intensely managed ecosystems. These coadaptive interrelations among the species provide the stabilizing and sustaining processes of the ecosystem. Symbiotic interactions between seed plants and fungi and between algae and animals, mimicry among butterflies, protective coloration in insects and the numerous defensive secretions of a wide variety of plants and animals attest to the ubiquity of such coadaptation. It remains to be learned to what degree man can disassemble these coadaptive complexes without incurring inordinate maintenance costs.

4.C. PROSPECTS AND PROBLEMS IN THE MANAGEMENT OF ECOLOGICAL SYSTEMS
Self-Maintaining Natural Ecosystems

Most natural or undisturbed ecosystems are characterized by low and sometimes intermittent flow of the mineral nutrients essential for plant, animal and microbial growth. These nutrients flow or move via the geochemical cycles (Chapter 3). This nutrient flow is literally carried by the hydrological (water) cycle, the nutrients returning to the land in the rain and snow. Under such circumstances biological communities evolved a reliance on internal nutrient cycling and self-regulation of ecosystem functions (4).

The cycling of whole complexes of nutrients has been elucidated for several ecosystems, particularly the north temperate forests (5, 6, 7). An example is shown in Figure 4.1 for a forest in Belgium (8). These data indicate that only 10% or less of the nutrient flow depends on inputs through rain and snow and that there are no other sizeable inputs. Thus the cost in nutrient input is exceedingly low for the 328 kg/ha in biomass (weight of living material) which it supports. It seems to be a universal condition in such undisturbed forests that the mineral nutrients are for the most part bound up in the living plants and animals. As a consequence, the recycling is very tightly controlled. A forest such as the one in Belgium is then almost self-contained or, put another way, it is weakly coupled with its external environment. Similar results have been reported for the second growth Douglas Fir ecosystem of the Pacific Northwest of the U.S.A. (see Table 4.1) (9).

The importance of the intact biological structure of an ecosystem in maintaining internal nutrient flow was demonstrated experimentally in the Hubbard Brook watershed ecosystem in New Hampshire (10). Here, again, the only important input of nutrients was in the rain; and the inputs were small, usually with an annual average of less than 1 mg of any specific nutrient per liter of rain for the ten nutrients measured. After the trees were cut and herbicides applied, a significant loss of nutrients was observed in the altered parts of the forest but not in the uncut parts (see Table 4.2).

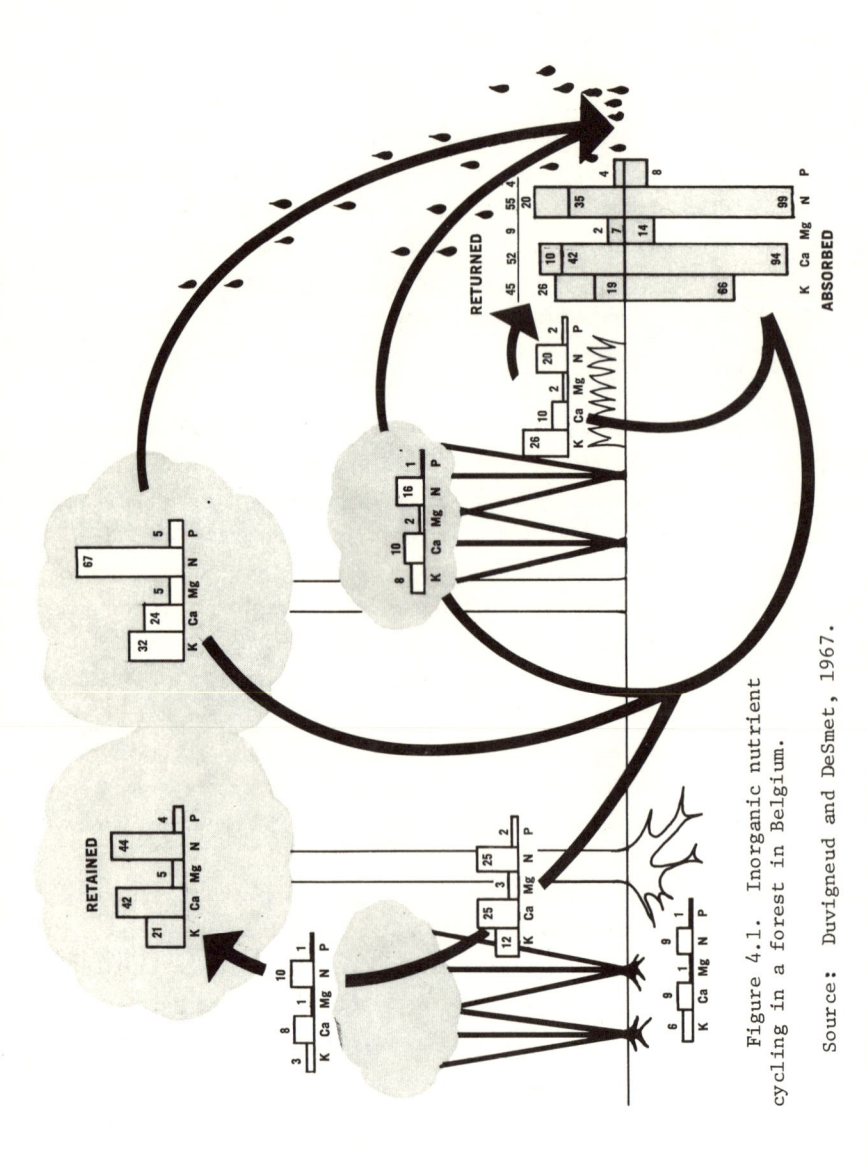

Figure 4.1. Inorganic nutrient cycling in a forest in Belgium.

Source: Duvigneud and DeSmet, 1967.

	N	P	K	Ca
Input (precipitation)	1.1	Trace	0.8	2.8
Uptake by forest	38.8	7.23	29.4	24.4
Total return to forest floor	16.4	0.64	15.8	18.5
Leached from forest floor	4.8	0.95	10.5	17.4
Leached beyond root zone	0.6	0.02	1.0	4.5

Table 4.1. Annual transfer of N, P, K, and Ca (kg/ha) between components of the Douglas-fir ecosystem.

Source: Cole, Gessel and Dice, 1967.

	1966-67		1967-68	
	Cut	Uncut	Cut	Uncut
Ca	-7.5	-0.8	-9.0	-0.9
K	-2.3	-0.1	-3.6	-0.2
Al	-1.7	-0.1	-2.4	-0.3
Mg	-1.6	-0.3	-1.8	-0.3
Na	-1.7	-0.6	-1.7	-0.7
NH_4	+0.1	+0.2	+0.2	+0.3
NO_3	-43.0	+1.5	-62.8	+1.1
SO_4	-0.5	-0.8	0	-1.0
HCO_3	-0.1	+0.2	0	-0.3
Cl	-0.1	+0.2	-0.4	0
SiO_2 aq	-6.6	-3.6	-6.9	-3.6
Total	-65.0	-4.6	-88.4	-5.9

Table 4.2. Comparative net gains or losses of dissolved solids in runoff following clear cutting in the Hubbard Brook Experimental Forest for the period 1 June to 31 May. In metric tons/km^2/year.

Source: Likens, Bormann, Johnson, Fisher, and Pierce, 1970.

Natural Ecosystems with High Nutrient Flow

Some natural ecosystems maintain high productivity due to high rates of nutrient flow from and to other ecosystems. Two examples, the salt marsh ecosystem and the marine anchoveta community of the Peruvian upwellings will serve as case studies. Coral reefs and flowing springs offer other examples.

Teal (11) presented an energy budget (see Table 4.3) for a Georgia salt marsh. About 45% of the organic material synthesized in the salt marsh is exported to the adjoining estuary.

The salt marsh community is simpler both in the number of species and the number of interconnections among the species (see Figure 4.2) than the forest ecosystems. Further, the fluctuations of biological processes within the marsh are considerable (12) as would be expected given the extensive climatic and tidal fluctuations which occur.

Nutrient budgets for the marsh are not available, but considerable evidence suggests that the tidal flows and runoff of fresh waters into the marsh provide a moderately strong coupling between the marsh and adjoining terrestrial and estuarine ecosystems. Stability is maintained through a pattern of nutrient renewal as dependable as the tidal cycle or stream flow across the marsh. Internal self-regulation of nutrients is replaced by a strong driving of nutrient flow from the outside. The maintenance cost of supplying nutrients to the marsh is paid by natural physical forces; and together the marsh and the estuary, though quite different ecosystems, are coupled to make a single relatively closed system.

The anchoveta fishery of the Peruvian current depends similarly on nutrients driven into the system by upwelling from 200 meters down in the ocean along a 320 km stretch off the Peruvian coast. Historically the anchoveta were preyed upon by marine animals and sea birds. Cormorants, gannets and pelicans alone removed an estimated 0.85 million metric tons annually. The growth of the anchoveta fishing by man since 1950 is shown in Table 4.4. Today this fishery produces two million metric tons of fish meal from a total annual harvest of nearly 20 mmt of

Input as light	600,000 kcal/m^2/yr.
Loss in photosynthesis	563,620 or 93.9%
Gross production	36,380 or 6.1% of light
Producer respiration	28,175 or 77% of gross production
Net production	8,205 kcal/m^2/yr.
Bacterial respiration	3,890 or 47% of net production
Herbivore/consumer respiration	596 or 7.0% of net production
Carnivore/consumer respiration	48 or 0.6% of net production
Total energy dissipation by consumers	4,534 or 55% of net production
Export	3,671 or 45% of net production

Table 4.3. Summary of salt marsh energetics.
Source: Teal, 1962.

Year	Thousands Metric Tons
1951	7.2
1954	16.5
1957	64.5
1960	558.3
1963	1,159.2
1966	1,470.5
1967	1,816.0
1968	1,922.0

Table 4.4. Fish meal production from annual Peruvian anchoveta catch.
Source: Paulik, 1971.

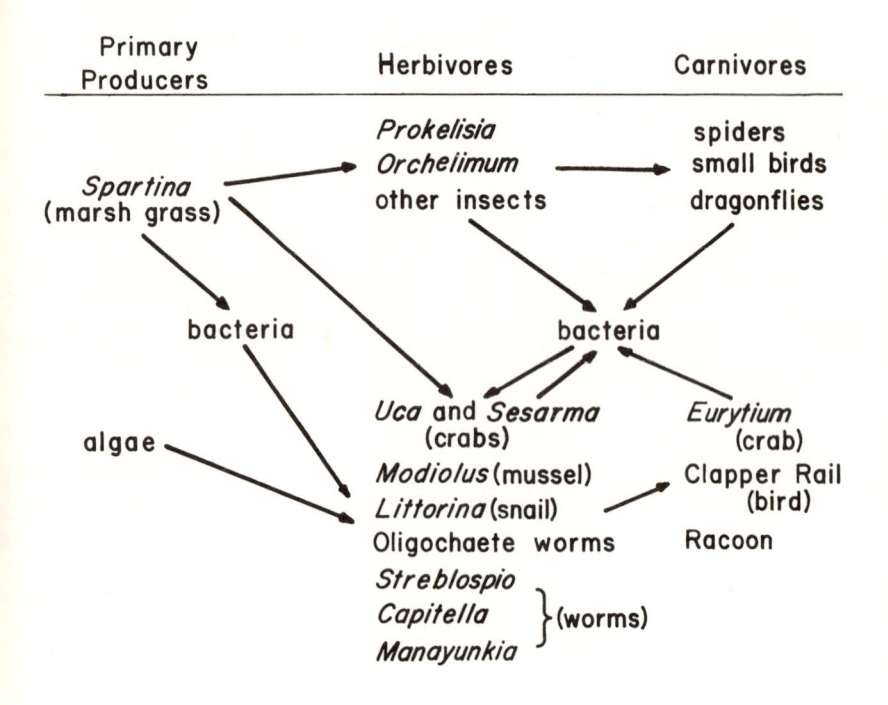

Primary Producers	Herbivores	Carnivores
Spartina (marsh grass)	*Prokelisia* *Orcheiimum* other insects	spiders small birds dragonflies
bacteria	bacteria	
algae	*Uca* and *Sesarma* (crabs) *Modiolus* (mussel) *Littorina* (snail) Oligochaete worms *Streblospio* *Capitella* *Manayunkia* } (worms)	*Eurytium* (crab) Clapper Rail (bird) Racoon

Figure 4.2. Food web (trophic structure) of the biological community in a Georgia salt marsh. The arrows indicate the passage of energy and nutrients from the producers (plants) through the herbivore and carnivore levels. The diagram is much simpler than the real situation which contains nearly 100 species of animals, two higher plant species and many algal, bacterial and protozoan species.

Source: Teal, 1962. © 1962 by the Duke University Press.

anchoveta. This currently represents about 20% of the world's total catch of marine fishes (13). Such an astoundingly productive system exists only because of its strong and consistent coupling with a vast and dependable nutrient and physical power source. There is here a situation similar to intensive human agriculture.

Strongly Driven Systems of Modern Agriculture

Human agricultural systems range from self-maintaining, subsistence systems to the strongly driven systems dependent on external power and nutrient sources.

The demands of increasing human populations and the economies of scale associated with mechanized farming have led man to design agricultural ecosystems using a single crop species (monoculture). Such systems are weak in self-regulatory capacity.

The procedures of industrial agriculture have greatly raised the photosynthetic conversion of solar energy into edible plant and animal tissues per unit area. This improved biological efficiency requires, however, a disproportionate increase in expenditures outside the agricultural ecosystem to maintain the nutrient flows required. FAO (3) data show the disproportionate ratios between some input increases, especially fertilizers and pesticides, and the consequent increase in agricultural yield (see Table 4.5).

Until the last decade rural landscapes could absorb the flow of wastes and unused nutrients from agriculture with little apparent environmental degradation. Now, conspicuous environmental degradation is beginning to impose localized reductions in real agricultural output, in addition to diminishing the aesthetic value of rural areas.

Modern agriculture is adequately stable only because it is strongly coupled with chemical and energy flows from a dependable external source--the industrial complex. Modern agriculture also depends on natural or partially managed ecosystems to absorb and remove chemical by-products, pesticides, domestic sewage, runoff of excess nutrients, etc., without cost.

Identified Current Inputs	Value 1962	Value 1985	Change 1962 to 1985 percent	Growth rates 1962 to 1985 percent per year
	Million dollars at 1962 prices			
Seed	1,673.1	2,473.6	+ 48	1.7
Feed	3,028.1	6,993.8	+ 131	3.7
Fertilizers	671.4	8,362.4	+1,146	11.6
Crop Protection	180.0	2,076.9	+1,054	11.2
Mechanization	797.1	2,610.2	+ 227	5.3
Irrigation	1,494.1	2,433.7	+ 63	2.1
Total Crop and Livestock	7,845.1	24,950.6	+ 218	5.2
Fishery	358.9	983.7	+ 174	4.5
Forestry	183.9	413.0	+ 125	3.6
Total Identified Inputs	8,387.9	26,347.3	+ 214	5.1
Total Output (Gross Value)	54,900.0	121,640.4	+ 122	3.5

Table 4.5. Identified inputs of agriculture.

Source: FAO, 1970.

The importance of an auxiliary energy source in human agriculture is made clear by the following series of ecosystem analyses (14, 15). Figure 4.3 is a diagram which shows part of the flow of energy in a rain forest system in which man is almost inconsequential. Figure 4.4 depicts energy flow in a tribal grazing system, managed by man but not designed by him in any substantial way. Figure 4.5 shows monsoon agriculture in India, a system designed and managed by man, but not dependent on mechanization, fertilizers, pesticides or a larger external energy source. All of these inputs become essential for modern industrial agriculture as shown in Figure 4.6. It is also clear that the ecological systems in this series become progressively simpler as human design and engineering of the system increase in importance.

Conclusion

The simple, highly productive systems of intensive agriculture are absolutely dependent on a reliable industrial base. As developing countries become more deeply committed to industrial agricultural practices, in order to feed their peoples, they will also acquire dependence on the industrial complexes of other nations. Eventually all the components of industrial agriculture may be transferred to the developing nations of the world. But during the transitional period a lack of cooperation and coordination between nations can produce severe disruptions in the agricultural systems of the developing nations. It must be accepted as a general principle that the coupling of industry in one country with the agriculture of another involves a direct sharing of responsibility for the welfare of the people dependent on that agricultural system.

RECOMMENDATION

We recommend that carefully worked out international accords be concluded for situations where the industrial base of one nation is used to promote and sustain modern agricultural practices in another nation.

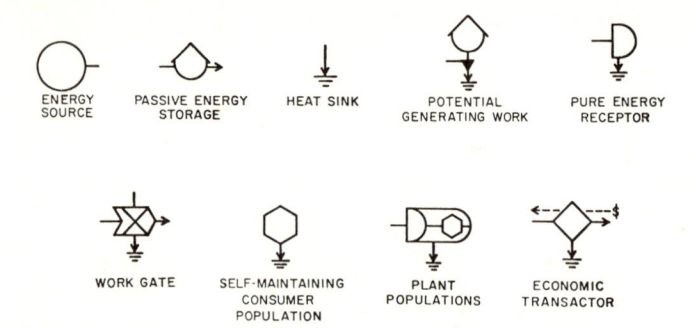

Energy network symbols, figs. 4.3--4.6. Symbols and figs. 4.3--4.6 all from Odum 1967; for full discussion, see that source.

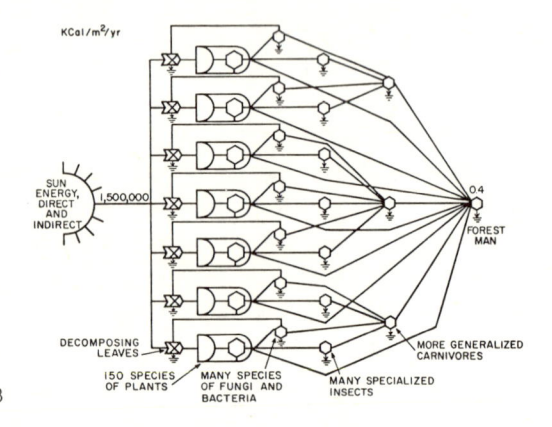

Figure 4.3

Figure 4.3 Complex energy transfer pattern in part of a rain forest ecosystem. Found where climate is relatively invariant. Man is found in low densities of about one person or less per square kilometer. Examples are the forests of the Amazon and Congo.

Figure 4.4 Energy transfer in a simple tribal grazing system in Uganda. Grains, meat, blood and milk are used as food. The cattle serve to smooth out fluctuations in climate. Supports about 25 people per square kilometer.

Figure 4.5. Energy transfer under monsoon agriculture in India. An agricultural system not subsidized with fossil fuels and in a climate which has sharp seasonal changes alternating between wet and dry. Supports about 230 people per square kilometer.

Figure 4.6. Energy transfer in fuel-subsidized industrial agriculture such as that in the United States. Sixty-one people per square kilometer support almost 2,000 people in the cities dependent on such an agricultural system.

Figure 4.4

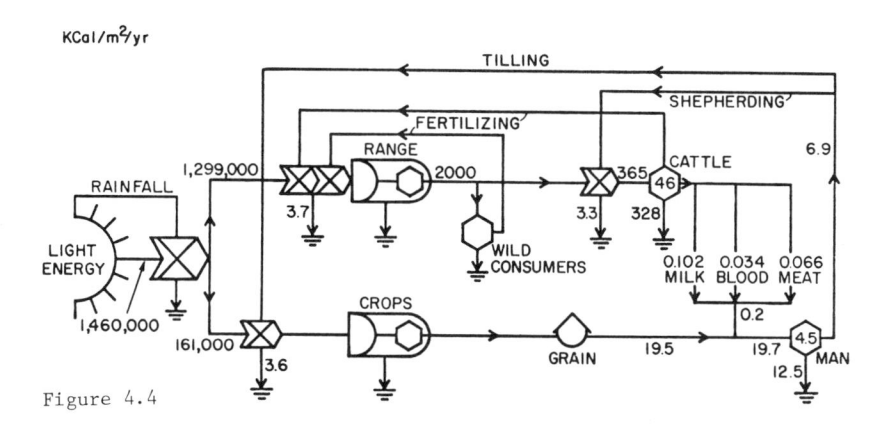

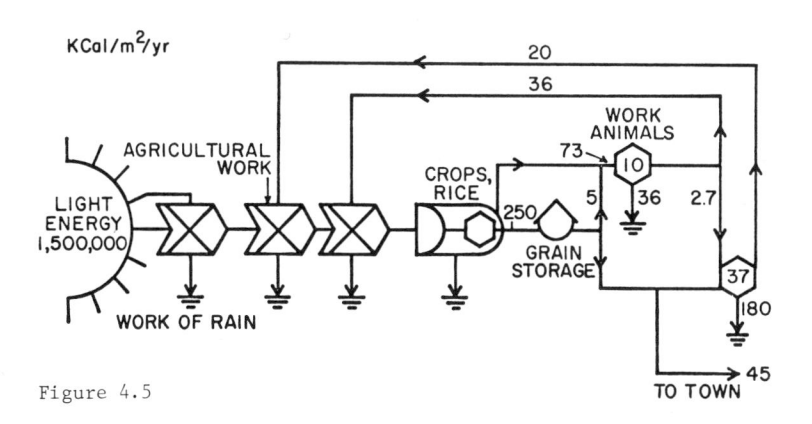

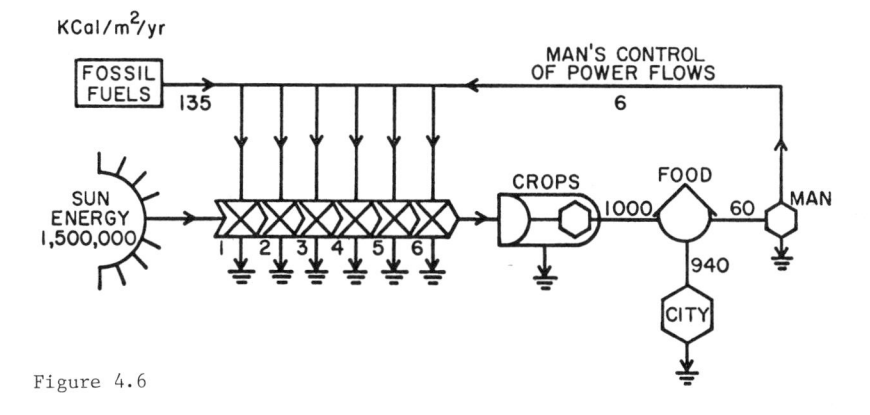

Figure 4.5

Figure 4.6

Conclusion

It is now essential that the one-way flow of nutrient materials from agricultural land to urban areas and to fresh and salt waters be altered by returning these nutrients to croplands or by diverting such nutrients to other productive uses such as aquaculture. All future designs for intensely managed ecosystems must involve such recycling of nutrients and wastes.

4.D. DIVERSITY AND STABILITY

It is a working hypothesis among ecologists that diversity enhances stability in an ecosystem (16-34). Two major questions involving the application of the diversity-stability hypothesis are examined here: 1) How good is the scientific evidence that diversity does in fact enhance stability? 2) What kinds of diversification of managed ecosystems would be effective in stabilizing production and still not interfere with harvesting and marketing or be uneconomical in other ways?

Evidence for the Relation Between Diversity and Stability

Diversity of Species

Two aspects of species diversity are generally considered together: 1) the number of species and 2) the degree to which a few of the species predominate numerically. Thus, a forest community which has ten species but which has 99 percent of all the individuals in one species is less diverse than one with five species all equally abundant.

There is evidence that reducing the diversity of communities can reduce stability. In balsam fir forests the lowest infestation by spruce budworm occurs in patches of forest made up of a mixture of species--conifers interspersed with several hardwood tree species (54). When the hardwood species were removed, the spruce budworm reached epidemic densities in these stands. On a local basis, the hardwood trees cause discontinuity between susceptible individuals of balsam fir, retarding the spread of the budworm epidemic. Species diversity in this example is thus combined with spatial heterogeneity.

Species diversity may also enhance stability by increasing the number of links between important commercial species and other species in the ecosystem. For example, it is important to have flowering plants present to provide nectar for the adults of parasitic insects that attack and help to control caterpillars which in turn feed upon plants of commercial value. This has been shown also for mite species (35). A good example of this kind of linking is provided by the successful biological control of the grape leaf hopper, Erythroneura elegantula. Its parasite, Anagrus epos, also feeds on another non-pest leaf hopper which in turn feeds on wild blackberries. Planting small patches of wild blackberries maintains the parasite in vineyards and so controls the pest Erythroneura (36).

Certain kinds of diversity may produce instability. There are a large number of examples in the literature indicating that pest species are very often exotic species. The instability here arises because the introduced pest species and other species in the community are not coadapted. Thus, in considering simple communities, we suggest that instability is generated, not so much by having fewer species than communities elsewhere, but by having species artificially and incompletely linked to one another.

The more species of actual or potential parasites, predators and pathogens each species has, the more likely it is that one or more will continue to operate and hold its population stable. Similarly, a species will be able to survive temporary fluctuation in one of their food sources if they have other sources available to them. In addition there must be flexibility in the interactions, so that if one link in the system cannot work, other links become more effective. An example is a predatory population that feeds upon several prey species and is able to "switch" from one prey to another as their abundances change (37). This stabilizing mechanism will operate more effectively where there is spatial heterogeneity (37-39).

There is no doubt that natural communities have such multiple predator-prey linkages. The average herbivore insect species in unmanaged terrestrial communities has dozens of species which prey on it (40). The deleterious effects of inadvertently removing or reducing predatory populations with insecticides is well documented (41). Pest epidemics recur when controlling predators are severely reduced, and new pests (upset pests) are created when hitherto harmless species increase in abundance after their predators have been reduced or eliminated (42, 43).

Many successful cases of biological control illustrate the effectiveness of such regulatory systems. Complex cases are known where a pest is controlled by having a number of predatory species that differ either in the area of the pest population over which they hunt or in the time of year at which they are most abundant (44). There are also examples to show that the presence of alternative prey species enhances the stability of biological pest control situations (45).

Spatial Heterogeneity

Spatial heterogeneity includes differences in biological and physical properties in space. It is a mosaic of patches either temporally out of phase with each other or qualitatively different in biological composition. There is evidence from laboratory studies of populations of predators and prey that the physical structure of the environment can enhance stability (46-48). The variations in structure provide refuges for part of the prey populations (39, 49). Spatial heterogeneity also introduces statistical elements into population interactions so that in different parts of the ecosystem different events are occurring. This prevents drastic fluctuations of animal and plant populations over large areas. Spatial heterogeneity is probably the most fundamental and important aspect of the relation between diversity and stability. From theoretical studies we know some possible mechanisms for such a diversity-stability relation (50-53).

The interaction between spruce budworm and fir trees in the forests of eastern Canada illustrates the importance of heterogeneity and discontinuity. Isolated stands were shown to have lower infestation rates than continuous stands (54). The persistence of mussel populations on the California coast in the face of great instability in local patches can be attributed to similar patterning (55, 39). Different events occur on different parts of the shore in turban snail populations attacked by starfish, and movement between areas seems important in stabilizing the system (56).

Detailed study of the insect species diversity of hedge rows, adjacent pastures and adjacent bean fields has shown that species diversity on vegetation and in the air above varies in a consistent way over spatially heterogeneous vegetation (see Figure 4.7). Diversity was greatest in and over the hedge, lowest in the pasture and intermediate in the bean field. It appears that a hedge row may enrich the insect species diversity for a distance of 3 to 10 times the height of the hedge to the leeward and 1 to 2 times the height of the hedge to the windward (57).

Differences Among Individuals of the Same Species

Variety within a population allows it to compensate for variation in the environment in time and space. Individual plants and animals vary in susceptibility to attack from diseases and "enemies" (predators and parasites), and a mixture of individuals of different susceptibilities is less likely to promote outbreaks of the disease or enemy.

One important variable is age. The best examples come from forests (58, 54). In balsam fir forests of eastern Canada, mature trees around 80 years old are more susceptible to attack from the spruce budworm than are younger trees. As a consequence, large tracts of forest that are made up of mature trees suffer up to 100% infestation. By contrast, areas with a mixture of ages suffer less infestation of the susceptible age groups.

We expect genetic differences among individuals in a population to provide stabilizing influences similar to those provided by

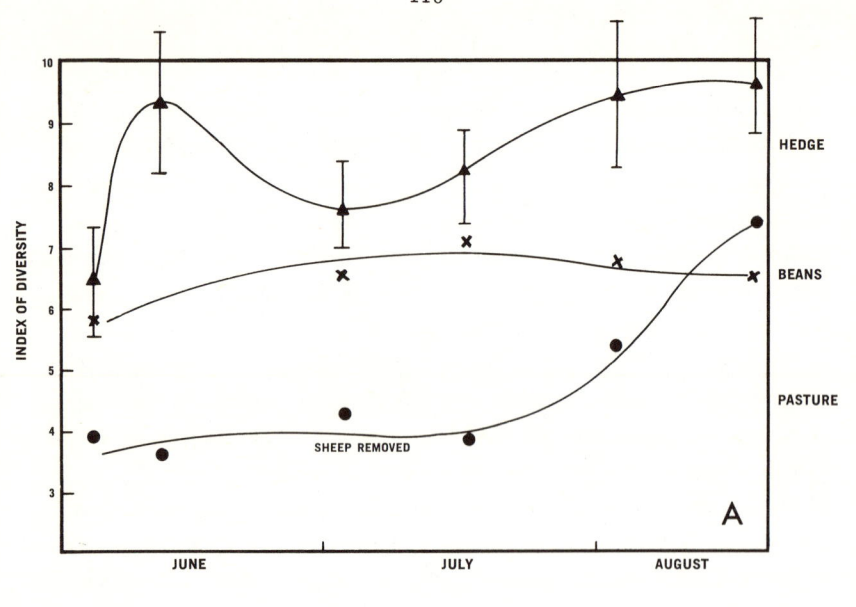

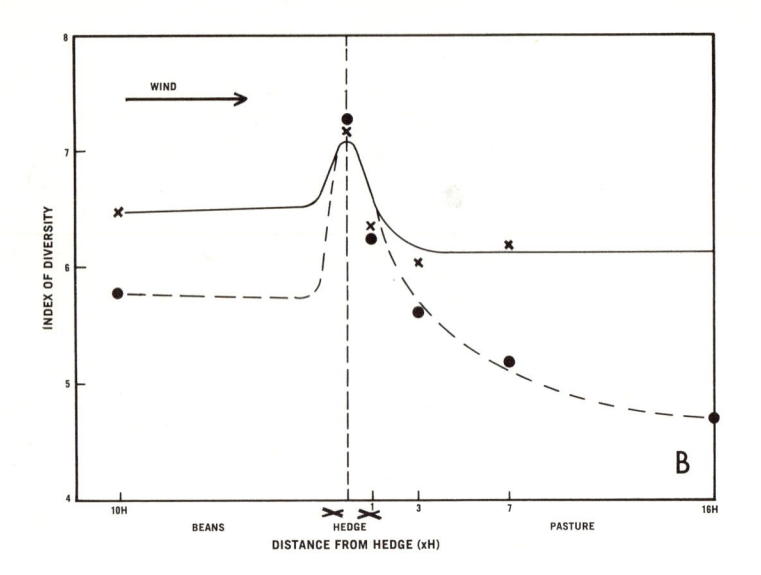

Figure 4.7. Patterns of species diversity on vegetation (a) and in the air (b) across three different patches of vegetation—beanfield, hedge, and pasture.

Source: Lewis, 1969.

differences in age, but we have not found clear examples of this. An example of the effect of individual differences, which may or may not be of genetic origin, occurs in the case of prickly pear plants (Opuntia) in Australia (59, 60). The plants in any small area vary in their attractiveness to the moths that eat them, and the resulting patchiness of the attacks on the plants leads to a stable interaction between the plants and the moth population.

Conclusions

There is abundant evidence for the idea that diversity of several kinds enhances the stability of populations, communities and ecosystems. Two specific conclusions are drawn. 1) For a strong relation between diversity and stability to exist, it is important that the biological community be made up of coadapted species. 2) Spatial heterogeneity, both in itself and in its interactions with other kinds of diversity, is a crucial component, yielding stability. At the same time, there is enough doubt over specific mechanisms that we cannot state the diversity-stability relationship as an invariant rule. In addition, since ecological diversity comprises a number of factors and mechanisms, one has to specify the particular aspect of diversity involved in any single case.

4.E. DIVERSITY, STABILITY AND PEST CONTROL

The degree and mode of application of the diversity-stability relationship varies among different types of managed systems. Along the gradient from natural systems to intensely managed systems, man intentionally reduces the diversity of the system in order to maximize the production of one or a few components. At the same time, the relationship between diversity and stability has applications even in intensely managed agricultural ecosystems.

Problems with Chemical Pest Control

The instability in agricultural pest species generated by simplification is largely controlled by two kinds of activities—crop breeding for pest resistance and large-scale use of pesticides. In spite of some problems, the system has been eminently successful at producing consistently high yields of food for more than 30 years.

There is, however, reason to suspect that major difficulties will develop in the next few decades—difficulties that may be surmounted only by starting now to develop alternative technologies. Two particular kinds of problems are evident. The first concerns the long-term dependability of agricultural systems based on chemical control. The second includes the broader environmental consequences of the widespread use of these chemicals (discussed in Section 4.G).

The problem of the breakdown of chemical control is perhaps best illustrated by the following quotation from Conway (41).

> Over a hundred species of insect and spider mite attack cotton in the United States. But only a few of these in any area are key pests in the sense that if not controlled they would, year after year, cause serious damage to the crop. Over most of the cotton-growing acreage in the United States the boll weevil (<u>Anthonomus grandis</u>) is the key pest, and before the use of organic pesticides it caused considerable losses of cotton. There are, in addition, a number of other pests of lesser importance, such as the American bollworm (<u>Heliothis zea</u>), the cotton fleahopper, the cotton leafworm, and the cotton aphid. In 1943 when DDT became available it was found to control the bollworm and the fleahopper, although not the boll weevil or the other pests. But then 2 years later benzene hexachloride (BHC), another organochlorine insecticide, was found to be effective against all the pests that DDT did not control. In the years that followed, cotton pest control came to rely very heavily on these two compounds and on a number of other organochlorine compounds. Although resistance by cotton aphid to BHC and by leafworm to toxaphene began to show up quite soon, in the early 1950's growers and entomologists felt confident that cotton pests were well under control.
>
> In 1955 this confidence was shattered by the development of high resistance to a range of organochlorine insecticides by

the boll weevil in the lower Mississippi Valley. This proved
to be the beginning of the development of widespread resistance
in nearly all the other major cotton pests. The change was
made to organophosphorus insecticides and then to carbamates,
but in each case it was not long before resistance occurred.
As a report of a panel of the President's Science Advisory
Committee has stated: "By the end of the 1963 season, almost
every major cotton pest species contained local populations
that had developed resistance to one or more of the chlorinated
hydrocarbons. Moreover, strains have developed in the laboratory that are resistant to all of these." In addition to this
resistance effect, the heavy insecticide spraying had severely
depleted the numbers of beneficial parasites and predators, and
upsurges occurred of many pests which had hitherto been considered of secondary or minor importance. The American bollworm
and other related bollworms, spider mites, and aphids were a-
mong the species which became considerably more important
than before.

The story of cotton as an illustration of the failings
of modern pesticides is by no means unique. Similar case
histories, although perhaps not quite so dramatic, could be
described for a number of crops, such as apples and citrus in
North America or cocoa in the tropics. There is also evidence
that throughout the world many cereal crops are following
the same pattern. The problem, then, is not a minor one nor
is it restricted to special situations. It is a general
and growing problem equal to, if not more important than, the
direct consequences of pesticide use on wildlife and man.

Resistance of insects to the insecticides used in agriculture is
increasing rapidly. The changes in pest species which allow them to
survive higher and higher concentrations of insecticides are genetic
changes due to natural selection. Thus the process proceeds by biological evolution in the usual Darwinian sense. Figure 4.8 records
the known increase in resistance over the last sixty years. However,
the graph does not tell the whole story. Large numbers of insect species which we do not examine because they are not now pests are being
subjected to similar selection for resistance so that when some of
these species erupt for the first time as agricultural pests it is
likely that they will already possess significant resistance to the
pesticides in use.

The problem of pesticide resistance among insects is further

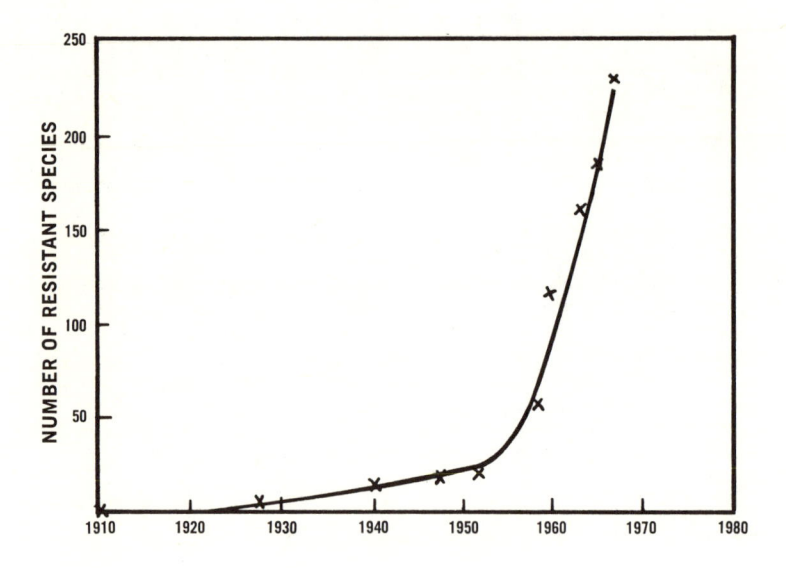

Figure 4.8. The rise in number of species of insects and mites resistant to one or more pesticides.

Source: Conway, 1971.

complicated by the phenomenon of cross-resistance, where a species
that acquires resistance to one specific insecticide will also possess
some degree of resistance to other pesticides. There are presently
four groups of pesticides within each of which cross-resistance is
known (41): 1) the DDT group of organochlorides; 2) the cyclodiene
derivative group of organochlorides, to which dieldrin belongs; 3) the
organophosphorus compounds used as insecticides; and 4) the carbamate
insecticides. Table 4.6 gives some indication of the degree of cross-
resistance shown by citrus red mites which had first acquired resistance to the insecticide Systox. As this table indicates, the phenomenon of cross-resistance among current and potential pest species
is amenable to experimental analysis. Furthermore, the appearance of
cross-resistance suggests that our ability to keep ahead of the development of resistance is limited by the agricultural chemist's inability
to generate safe insect poisons of sufficiently great variety. Data
from extensive studies of cross-resistance in houseflies reveal that
resistance is often greatest for some insecticide other than the one
used to induce resistance (see also Table 4.6) (61). Available data
suggest that the genetic basis for insecticide resistance is not
usually simple. Cross-resistance casts doubt on the future effectiveness of sequential applications of different pesticides to overcome
resistance.

Conclusion

The phenomenon of insecticide cross-resistance should be subjected
to extensive study using both current and potential pest insects. A
diagnosis of the present state of cross-resistance is required in order
to predict the effectiveness and subsidiary consequences of chemical
control programs. Further, because different geographical areas have
different pest species and because populations of the same species
usually display genetic differentiation in different geographical
areas, it may be necessary to conduct studies of cross-resistance
in most agricultural areas separately.

Compound	Times increase in resistance over a normal population
Trithion	15,000
Iso-Systox	8,570
Methyl Systox	8,000
Schradan	2,000
EPN	1,400
Parathion	883
Phosdrin	350
Pyrazoxon	300
Systox	266
Tetram	111
Delnav	100
Disyston	25
Diazinon	12
Malathion	8
Ethion	8

Table 4.6. Cross-resistance of citrus red mites to various organophosphorous pesticides.

Source: O'Brien, 1960.

Integrated Pest Control

Integrated pest control rests on the view that a crop and its pests form an ecological system. No single control mechanism is considered a panacea. Natural controls are recognized as potentially powerful agents and are manipulated as required. Pesticides are considered as ultimate weapons, to be used only when necessary and in as small a quantity as is needed.

The components of integrated control are shown below. In any given situation some or all of these components may be needed.

Integrated Control

Field population dynamics and systems analysis for decision-making	Crop and habitat management ("cultural control")	Biological control	Crop Breeding for pest resistance	Pesticide use

The development of integrated control techniques is only beginning. Possibly the most fully developed example is in several cotton growing valleys in Peru. In the Canete valley a number of changes were made after a disastrous experience created by heavy use of pesticides. Cotton production on marginal lands was forbidden. Ratooning, that is allowing the crop to persist for two to three years, was stopped because it allows more pest individuals to complete their life cycles, thus increasing pest population growth in the second year. The soil was "dry-cultivated" to kill bollworm pupae. Uniform planting dates, timing and methods of plowing were established, and a cotton-free fallow period was introduced. The valley was repopulated by beneficial insects from neighboring valleys that had not been sprayed, and beneficial insects were fostered in a variety of other ways.

(Notice that the nearby pool of diversity was needed for this technique.) Synthetic organic pesticides were prohibited except by dispensation of a special commission. Doutt and Smith (36) point out that: "As a result of this new integrated control program, there was a rapid and striking reduction in the severity of the cotton pest problem. The whole complex of formerly innocuous species, which cropped up in the organic insecticide period, reverted to their innocuous status. Furthermore, the intensity of the key pest problems also diminished, and there was an overall reduction in direct pest control costs. By the next year, the yield was back to 526 kilograms per hectare [after plummeting to 300 kg/ha just before the shift to integrated control] and since has varied from 724 to 1,036 kilograms per hectare. These are the highest yields in the history of the Valley."

Biological Control

Biological control involves the use of predatory, parasitic or pathogenic species which attack a pest species. It has been most successful in controlling exotic pest species.

Efforts at biological control have ranged from spectacular success to total failure. One of the most famous success stories is the control in California citrus orchards of the cottony-cushion scale insect (Icerya) by the lady-bug Rhodalia. Another is control of the prickly pear Opuntia in Australia by the moth Cactoblastis. Huffaker (44) records 70 complete successes and a total of 250 cases of complete or partial control.

Microbial organisms (pathogens) can be effective in biological control. One early example was the successful use of the milky spore disease to control the Japanese beetle. More recently, much work has been done on a bacterium Bacillus thuringiensis, and it is now registered in the U.S.A. for the control of such insects as the imported cabbage worm, tobacco budworm and the alfalfa caterpillar. A polyhedral virus is also used for control of the alfalfa caterpillar in California, and encouraging results have been obtained for the control of cabbage looper. In the field of weed control, a rust (Uromycis rumicis) appears promising for the control of certain plant species of the genus Rumex.

Another mechanism, less widely used, involves the release of vast numbers of sterile males of a pest species. This decreases the mating success of native, fertile males and reduces the pest's population (127). The sterile male technique has considerable potential. The screw-worm fly, a major pest of livestock, was the first insect controlled in this manner. Sufficient information has now been obtained to indicate that sterile male release may prove useful in controlling the Mediterranean fruit fly, oriental fruit fly, Mexican fruit fly, pink bollworm, boll weevil, tobacco hornworm, codling moth and fruit flies of the genus Drosophila. The technique is most likely to be effective where the pest population is isolated. This suggests that it may be more effective where large monocultures are replaced by more diversified crop patterns.

The fact that biological control has met with only modest success is no real measure of its future potential within integrated control. Biological control has generally operated as an isolated mechanism rather than as part of a comprehensive plan. Biological control using natural enemies is less likely to work in an ecological "island" surrounded by chemical pest control. Furthermore, the financial support of biological control research, compared with that for pesticide research from all sources, has been small. We must expect a long lag in the development of this rather complex ecological technology. Pesticide research rests on a large body of fairly straightforward chemistry and physiology. Biological control workers are still developing the general techniques of biological control (63).

Crop and Habitat Management

Crop and habitat management both have a variety of purposes, but in general the idea is to manage things so that we take advantage of the biology of the crop, its pests, and their enemies. By managing the crop properly we may be able to obtain high yields and at the same time attack the pest at "weak points" in its life cycle, prevent it from spreading through the crops or obtain other aids to control. By manipulating the habitat surrounding the crop, parts of the pest life cycle can be broken or natural enemies can be augmented. All of these reduce the use of pesticides and clearly fit in with the use of other techniques, such as biological control. Crop and habitat management provide good examples of the application of the ecological findings concerning spatial heterogeneity and species diversity.

A good example is provided by alfalfa management (64) in the Great Central Valley of California. Here alfalfa covers 20 percent of the land under irrigation. About 1,000 insects and mites, of which more than half are parasites and predators, are associated with the alfalfa. One pest, a bug Lygus, increases in alfalfa and moves into other crops such as cotton. The practice of strip cutting of the alfalfa has been introduced in several areas with great success. Alternate strips are cut so that half the crop remains standing at any one time. This controls Lygus populations by killing the nymphs, causing adults to migrate and suffer high mortality, and at the same time allows too little time for a new generation of migrants to develop before the remaining strips are cut. The predator and parasite populations are favored by the strip cutting, which improves their synchrony with the pest.

Another instance of successful habitat management was demonstrated by Stern (65). Here alfalfa was planted between cotton strips. The cotton served as a trap for the Lygus pest and as a source of natural enemies.

Other examples of crop and habitat management are collected in the Proceedings of Tall Timbers Conference in 1969 and 1970 (66), and in Huffaker (44).

Crop Breeding

An important method of pest control is the development of resistant crop varieties. Most of the success in this field has been in breeding for resistance to plant diseases, but some notable successes have been recorded for resistance to insects. Resistant varieties of wheat are virtually immune to the Hessian fly; resistant strains of alfalfa have been developed that preclude attack by the spotted alfalfa aphid; and good progress has been made in developing sweet corn varieties resistant to the corn earworm.

Unfortunately, pest organisms can evolve to overcome such resistance in plants, so the process may be a continual one of keeping ahead of the pest. This is especially the case with fungi and bacteria, which have short generation times. For example, a new variety of rust disease appears every three or four years in the United States.

Pesticide Use with Field Monitoring of Pests

The first prerequisite for better pesticide use is accurate measurement of pest distribution and abundance in each situation. The current widespread practice of applying pesticides by the calendar, rather than in response to real pest population buildup, not only wastes pesticide but also endangers the remainder of an integrated program. When the pest is monitored, more efficient control can be obtained by fewer, well-timed applications. In addition, many pests change in numbers in response to the weather, so that we can forecast imminent pest increases. In cotton crops in Colombia, the number of applications per season was reduced from 18 to 20, to 9 or 10 by monitoring the pests.

Pests can be sprayed at times or places where it will not affect their natural enemies. For example, cockchafer beetles which are pests on rubber trees in Malaya can be sprayed in the soil when they are pupae at times when their parasites are not in the soil (41). Selective pesticides are preferable, where they are available.

The less frequently pesticides are used, the more likely they are to be effective since resistance will develop more slowly.

Pest Control in Developing Nations

Great expansion of chemical control of pests will be necessary to meet world food needs in the future. In particular there will be much expansion of pesticide use in the tropics and subtropics. At the same time, we must recognize that the massive application of such poisons can only be a temporary stop-gap rather than a long-term or permanent solution. The problems of continual development of resistance by pests, the creation of "upset" and "resurgence" pests (when beneficial predators are reduced) and the widespread simplifying of biological communities due to pesticides all create the possibility that in the future our agricultural system will become undependable. These problems are likely to be more intense in the tropics and subtropics where pests have more generations per year and sometimes no season of adverse weather and in addition where there is less scientific expertise to cope with increased problems. It would be unwise to assume that the successes of the last few decades in the temperate zone and the last few years in the tropics guarantee continued success.

In the tropics in particular we face additional problems (67-69 and Chapter 5). Most of the herbicides developed for temperate regions do not work well in the tropics. High rainfall further reduces their effect by diluting them and moving them from the site of application. The soil is often highly variable from place to place and so the response of a single crop, or crop strain, varies enormously. These differences have resulted in an indigenous agriculture which is a mosaic pattern. This suggests that it would be wise to continue to incorporate spatial heterogeneity in tropical agriculture.

Another important factor is that large areas of the tropics may not be suited to cereal production and would be much better used for maintaining either semi-natural forest or tall crops. These are circumstances where ecological ideas of diversity and stability are most applicable. In addition, since such crops are long-lived, the technique of integrated control (particularly biological control) can be most easily applied because the pest and control populations can persist together continuously in one place as a stable interaction without the periodic interruption caused by complete harvests.

We must make certain that our temporary reliance on chemical control does not prevent the development of other options. The developed nations are both at an advantage and at a disadvantage in this regard. Successful programs of integrated control have been developed to some extent, but much of the raw material needed for the successful use of natural biological diversity in biological control has already been removed.

In the developing nations, particularly in the subtropics and tropics, much of the diversity still exists; but there is as yet no strong local development of the alternatives to chemical control. It is crucial, therefore, that some large areas of tropical agriculture be used specifically to develop a combination of high yield crops and integrated pest control and tree crops with integrated control. To achieve this, large scale experimental agricultural projects should be started now and kept separate from areas in which pesticides are used extensively.

There is an additional reason why integrated control should be widely developed in the tropics. We noted earlier that modern temperate agriculture depends upon an industrial base. There is considerable doubt that the necessary industrial base can be developed in the poorer countries in the next decade or so. The great advantage of integrated control is that the industrial (and environmental) maintenance costs are low, while at the same time it is more labor-intensive than chemical control.

The following considerations should be part of the overall planning process in agricultural management.

1) What kind of landscape pattern is best for a combination of high crop yield and integrated control? There is evidence (70) that biological control is more effective on geographic or ecological "islands," though these "islands" might be quite large as in California

vineyards. Experimentation is required to find out the optimal size of such islands for various agricultural lands and the proper size and kind of barriers between islands. Such barriers could be native bush or forests.

2) What is the optimal size and arrangement of mosaics of different crops?

3) Work is needed on the entire range of biological control agents. In intensely managed systems where the crops are short-lived, such techniques will require research on intensive management and culture of pest control species. By contrast, experience in California vineyards and with citrus scale insects suggests that less intensive management is needed for longer-lived crops.

There is a particularly great need to develop competent institutions in the tropics to carry out the work proposed here.

Conclusions

Dependence on chemical pest control may endanger the long-term dependability of our agricultural ecosystems, cause serious environmental degradation and sometimes pose a health hazard (125). Large scale monoculture exacerbates the problems. Every effort should be made to replace chemical pest control with other methods and in particular with an integrated approach that will develop and use ecological diversity.

In the developing nations in the tropics, in particular, much of the necessary ecological diversity remains. But great effort is needed to develop competence in integrated control; local expertise is especially needed. A strongly experimental approach is needed to determine for each type of agriculture the optimal scale and kind of diversity that results in high yields sustainable into the indefinite future. The new UNESCO program for Integrated Natural Resources Research is a small but promising step toward solving many of the problems we have outlined here.

RECOMMENDATIONS

We recommend that agricultural research agencies in all countries initiate experiments on the effects of increasing the spatial heterogeneity of agricultural landscapes. The first problem will be to determine feasible scales and geometrical patterns applicable to modern agriculture.

We recommend the creation, with continuing international support, of several centers in the tropics for the development of integrated pest control and crop management techniques. Support for such work should also be given to existing research or agricultural centers.

Conclusion

With the emerging concerns over complex environmental problems considerable emphasis will be placed on the development of planning for large heterogeneous landscapes. Management techniques required to control such complex systems must also be developed. Tradeoffs between technical feasibility, economic viability, social acceptability and ecological stability will require decision processes other than those we now use. Our current education programs are not fulfilling such needs.

RECOMMENDATION

We recommend that the United Nations initiate and fund a program to encourage institutions of higher learning to provide training in the planning and management of environmental systems. These programs should impart understanding of the ecological constraints, life styles, social institutions and political and economic interrelations of the major geographical areas of the world.

4.F. INTENSITY OF DEMANDS ON ECOSYSTEMS
Diversity, Stability and Maintenance Costs

The productivity of natural ecosystems is related to species diversity or its converse, species dominance. The relation is not simple. Sometimes diversity is positively related to natural (net) productivity, and sometimes the relation is negative (16, 17, 71). Increase in the productivity of natural ecosystems requires an increase in maintenance cost (72), just as it does in ecosystems managed intensely by man.

The intensity of ecosystem use by man is perhaps best defined as demand for a specific output (yield) or a specific service (waste removal or nutrient uptake). Intensifying the demand on an ecosystem will usually decrease diversity. This happens because the productivity of the population(s) on which the demand is made is enhanced, creating a shift toward effectively greater dominance by that species--at least in a functional sense. The total net productivity of the entire ecosystem may increase or decrease.

In general, the relation between maintenance costs and intensity of use will approximate Figure 4.9. This also implies an increasing requirement for human management to guarantee that the specific use will remain possible. In order to decide with what intensity to use an ecosystem we must know the marginal costs of any increase in outputs. Such economies of scale will permit sustainable benefits, say gross yield, as illustrated in Figure 4.9. Eadie (73) shows part of this process for a grazing system (see Figure 4.10).

If we combine these relations involving the intensity of use, we find that there is some intensity at which diminishing returns in net yield (gross yield minus maintenance cost) per unit effort results when net yield per unit effort is maximum; and we anticipate a lowering of diversity as this maximum is approached. We must ask, further, at what intensity of use can we hope to continue the process indefinitely?

This is the optimum, sustainable yield problem. The problem is well illustrated by the management of fisheries. The optimum yield solution is usually sought by analyzing the population processes of the exploited species. Two major weaknesses arise from this approach.
1) The relation between a breeding stock of any given size and the

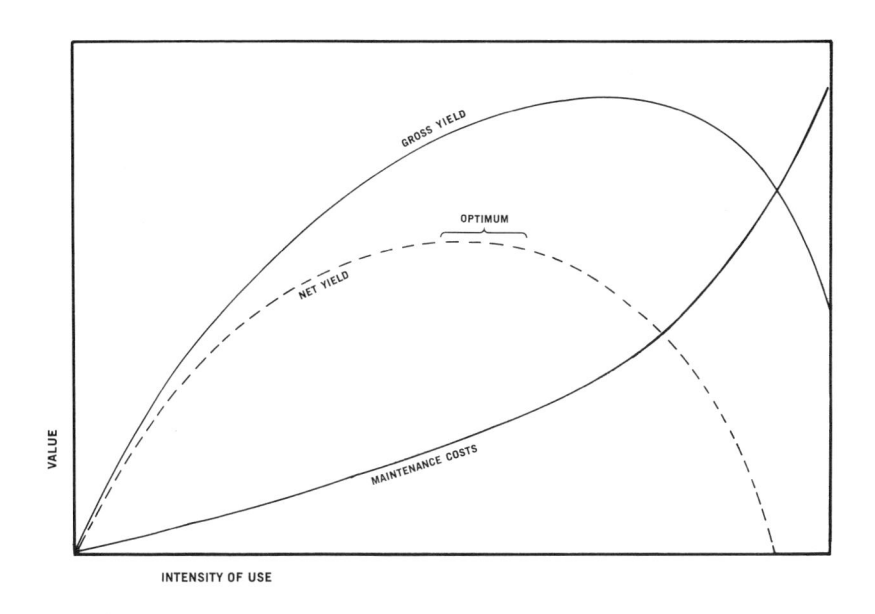

Figure 4.9. Trends in gross yield, maintenance costs and net yield with increasing intensity of use.

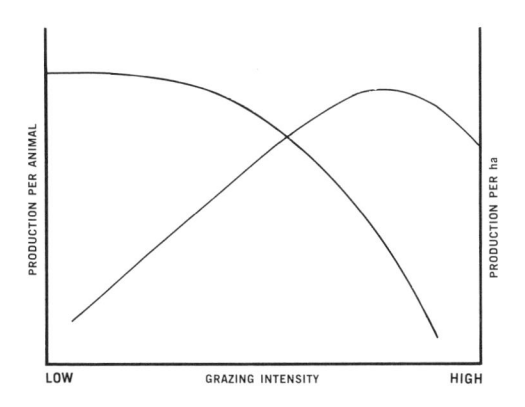

Figure 4.10. Changes in production per animal and production per hectare with increasing grazing intensity.

Source: Eadie, 1970.

number of new recruits by birth from that stock is not simple (74). In the case of some sea fisheries there appears to be no relation between stock and recruitment (75-78). This lack of relation may stem from temporal (say year to year) variation in physical-chemical conditions and variations in population responses to changing density. In short, there is a great deal of statistical variation in the system, and the reliability of any calculated optimum yield cannot be determined. 2) Even if the optimum yield were dependable on the basis of short-term population analyses, uncertainty still arises because the supporting interactions between the exploited population and the rest of the ecosystem must also be reliable. Even small alterations in the quantitative relations of the exploited population to other parts of the ecosystem could lead to long-term change (instability) in the entire ecosystem and the eventual collapse of any industry dependent on a sustained yield.

The collapse of the Alaskan salmon fishery is a recent example attributed to overfishing. Between 1878 and 1935 the annual yield from this fishery grew steadily to over 170 thousand metric tons. Between 1935 and 1967 the intensity of fishing continued to increase, but the annual yield fell to less than 40 thousand metric tons (79).

Extensive ecosystem alteration due to both the intentional and unintentional intervention of man is well illustrated by changes in deep-water fish species in Lake Michigan, U.S.A. (80). The natural assemblage (see Figure 4.11a) was characterized by a dominant predator, the Lake Trout, and seven species of deep-water whitefishes (chubs). This system sustained a fishery (see Figure 4.11b) of about four million kilograms per year from 1910-1940. With the completion of the Welland canal to allow navigation around Niagara Falls, the sea lamprey became established in the upper Great Lakes (see Figure 4.11c). This, combined with an increase in the intensity of fishing (see Figure 4.11d), brought a sharp reduction in the abundance of the larger fish species in the 1950's and an end to their commercial importance.

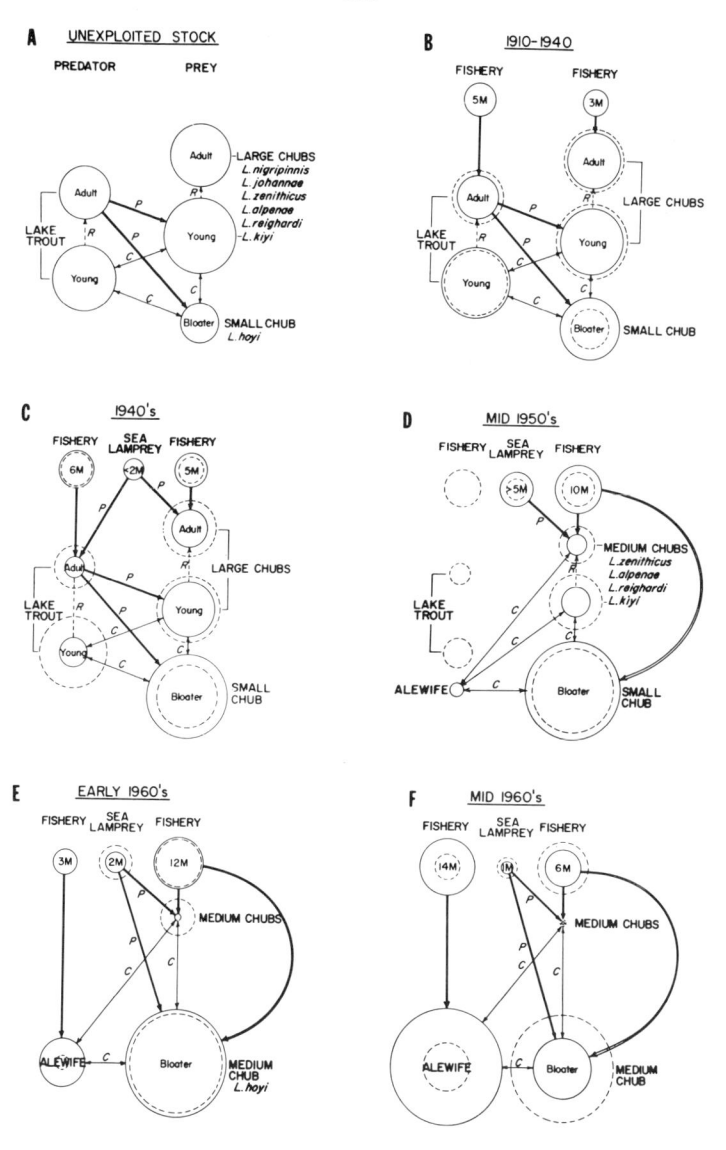

Figure 4.11. Interrelations of major deep-water species of Lake Michigan before exploitation (A) and during the following periods: stable exploitation, 1910-40 (B); early influence of the sea lamprey, 1940's (C); maximum abundance of the sea lamprey, mid-1950's (D); maximum abundance of bloaters, early 1960's (E); maximum abundance of the alewife, mid-1960's (F). P = predation; C = food competition; and R = recruitment.

Source: S. H. Smith, 1968.

The lamprey populations were subsequently brought under control by the use of a lampricide (poison) applied in tributary streams (see Figure 4.11e), but the concurrent natural invasion of a marine fish, the alewife, resulted in a further alteration of the native biological community (see Figure 4.11f). Recent introductions of salmon have established spectacular sport fisheries dependent on the alewife (81), but the reestablishment of a stable biological community has not taken place.

Conclusion

There is an important difference between an intensely managed ecosystem and a moderately managed ecosystem. In an intensely managed system, yield and stability depend on heavy subsidizing of maintenance costs from outside the ecosystem, and the highest possible yield will be sought only if that yield is desirable enough and the outside energy and material are available. Then the tradeoffs involved are open almost entirely to human decision barring some lack of critical knowledge (as happens frequently in pest control). In the moderately managed situation the tradeoffs are in part determined by responses within the large semi-natural parts of the ecosystem necessary to sustain the process of exploitation.

Benefits from Natural Species Diversity

Taken together all the preceding information on diversity and stability (Sections 4.D, 4.E, 4.F) suggest strong reasons for preserving local and global species diversity.

Conclusions

1) Many pest species can be brought under biological control only if their original parasites and predators remain extant or if a very large number of potential (though not coadapted) parasites and predators remain available, among which control species may be sought.

2) Genetic variation in wild populations of crop species and related species serves as a long-run resource for future development of desirable properties in crop species. Diseases and pest resistance, adaptation to various physical and chemical conditions of husbandry and higher yields are examples of properties for which such genetic resources serve as raw material.

3) Locally diverse ecological assemblages harbor the controlling species whose interspecies relations check the growth of many potential pest species. The problems of pest control will be increased in most areas of the world if local natural diversity is reduced. Care must be exercised to assure that semi-wild assemblages of plants, animals and microbes do not serve as foci for the continual eruption of pest species into adjoining agricultural fields. But this seems a less serious problem than that created by the loss of diversity because semi-wild patches of indigenous species are usually closed to invasion by the exotic pests of importance in agriculture.

4) Wild species of the present may in the future be domesticated by man as crop species or for other uses. The loss of wild species would thus reduce future opportunities for agricultural development. Perhaps a biological species should be viewed as non-renewable, or better, a non-retrievable resource. Even if a species does not become completely extinct, a great reduction of its global population will serve to eliminate much of its genetic variation and, thus, much of its value as a natural resource.

5) Many partially managed ecosystems require much of the structure of a preexisting natural ecosystem to sustain the populations of exploited species. Thus it is necessary that the natural ecosystems be preserved. It is not only the biological species which are irreplaceable, but also to a large extent the quantitative framework of exchanges, interactions and organization which must be preserved and which underlies the ecological stability of such exploited ecosystems.

6) Aesthetic aspects of diversity will remain essential to man. Many pleasures of life and opportunities for individual human enrichment cannot exist without a varied and lovely landscape.

Clearly, the ecological concepts of diversity and stability are directly applicable to the maintenance of all unmanaged ecosystems. More study is required to determine the best procedure for selecting representative natural areas to be preserved. Where the amount that can be preserved is limited, should we have one large tract or a number of smaller areas? What is the minimum size of each kind of ecosystem that is in some sense "worth" preserving?

4.G. TOXIC SUBSTANCES IN ECOSYSTEMS

Earlier sections of this chapter have explored the importance of industrialization in the maintenance of stability in simple, high-yield agricultural systems. The industrial processes of today, however, release many toxic substances into air, soil and water. Some of these, the pesticides, are released directly during use in agriculture or forestry. Others, such as heavy metals; oil; carbon, sulfur, and nitrogen oxides; and polychlorinated biphenyls are released as a consequence of manufacturing, heating, transportation, power generation, construction and waste disposal. Many of these substances now enter the food chains of ecosystems in a wide variety of chemical forms and through many different routes. Some have reached concentrations directly deleterious to human health. For example, mercury contaminated fish and shellfish have caused illness and death at Minimata Bay and Niigata in Japan (1). In other cases, involving some insecticides, we know of lethal and sub-lethal effects on wild species of animals. However, we are for the most part ignorant of the long-term effects upon humans, other species and ecosystems from chronic low-level exposure to toxic materials in the environment. Thus, the control of toxic substances has become an important and difficult aspect of ecosystem management. Despite widespread expressions of concern over toxic materials in the environment, the difficulties posed for the management of ecosystems have apparently not been widely appreciated. Extreme difficulties arise because industrialized societies are now thoroughly dependent on the processes which lead to release of toxic materials (82) and because the solutions to problems posed by these aspects of ecosystem management will, in general, be far more comprehensive than those with which present day planning and social decision procedures usually contend (83).

We have chosen pesticides, lead, mercury, cadmium and polyclorinated biphenyls for detailed treatment because these are critical toxic substances entering the environment at present. There are numerous other toxic substances being continuously introduced into the environment, and we will briefly discuss a few of these. Pollution due to oil spills, carbon dioxide emission, general release of particulate matter to the atmosphere and others are discussed in the SCEP report (1)

Pesticides

Pesticides are chemical compounds used to restrict the population size of unwanted species. Modern, chemical pest control began in the 1940's with the development and widespread use of organochlorine insecticides and phenylacetic acid herbicides. There are now about 300 insecticides, herbicides and fungicides in use containing such chemical compounds as organochlorines, phenylacetic acids, carbamates, organic phosphates, acylanilides, organometalic complexes, substituted ureas, triazines and many others. They are used widely; but the pests affecting man, either directly or indirectly, are still with us. Pesticides are effective tools for pest control, but they do not offer a permanent solution to the many pest problems with which man has to deal (128).

Benefits of Pesticide Use

Agriculture is one of the principal users of pesticides (2). The range of annual losses in production of food crops in the U.S.A. from 1951 to 1960 was 2 to 38 percent due to plant diseases, 2 to 31 percent due to insects, and 3 to 25 percent due to weeds. Reduced production because of pests in the U.S.A. is now estimated to be at least 30 percent annually.

Annual losses caused by forest insects and diseases are estimated at 4.8 billion cubic feet of lumber. Insect and disease control activities prevent an additional loss of about 1.2 billion cubic feet. Competing woody vegetation is often controlled by the use of herbicides during reforestation.

Pesticides have been widely used in operations against vector-borne diseases (diseases in which the human pathogen depends on another organism, often an insect, to spread the disease from person to person). DDT was the principal insecticide used in control of most vector-borne diseases.

Over 1,000 million people have been freed from the risk of malaria during the 12 years from 1959 to 1970 largely through the use of DDT (84). The effectiveness of the malaria program is attested by the data in Table 4.7, and similar success has been experienced in other places (117).

If starvation and disease are to be avoided, the continued use of pesticides seems inescapable.

Risks of Pesticide Use

There is concern about insecticide use because compounds such as DDT are highly persistent and are concentrated in the fatty reserves of animals (125). Fungicides cause considerable concern because some of them contain toxic heavy metals. Herbicides have been of less concern because they are relatively non-persistent and are not as frequently used as insecticides and fungicides.

Persistence of pesticides is at once a curse and a blessing: a curse because of the potential for distribution throughout the environment with attendant effects on non-target organisms (85-87, 126), a blessing because the residual activity against pest species decreases the frequency of application.

Area	Year	Number of Cases
Mauritius	1948 1969	46,395 17*
Cuba	1962 1969	3,519 3
Dominica	1950 1969	1,825 Nil
Dominican Republic	1950 1968	17,310 21
Grenada and Carriacou	1951 1969	3,233 Nil
Jamaica	1954 1969	4,417 Nil
Trinidad and Tobago	1950 1969	5,098 5
Venezuela	1943 1958	817,115 800
India	1935 1969	more than 1,000,000 286,962
Bulgaria	1946 1969	114,631 10*
Italy	1945 1968	411,602 37
Romania	1948 1969	338,198 4*
Spain	1950 1969	19,644 28*
Turkey	1950 1969	1,188,969 2,173
Yugoslavia	1937 1969	169,545 15*
China (Taiwan)	1945 1969	more than 1,000,000 9

*Imported or induced cases.

Table 4.7. Changes in malaria morbidity in countries before and after mosquito control.

Source: World Health Organization, 1971.

DDT from water can be concentrated a million times by gill filtration of some fish and shellfish. Earthworms concentrate chlorinated hydrocarbons in their fatty tissue up to 10 times that occurring in the soil. Bird species subsisting on fish, shellfish and earthworms may suffer injury from the DDT they ingest with their food.

In a natural system there is always some biological control. Where a pesticide destroys not only the pest but also its predators the natural checks on the pest operate with reduced efficiency, if at all. Moreover, beneficial insects such as bees may have their populations reduced to a level where they are no longer effective in the pollination of certain plant species (89).

Insecticides have been effectively and widely used for the last 20 years in the control of soil insects. However, the aeration of soils and degradation of plant debris by organisms such as earthworms and collembola (springtails, insects) is important for the maintenance of soil fertility. Earthworms are not seriously affected by some chlorinated hydrocarbons and organophosphates. However, haptachlor, chlordane and the carbamate insecticides are toxic to earthworms and collembola (88).

Studies to date indicate that pesticides have little effect on either soil fungi or bacteria. Soil microorganisms are important in the degradation of pesticides (90). Were it not for these organisms, there would be many more persistent pesticides. The information available indicates that soil microorganisms capable of degrading pesticides are widespread.

The effect of DDT and possibly other chlorinated hydrocarbons on the mortality and reproductive potential of certain birds is a matter of concern and some confusion (91). There is clear evidence that DDT and its metabolites have adverse effects on predatory birds such as hawks, owls and eagles, and on the brown pelican (87, 93). There is a clear relationship between the accumulation of DDT residues in birds and reduced eggshell thickness. It is suspected that polychlorinated biphenyls (PCB's), mercury and lead can have similar effects. In some cases PCB's have been mistakenly identified as DDT because of similar retention times in gas chromatographic analyses (92). Analytic procedures which separate the PCB's from chlorinated hydrocarbons are now available and these techniques should be applied in the future (93, 116).

The pesticides offer no easy solutions. There have been, and will continue to be, both benefits and risks involved with their use. Balancing the benefits and risks demands responsible judgments based on the best scientific evidence available. These judgments will not be easy ones for individual nations and will be even more difficult on a worldwide basis. Severe restrictions placed on the use of a specific pesticide in a wealthy nation such as the U.S.A. may have no serious consequences. However, it may be more serious to restrict use in a country whose food production or public health is currently below an acceptable level.

A comprehensive review of pesticides in relation to environmental health can be found in the report to the Secretary of the U.S. Department of Health, Education and Welfare (94). The fourteen recommendations within that report should be given extensive consideration, particularly the last recommendation which calls, as we do, for "participation in international cooperative efforts to promote safe and effective usage of pesticides."

Conclusions

Increasing demand for the use of pesticides and increasing pesticide levels in the environment offer cause for concern. The various pesticides, however, differ in toxicity to man, toxicity to non-target species and the length of time that they persist in soils and water. Therefore, considering the current dependency of high agricultural yields and disease control on the use of pesticides, it becomes essential to differentiate among the various pesticides available and use them in quite complex ways. This also complicates the problem of achieving adequate control over pesticide use through legislation. It is clear that there is no simple solution to the problems engendered by pesticides.

In the case of DDT, we agree with SCEP (1) that all uses should be reduced as rapidly as possible, that subsidies should be available to developing countries to allow use of less persistent alternatives, that DDT levels in the environment should be monitored and that increased research effort should be devoted to devising non-chemical and integrated control procedures.

Further, we suggest that the analytical procedures used to monitor pesticides should be standardized so that valid biological, geographical and temporal determinations and comparisons can be made.

RECOMMENDATION

We recommend that all pesticides suspected of causing environmental damage or hazards to human health be subject to international restrictions and that when adequate alternatives are available the use of such pesticides be banned by international agreement.

Heavy Metals

Lead

The major reasons for concern over the long-term human health effects due to lead from environmental sources are: its ubiquity in nature, increases from lead additives in gasoline and evidence of increasing lead accumulation in human populations (95-97).

In 1968, 180,000 tons of lead were emitted from combustion of leaded gasoline in the U.S.A alone (96). This amounted to 14% of the lead consumed by the U.S.A. during that year. Lead pollution has now reached global proportions. Between 1904 and 1964 lead concentrations in Greenland snow have increased 16-fold (98, 99). Consumption of lead in the U.S.A. during 1968 for various purposes is shown in Table 4.8.

Use	Thousand Metric Tons	% of Total Use
Storage batteries	467	38.6
Tetraethyl lead	238	19.8
Total Automotive Use	705	58.4
Metal products	160	13.3
Paints and pigments	100	8.3
Ammunition	75	6.2
Solder	67	5.6
Typemetal	25	2.1
Brass and bronze	19	1.6
Bearing metals	17	1.4
Weights and ballast	15	1.3
Annealing	3.8	0.3
Galvanizing	1.6	0.1
Terne metal	1.3	0.1
Total	1,189.7	

Table 4.8. Primary uses of lead in the U.S.A., 1968.
Source: USDA, personal communication.

Global patterns of lead usage are somewhat similar to those of the U.S.A. except that more is used in metals, alloys and pigments and less in automotive applications.

Since economic sources of lead are being rapidly depleted, it is necessary to recycle existing supplies. Lead storage batteries are an excellent example of a case where recycling has resulted in nearly complete return of lead to manufacturers for reuse on a relatively short cycle (two to three years). This is important for two reasons--it significantly extends natural lead resources and it precludes release of lead, particularly lead oxides, to the environment.

Lead from gasoline follows two major environmental pathways leading to man: direct inhalation of small particles from motor exhausts (95, 100, 101) and introduction into food chains by deposition of lead particles on vegetation and soil, particularly along major highways. There are, in fact, gradients of particulate lead deposit with distance away from highways (102, 103).

Lead also enters a man-linked food chain from lead shot used in game hunting (104). Waterfowl ingest these shots as grit, and subsequent lead absorption results in the death of an estimated two to three percent of the American waterfowl population. In England there are areas where hunting has been eliminated for a generation, yet lead poisoning of waterfowl continues due to lead shot coming from eroding banks.

Human clinical disorders caused by internally deposited lead include abdominal pains, distributed peristalsis, blood damage via hemoglobin synthesis inhibition and red blood cell breakdown, and renal and brain injuries. Environmental lead concentrations are not usually high enough to produce the classical toxic symptoms--although such severe cases do occur when small children eat lead-base paint chips which fall from the walls of old buildings (105). We do not know what effect current ambient lead levels will have on animal populations. Neither are we able to correlate specific groups of people having high lead body burdens with areas of high lead pollution. We do know that lead has considerable reactivity in biochemical processes. It will affect cell membrane permeability which can in turn cause very subtle changes in intercellular metabolism. Lead passes the placenta and may be secreted in mother's milk. Additionally, alkyl leads are ten times more toxic to animals than is inorganic lead; there may be conversion in nature from inorganic to organic forms thereby increasing the danger to man. The critical question today is whether the body burden of lead derived from ingestion and inhalation is sufficient to cause adverse effects. The general opinion today is that with our present rate of lead pollution, we will incur diseases related to lead toxicity (106).

Conclusions

Research should be done immediately to determine the effects of chronic low-level lead poisoning in man. At the same time research on the passage of lead through food chains and the chronic effects of lead in ecosystems should be expanded. We support the SCEP recommendation that lead be monitored on a global scale.

RECOMMENDATIONS

We recommend that all use of tetraethyl lead in gasoline be eliminated and that international regulations be established which guarantee that only gasoline free of heavy metals will be marketed in all countries. Where substitution of cyclic organic compounds and other additives are envisaged, we recommend sufficient screening to ensure that one form of air pollution is not replaced by another.

We recommend that where possible lead-containing products be recycled in order to extend natural lead resources and that the release of lead, particularly lead oxide, to the environment be curtailed.

Mercury

Mercury has many uses, some of which are shown in Table 4.9 (107).

	1968	1969	1975
Agricultural use	118	93	92
Amalgamation	9	6	8
Catalyst	66	102	81
Dental	105	105	131
Electrical equipment	677	644	783
Chlor-alkali plants	602	715	788
Laboratory use	68	71	71
Industrial controls	183	240	318
Paints	364	336	369
Paper and pulp	15	19	8
Pharmaceuticals	15	25	23
Other uses	274	334	205
Not accounted for	11	38	–
Total U.S.A.	2,597	2,727	2,878
Total World	8,923	9,875	–

Table 4.9. U.S. production of mercury (metric tons).
Source: Nelson, et al., 1971.

Until recently, the greatest mercury loss to the environment occurred from caustic-chlorine mercury cells. In the past several years, much has been done to correct this problem and some industries have been able to reduce their losses by 95%, at significant economic gains to themselves.

Mercury is present in all ecosystems, although generally in small amounts, and it has a toxic effect on man (96, 107, 108). The most important release of mercury (methyl, alkyl, alkoxy and aryl mercury) into terrestrial ecosystems is from fungicides used on crop seeds (96, 97). Other important uses include mildew proofing and pulp, paper and paint manufacturing (109). Suspension of methyl mercury seed treatment in Sweden brought about noticeable decreases of mercury levels in seed-eating and predatory birds (110). However, recent evidence indicates that methyl mercury (the most toxic form of mercury) can be formed in animal bodies from other mercury compounds (111). Conversion to methyl mercury also occurs in aquatic sediments (121). With this in mind, it becomes evident that substitution of supposedly less toxic mercury compounds for methyl mercury is not a solution.

Conclusions

We endorse SCEP's (1) recommendations that: 1) all uses of mercury-containing pesticides be curtailed; 2) much more extensive data on concentrations in food organisms and on ecosystem effects be obtained; 3) industrial wastes and emissions be controlled by recovery of released mercury to the greatest extent possible; and 4) that world mercury production and consumption figures be obtained.

It matters little whether or not global environmental levels of mercury have risen greatly during the recent past. Actual experience with hazardous levels of mercury in the environment is sufficient to justify efforts to prevent further addition of mercury to soils and waters.

Cadmium

Cadmium is a by-product of zinc production. Cadmium products in use include storage batteries, plastics, pigments, plating and petroleum products (112). Patterns of use for cadmium are much simpler than for mercury or lead. In the U.S.A., 65% is used in providing an attractive rust-resistant plating on numerous small steel items, 20% is used as an additive in plastics, storage batteries and petroleum products and the remaining 15% is used in yellow and orange pigments. Since cadmium and zinc are associated in natural ores, cadmium is found as a trace contaminant in nearly all zinc products, the most prominent being galvanized steel products.

A significant source of cadmium for environmental pollution is super-phosphates. Food grown on soils fertilized with super-phosphates--including coffee, tea, grapes, lemons, cereals and sugar--have been found to contain significant levels of cadmium (113). Eggs and seafoods may also contain cadmium. High levels of cadmium contamination have also been recorded for meats (beef kidney, 40 ppm, 114) and game animals (grouse, 51 ppm, 115). The processing of foodstuffs may occasionally increase cadmium concentrations. An additional source of cadmium contamination is from galvanized and black polyethylene pipes used in housing (116). Incineration of cadmium-coated hardware, cadmium-containing plastics and cadmium-painted materials releases cadmium by volatilization directly to the atmosphere and subsequently to water and land. Schroeder (117) linked human deaths from hypertension with increased concentrations of cadmium in the kidneys. Similar results have been shown for other animals (118). Apparently, cadmium enters the food chain and moves rapidly to biological consumers, including man, where it accumulates because of a low rate of excretion. Cadmium has a peculiar affinity for sulfhydril and hydroxyl groups and inhibits several enzymatic systems (119).

Most countries including the U.S.A., Japan and Sweden have adopted a value of 0.1 mg/m^3 as the maximum allowable concentration in air for occupational exposure. Available data indicate that this concentration in air affords protection against serious pulmonary diseases but does not afford a sufficient margin of safety against chronic cadmium poisoning (116). Currently, a maximum food level of 5 ppm cadmium is given as acceptable by the USFDA and the WHO. This value is not founded upon thorough toxicological data (116). It is apparent that most humans accumulate a certain amount of cadmium.

We also know little of the pathways of cadmium movement through ecosystems. Specifically, we are uncertain of the chemical forms present in ecosystems and their movements through successively higher links in food chains.

Conclusions

A worldwide monitoring of cadmium should be initiated. Further study should be given to: the fate of cadmium within ecosystems, the toxicology of cadmium in general and the effects of chronic low-level intake of cadmium so that maximum allowable concentrations can be established. The present maximum permissible levels of cadmium in air, water and food should be reduced until better knowledge of low-level effects becomes available.

Polychlorinated Biphenyls (PCB's)

Polychlorinated biphenyls (PCB's) resemble DDT in chemical structure (93). Like DDT they are fat soluble leading to their accumulation in fatty tissues. They are also extremely persistent in the environment (123).

PCB's are used as additives in plastics, paints and electrical equipment, and as insecticide carriers. Sources of environmental pollution by these materials include leakage of heat exchange fluids from industrial plants (120) and release of PCB additives from plastics.

Trace quantities of PCB's have been observed in fish and wildlife around the world. Tests have shown 0.1 ppm to be fatal to juvenile shrimp in 48 hours and the same dose to cause cessation of shell growth in oysters (96). Lethal effects of PCB's on game animals have been directly correlated with chlorine composition of the PCB.

PCB's have also been detected in fish (Great Lakes) and human fatty tissue (122). Concentrations in human tissue ranged from 1 to 250 ppm. Another study showed that more than 50% of an urban population had trace quantities of PCB's in blood samples (88). There is little data concerning toxicological aspects of PCB's.

Because of the widespread use of PCB's in disposable products and because PCB's are not decomposed by burning, but merely volatilized, incineration of unsorted waste leads to their release to the environment (123, 124). This method of release is global. Further, separation of PCB-containing materials from other wastes prior to incineration would be a difficult, if not impossible, task.

Conclusion

The use of PCB's should be limited to those applications for which there is no substitute. Methods of incineration or stack gas cleanup should be developed which effectively decompose or remove PCB's before release to the atmosphere. There is also danger of release to groundwaters by leaching from solid waste landfills. Data on the world production of PCB's should be made public by manufacturers.

Additional Toxic Materials

Arsenic

Major sources of arsenic intake are food (crustacea) and beverages (wine). Some arsenic may be inhaled in tobacco smoke. Agricultural uses of arsenic-containing herbicides are a potential future threat in the form of phytotoxicity from increasing arsenic levels in treated soils. The trioxide form is the most toxic, requiring concentrations of only 2 to 10 ppm to kill aquatic life. Present maximum allowable levels of arsenic in food and water are 3.5 mg/kg and .05 ppm respectively.

Beryllium

This material is used as a hardening agent in copper and as a moderator for nuclear reactors. Beryllium was once used in fluorescent lighting tubes, but this use has been abandoned due to health hazards. Economically significant world reserves total 12 to 15 thousand metric tons; therefore, a large increase in beryllium use is unlikely. The chief mode of entry into the body for beryllium is by airborne pollution. Beryllium metal is extremely toxic to living tissues. Very little absorption occurs in the gastrointestinal tract. The potential health threat from beryllium is a localized phenomenon. However, due to its high toxicity, it should be closely regulated.

Nickel

Nickel has been suggested as a substitute for lead in anti-knock additives in gasoline. The environmental pathways leading to man would be: direct inhalation of metallic nickel from automotive exhausts and ingestion of food stuffs which have been contaminated, either from nickel deposited on plants or by uptake from soil. In either instance the danger to man is tumor formation. Cancer has been shown to occur following continuous exposure of animals to nickel-containing compounds

Ozone

Ozone is the dominant constituent of photochemical smog. Toxicologically, O_3 is an extremely active free radical. There is no threshold concentration below which biological damage will not occur. The maximum allowable concentration in the U.S.A. is 0.05 ppm for not more than two hours per day. Ozone has been connected with acceleration of the onset of emphysema and lung cancer. It is also involved in accelerated aging, interference with reproduction and teratogenic effects. Ozone is undoubtedly the most hazardous of all gaseous air pollutants; therefore, all efforts must be made to keep exposure levels below the recommended limits.

RECOMMENDATIONS

We recommend that an international pollution control commission be established by the United Nations. Subsidies and loans should be made available to allow newly established industries in developing nations to operate from the outset under the same pollution emission standards applied in the industrialized nations. The Commission should maintain a program of emission inspection for all global, industrial pollutants.

We recommend that all nations adopt comprehensive regulations to control the manufacture and release of toxic materials within their boundaries.

REFERENCES

1. Study of Critical Environmental Problems (SCEP). 1970. Man's impact on the global environment. MIT Press, Cambridge, Mass. 319 p.

2. Nelson, L. B., and R. Ewell. 1967. Fertilizer requirements for increased food needs. Also, Giles, G. Agricultural power and equipment. In PSAC, World food problem. U.S. Supt. of Documents, Wash., D.C.

3. Food and Agricultural Organization (FAO). 1970. A strategy for plenty. United Nations.

4. Odum, E. P. 1969. The strategy of ecosystem development. Science 164:262-270.

5. Whittaker, R. H. 1970. Communities and ecosystems. Macmillan Co., London. 158 p.

6. Ovington, J. D. 1965. Organic production, turnover and mineral cycling in woodlands. Biol. Rev. 40:295-336.

7. Bormann, F. H., and G. E. Likens. 1967. Nutrient cycling. Science 155:424-429.

8. Duvigneaud, P., and S. Denaeyer-DeSmet. 1967. Symposium on Primary Productivity and Mineral Cycling in Natural Ecosystems. p. 167-186.

9. Cole, D. W., S. P. Gessel, and S. F. Dice. 1967. Symposium on Primary Productivity and Mineral Cycling in Natural Ecosystems. p. 197-232.

10. Likens, G. E., F. H. Bormann, N. M. Johnson, D. W. Fisher, and R. S. Pierce. 1970. Effects of forest cutting and herbicide treatment on nutrient budgets in the Hubbard Brook Watershed-Ecosystem. Ecol. Monogr. 40:23-47.

11. Teal, J. M. 1962. Energy flow in the salt marsh ecosystem of Georgia. Ecology 43:614-624.

12. Odum, E. P., and A. E. Smalley. 1959. Comparison of population energy flow of a herbivorous and a deposit-feeding invertebrate in a salt marsh ecosystem. Nat'l. Acad. Sci. U.S., Proc. 45:617-622.

13. Paulik, G. J. 1971. Anchovies, birds and fishermen in the Peru current, p. 156-189. In W. W. Murdoch (ed.), Environment.

14. Odum, H. T. 1967. Energetics of world food production. The World Food Problem 3:55-95.

15. Odum, H. T. 1971. Environment, power and society. Wiley Interscience.

16. Loucks, O. L. 1970. Evolution of diversity, efficiency, and community stability. Amer. Zool. 10:17-25.

17. McNaughton, S. J. 1967. Relationship among functional properties of California grassland. Nature 216:168-169.

18. Connell, J. H., and E. Orias. 1964. The ecological regulation of species diversity. Amer. Nat. 98:399.

19. Fischer, A. G. 1959. Latitudinal variations in organic diversity. Evolution 14:64.

20. Hairston, N. G., J. K. Allan, R. K. Colwell, D. J. Futuyma, J. Howell, M. D. Lubin, J. Mathias, and J. H. Vandermeer. 1968. The relationship between species diversity and stability; an experimental approach with protozoa and bacteria. Ecology 49:1091.

21. Janzen, D. H. 1967. Differences in insect abundance and diversity between wetter and drier sites during a tropical dry season. Ecology 49:98.

22. Janzen, D. 1970. Herbivores and the number of tree species in tropical forests. Amer. Nat. 104:501-528.

23. Lloyd, M., and R. J. Chelardi. 1964. A table for calculating the equitability component of species diversity. Journal of Anim. Ecol. 33:217-225.

24. Lloyd, M., J. H. Zar, and J. R. Karr. 1968. On the calculations of information--theoretical measures of diversity. Am. Midl. Nat. 79:257-272.

25. Margalef, R. D. 1958. Information theory in ecology. Gen. Systems 3:36-71.

26. MacArthur, R. H. 1955. Fluctuations of animal populations and a measure of community stability. Ecology 36:533-536.

27. MacArthur, R. H. 1964. Environmental factors affecting bird species diversity. Amer. Nat. 98:387-397.

28. MacArthur, R. H. 1965. Patterns of species diversity. Biol. Rev. 40:510-533.

29. McIntosh, R. P. 1967. An index of diversity and the relation of certain concepts to diversity. Ecology 48:392.

30. Pianka, E. R. 1966. Latitudinal gradients in species diversity: a review of concepts. Amer. Nat. 100:33-46.

31. Recher, H. F. 1969. Bird species diversity and habitat diversity in Australia and North America. Amer. Nat. 103:75.

32. Simberloff, D. S. 1969. Taxonomic diversity of island biotas. Evolution 24:23-47.

33. Watt, K. E. F. 1964. Comments on fluctuations of animal populations and measures of community stability. Canad. Ent. 96:1434-1442.

34. Williams, C. B. 1943. Area and number of species. Nature 152:264-267.

35. McMurty, J. A., and G. T. Scriven. 1966. Studies on predator-prey interactions between *Amblyseius hibisci* and *Oligonychus punicae* under greenhouse conditions. Ann. Entomol. Soc. Amer. 59:793-800.

36. Doutt, R. L., et al. 1966. Dispersal of grape leafhopper parasites from a blackberry refuge. Calif. Agr. 20:14-15.

37. Murdoch, W. W. 1969. Switching in general predators: experiments on predator specificity and stability of prey populations. Ecol. Monogr. 39:335-354.

38. Tinbergen, L. 1960. The natural control of insects in pine woods. Arch. Neerl. Zool. 13:265-343.

39. Landenberger, D. E. 1967. Studies on predation and predatory behavior in the Pacific starfish (Pisaster). Doctoral Dissertation. Univ. of Calif., Santa Barbara.

40. Evans, F. C., and W. W. Murdoch. 1968. Taxonomic composition, trophic structure and seasonal occurrence in a grassland insect community. J. Anim. Ecol. 37:259-273.

41. Conway, G. R. 1971. Better methods of pest control. In W. W. Murdoch (ed.), Environment: resources, pollution and society. Sinauer, Stanford, Conn.

42. Ripper, W. E. 1956. Effect of pesticides on balance of arthropod populations. Ann. Rev. Entomol. 1:403-438.

43. Massee, A. M. 1958. The effect on the balance of arthropod populations in orchards arising from the unrestricted use of chemicals. Tenth Intern. Congr. Entomol., Proc. 3:163-168.

44. Huffaker, C. B. (ed.). 1971. Biological control. Plenum Press, New York. (In press).

45. Flaherty, D. L. 1969. Ecosystem trophic complexity and densities of the Willamette mite, Eotetranychus willamettei Ewing (Acarina: Tetranychidae). Ecology 50:911-915.

46. Huffaker, C. B. 1958. Experimental studies on predation. II. Dispersion factors and predator-prey oscillations. Hilgardia 27:343-383.

47. Flanders, S. E., and M. E. Badgley. 1963. Prey-pradator interactions in self-balanced laboratory populations. Hilgardia 35:145-183.

48. Crombie, A. C. 1946. Further experiments on insect competition. Roy. Soc. London, Proc. B132:362-395.

49. Connell, J. H. 1970. A predator-prey system in the marine intertidal region. I. Balanus glandula and several predatory species of Thais. Ecol. Monogr. 40:49-78.

50. St. Amant, J. 1969. The mathematics of predator-prey interactions. M.A. Thesis. Univ. California, Santa Barbara.

51. Smith, F. E. 1971. Spatial heterogeneity, stability and diversity in ecosystems. (In press).

52. Levins, R. 1969. Some demographic and genetic consequences of environmental heterogeneity for biological control. Bull. Entomol. Soc. Amer. 15:237-240.

53. Skellam, J. G. 1951. Random dispersal in theoretical populations. Biometrika 38:196-218.

54. Morris, R. F. (ed.). 1963. The dynamics of epidemic spruce budworm populations. Mem. Ent. Soc. Canada 31:1-332.

55. Harger, R., and D. E. Landenberger. 1971. The effect of storms as a density-dependent mortality factor in populations of sea mussels. The Veliger. (In press).

56. Paine, R. T. 1969. The *Pisaster-Tegula* interaction: prey patches, predator food preference and intertidal community structure. Ecology 50:950-961.

57. Lewis, T. 1969. The diversity of the insect fauna in a hedgerow and neighboring fields. J. Applied Ecol. 6:453-458.

58. Morris, et al. 1956. The population dynamics of the spruce budworm in eastern Canada. Tenth Intern. Congr. Entomol., Proc. 4: 137-149.

59. Birch, L. C. 1970. The role of environmental heterogeneity and genetical heterogeneity in determining distribution and abundance. Advanced Study Institute, Dynamics of Numbers in Populations. Oosterbeek, Netherlands.

60. Monro, J. 1967. The exploitation and conservation of resources by populations of insects. J. Anim. Ecol. 36:531-547.

61. O'Brien, R. D. 1960. Toxic phosphorus esters. Academic Press.

62. Doutt, R. L., and R. F. Smith. 1971. The pesticide syndrome--diagnosis and suggested prophylaxis. *In* C. B. Huffaker (ed.), Biological control. Plenum Press, N. Y.

63. Messenger, P. S., and R. Van den Bosch. 1971. The adaptability of introduced biological control agents. *In* C. B. Huffaker (ed.), Biological control. Plenum Press, N. Y.

64. Van den Bosch, R., and V. M. Stern. 1969. The effect of harvesting practices on insect populations in alfalfa. Tall Timbers Conf. on Ecological Animal Control by Habitat Management 1:47-54.

65. Stern, V. M. 1969. Interplanting alfalfa in cotton control Lygus bugs and other insect pests. Tall Timbers Conf. on Ecological Animal Control by Habitat Management 1:47-54.

66. Tall Timbers Conf. on Ecological Animal Control by Habitat Management. 1 and 2. 1969 and 1970.

67. Gómez-Pompa, A., L. Hernández, and M. Sousa. 1964. Estudio fitoecológico de la cuenca intermedia del rio Popaloapan. Bol. Esp. Inst. Nac. Inv. For. Mexico 3:37-90.

68. Martinez, M. A. 1970. Ecologia humana del Ejido. Benito Juárez, Oax. Bol. Esp. Inst. Nac. Inv. For., Mexico 5.

69. Hernández, X. E. 1955. La agricultura. In Recursos naturales del Sureste y su aprovechamiento. Edic. Inst. Mex. Recursos Nat. Renov.

70. Hansberry, R. 1968. Prospects for nonchemical insect control--an industrial view. Bull. Entomol. Soc. Amer. 14:229-235.

71. Singh, J. S., and R. Misra. 1968. Diversity, dominance, stability and net production in the grasslands at Varanasi, India. Can. J. Botany 47:425-427.

72. Engelmann, M. D. 1966. Introduction to energetics, terrestrial field studies and animal productivity. Advances in Ecol. Res. 3:73.

73. Eadie, J. 1970. Sheep production and pastoral resources. Animal Populations in Relation to Their Food Resources 10:7-25.

74. Paloheimo, J. E., and L. M. Dickie. 1970. Production and food supply. In J. H. Sheele (ed.), Marine food chains. Univ. of California Press, Berkeley.

75. Ricker, W. E. 1954. Stock and recruitment. J. Fish. Res. Bd. Canada 11:559-623.

76. Ricker, W. E. 1958. Handbook of computations for biological statistics of fish populations. Fisheries Research Board of Canada 119:26-30.

77. Ricker, W. E. 1958. Maximum sustained yield from fluctuating environments and mixed stocks. J. Fish. Res. Board of Canada 15:991-1006.

78. Beverton, R. J. H. 1962. Long term dynamics of certain North Sea fish populations. In E. D. LeCren, and M. W. Holdgate (ed.), The exploitation of natural animal populations. Blackwell Scientific Publication Ltd., Oxford. p. 242-259.

79. Lyles, C. H. 1969. Fishery statistics of the U.S. (1967). U.S. Govt. Printing Office, Wash., D.C.

80. Smith, S. H. 1968. Species succession and fishery exploitation in the Great Lakes. The J. Fish. Res. Bd. Canada 25:667-693.

81. Ellefson, P. V., and G. C. Jamsen. 1971. Economic appraisal of Michigan's sport fisheries, January 1-April 24. Mich. Dept. of Nat. Res., Research and Development Report No. 227.

82. Istock, C. 1969. A corollary to the dismal theorem. Bioscience 19:1079-1081.

83. Istock, C. A. 1971. Modern environmental deterioration as a natural process. Intern. J. Envir. Studies 1:151-155.

84. World Health Organization (WHO). 1971. The place of DDT in operations against malaria and other vector-borne diseases. (Offprint from official records of the WHO, No. 190).

85. Moore, N. W. 1966. Pesticides in the environment and their effects on wildlife. Suppl. J. Appl. Ecol. Blackwell.

86. Menhinick, E. J. 1962. Comparison of invertebrate populations of soil and litter of mowed grasslands in areas treated and untreated with pesticides. Ecology 43:556-561.

87. Moore, N. W. 1967. A synopsis of the pesticide problem. Adv. in Ecol. Res. 4:75-129.

88. Harris, C. R. 1970. Persistence and behavior of soil insecticides. In Pesticides in the soil: ecology, degradation, and movement. Mich. State Univ., East Lansing, Mich.

89. Swift, J. E. 1970. Unexpected effects of substitute pest control methods. In J. W. Gillett (ed.), The biological impact of pesticides in the environment. Oregon State Univ., Corvallis, Oregon.

90. Kaufman, D. D. 1970. Pesticide metabolism. In Pesticides in the soil: ecology, degradation, and movement. Mich. State Univ., East Lansing, Mich.

91. Edwards, J. G. 1971. In Testimony before the Committee on Agriculture, U.S. House of Representatives.

92. Menzel, D. B., and M. B. E. Abon-Donia. 1970. Analytic validation of environmental residues. In J. W. Gillett (ed.), The biological impact of pesticides in the environment. Oregon State Univ., Corvallis, Oregon.

93. Risebrough, R. W., P. Rieche, D. B. Peakall, S. G Herman, and M. N. Kirven. 1968. Polychlorinated biphenyls in the global ecosystem. Nature 220:1098-1102.

94. U.S. Department of Health, Education, and Welfare. Report of the Secretary's Commission on Pesticides and Their Relationship to Environmental Health. December 1969.

95. Stokinger, H. E. 1969. The spectre of today's environmental pollution--U.S.A. brand: new perspectives from an old scout. Amer. Ind. Hyg. 30:195-217.

96. Train, R. E., R. Cahn, and G. J. MacDonald. 1971. Toxic substances. Council on Environmental Quality, U.S. Gov't. Printing Office.

97. Craig, P. O., and E. Berlin. 1971. The air of poverty. Also, Magidson, D. T. Half step forward. Also, Human, M. H. Timetable for lead. Environment 13:2-29.

98. Murozumi, M., T. C. Chow, and C. Patterson. 1965. Concentrations of common lead in Greenland snows. In D. R. Schink and J. T. Corless (ed.), Marine geochemistry. Symp. held at the Univ. of Rhode Island, Proc. Oct. 1964. Also, Univ. of R. I., Grad. School of Oceanography. Narragansett Marine Lab. Occasional Pub. No. 3. p. 213-215.

99. Patterson, C. C., and J. D. Salvia. 1968. Lead in natural environment. How much is natural? Environment 10:66-79.

100. Rehoe, R. A. 1968. Lead intake from food and water. Science 159:1000.

101. Schroeder, H. A., J. J. Balassa, and W. H. Vinton. 1965. Chromium, cadmium and lead in rats: effects on life span, tumors and tissue levels. J. of Nutrition 86:51.

102. Creason, J. H., L. T. McNulty, L. T. Heiderscheit, D. H. Swanson, and R. W. Buechley. Roadside gradients in atmospheric concentrations of cadmium, lead, and zinc. In Fifth Annual Conference on Trace Substances in Environmental Health. (To be held June, 1971.) Univ. of Mo., Columbia, Mo.

103. Chow, T. J. 1970. Lead accumulation in roadside soil and grass. Nature 225:295-296.

104. Stickel, W. H. 1969. Lead shot poisoning of American birds. In Swedish Nat. Sci. Res. Council, Ecol. Res. Committee, Metals and ecology, Symp. Bull. No. 5. Stockholm, Sweden. p. 24-30.

105. Fristedt, B. 1969. Metal toxicity. In Metals and ecology. p. 64-66.

106. Schroeder, H. A. 1970. Trace elements in the human environment. Entered into the record of the Senate Committee on Commerce, Subcommittee on Energy, Natural Resources, and Environment, Aug. 27.

107. Nelson, N., T. C. Byerly, A. C. Kolbye, L. T. Kurland, R. F. Shapiro, S. L. Shibko, W. H. Stickel, J. E. Thompson, L. A. Van den Berg, and A. Weissler. L. J. Selikoff (ed.). 1971. Hazards of mercury. Environmental Research 4:3-69.

108. Johnels, A. G., and T. Westermark. 1969. Mercury contamination of the environment in Sweden. In M. W. Miller and G. C. Berg (ed.), Chemical fallout. C. C. Thomas, Springfield.

109. Westoo, G. 1969. Methylmercury compounds in animal foods. In M. W. Miller and G. C. Berg (ed.), Chemical fallout. C. C. Thomas, Springfield.

110. Smart, N. A. 1968. Use of residues of mercury compounds in agriculture. Residue Rev. 23:1-36.

111. Fowler, D. L., J. N. Mahan, H. H. Shepard. 1969. Pesticide rev. U.S. Dept. Agri. p. 30.

112. U.S. Bureau of Mines. 1968. Minerals yearbook.

113. Schroeder, H. A., and J. J. Balassa. 1963. Uptake by vegetables from superphosphates in soil. Science 140:819.

114. Kropf, R., and M. Geldmacher. 1968. Arch. f. Hug. u. Bakteriol. 152:218.

115. Schroeder, H. A., and J. J. Balassa. 1961. J. Chron. Dis. 14:236.

116. Nilsson, R. 1970. Aspects on the toxicity of cadmium and its compounds. Swedish Natural Science Research Council Bull. 7. Stockholm, Sweden.

117. Schroeder, H. A. 1965. Cadmium as a factor in hypertension. J. Chron. Dis. 18:647.

118. Schroeder, H. A. 1964. Cadmium hypertension in rats. Amer. J. of Physiol. 207:62.

119. Hewitt, E. J., and D. J. D. Nicholas. 1963. In R. M. Hochster and J. H. Quastel (ed.), Metabolic inhibitors. Academic Press, N. Y. p. 311.

120. Duke, W. H., J. L. Lowe, and A. J. Wilson. 1970. A polychlorinated biphenyl [Aroclor 1254 (R)] in the water sediment, and biota, of Escambia Bay, Florida. Bull. Environ. Cont. and Tech. 5:171-180.

121. Jernelöv, A. 1969. Conversion of mercury compounds. In M. W. Miller and G. C. Berg (ed.), Chemical fallout. C. C. Thomas, Springfield.

122. Price, H. A. 1970. Occurrence of polychlorinated biphenyls in humans. Presented at a President's Cabinet Committee on the Environment. Subcommittee on Pesticides meeting, Patuxent Wildlife Research Center, Laurel, Maryland. May 22.

123. Gustafsen, C. G. 1970. PCB's--prevalent and persistent. Environmental Science and Technology. Vol. 4.

124. Peterson, A. 1970. PCB--possibilities of destruction. PCB Conference, Wenner-Gren Center, Stockholm.

125. McCaull, J. 1971. Questions for an old friend. Environment 13:2-9.

126. Nisbet, I. C. T., and D. Miner. 1971. DDT substitute. Environment 13:10-17.

127. Knipling, E. F. 1963. Opportunities for development of specific methods of insect control. XVI Intern. Cong. Zool. Proc. Vol. 7.

128. U.S. Department of Agriculture. 1963. Research on controlling insects without conventional insecticides. ARS Special Report 22-85.

Chapter

5

Ecological Aspects of Land Management

TASK GROUP:

Boyd R. Strain, Chairman
Jean Lang, Reporter
Arturo Gómez-Pompa
Larry D. Harris
S. Blair Hutchison
Harold Jorgenson
Stephen Stephenson
Carol G. Wells

5.A. MAJOR FINDINGS

1) Many cases of environmental degradation may be related to poor land management practices. A primary responsibility for this rests with land management authorities who, too often, fail to consider the full range of effects of man's activities on the integrity of natural ecosystems.

Conclusion

There is a great need to increasingly consider ecological factors before making land management decisions.

RECOMMENDATIONS

We recommend that integrated land use planning, including an interdisciplinary consideration of physical, biological and human (social and economic) factors, should precede all future land management actions.

We recommend that ways be sought within the political and economic structure of each nation to incorporate ecological knowledge into land use planning and action.

2) We have inherited present patterns of land use from our ancestors. By modifying these methods, we have increased food productivity but, at the same time, have caused extensive damage to the environment. It is time to reevaluate our present land use practices.

Conclusions

Land use within a region should be balanced between intensely managed, moderately managed and wilderness ecosystems in order to assure the preservation of resources and the most efficient use of the land.

The cultural traditions of native peoples and their impact on ecosystems should not be overlooked in land planning or settlement programs.

RECOMMENDATIONS

We recommend the development and implementation of innovative methods of land use such as multi-purpose forestry and intensive, closed system agriculture.

We recommend that older forms of land use, such as slash-burn and nomadism, be evaluated, and their desirable factors be applied in present land management programs.

3) Under pressure of expanding utilization, natural ecosystems in many previously undeveloped parts of the world are rapidly disappearing. Many of these systems are, as yet, poorly understood by ecologists.

RECOMMENDATIONS

We recommend international cooperation in expanding knowledge of recovery and succession patterns in ecosystems under man's use, particularly those systems not suited to intensive management.

We recommend preservation of rapidly disappearing ecosystems which are sources of genetic diversity and of information vital to an understanding of ecosystem processes.

4) Growing human population is forcing the settlement and intensive use of relatively undeveloped lands like tropical forests, deserts, and semi-arid grasslands. Intensive agricultural use of these ecosystems requires an extensive support system (irrigation, fertilizers, pesticides, etc.), which can be both economically and ecologically expensive.

Conclusions

High risks of ecosystem degradation are involved in the human settlement of some lands. Therefore, land development programs should carefully consider all the alternative uses of these lands and take into account the ecological costs and benefits of each.

<u>Unless the explosive human population increase is eventually brought under control, global environmental degradation appears inevitable</u>.

5.B. INTRODUCTION

The earth may be divided into distinctive ecological systems, each of which is populated by a uniquely diverse array of organisms (1). Since prehistoric times these systems have been modified by man. But in recent times, man's use of land has increased in intensity. With the globe becoming more populated, less desirable lands are being settled; and the modification of natural systems has become more extreme.

While no reasonable individual intends to destroy his own environment or source of livelihood, collectively, man has greatly disrupted the natural ecological systems of which he is a part.

Much of the observed environmental disruption can be related to improper land use. Short-term plans for land use may offer solutions to the immediate problems of a growing population and its demands for more space, food, jobs and resources; but long-term expenses may be high if excessive environmental degradation occurs.

Environmental degradation is defined as a regressive change in land quality which makes it less capable of supplying man's needs for food, fiber, living space, recreation and mineral resources. This change can disrupt global as well as regional economics if it proceeds to the point of lowered productivity over a significant land area. Even countries not directly affected by ecological catastrophes like floods and contagious diseases, which often occur in heavily populated areas, become involved for humanitarian reasons. Many of these unfortunate events could be avoided if ecological principles were understood and stringently applied in managing the land.

In addition, we have recently become aware of man's need for and dependence upon intact, stable ecosystems. Consequently, to assure that we do not eliminate natural species and weaken the resilience of these systems or lose species which may provide characteristics not yet determined desirable, it is important that we preserve representative samples of the world's ecosystems. Such environmental preservation, maintaining existing environmental quality, assumes that man's needs are best supplied by prevailing conditions.

There can be little doubt that man is having an effect on the global ecosystem. Our effluents are reaching the upper atmosphere and the depths of the ocean. Human populations are penetrating the tropics, the deserts and the tundra in increasing numbers. Since we are part of the global ecosystem and since our activities often cause regional and perhaps even global environmental changes, there can be little doubt that the world is in immediate need of land management schemes based on ecological as well as economic considerations. The matching of land uses with the natural capabilities and limitations of each area to absorb man's effects is essential in future land management decisions (2, 3)

Many commendable programs have already been launched by various agencies, including the United Nations, for the development and conservation of natural resources. However, a review of U.N. Programs (4) reveals that most of them have a definite bias toward single factor management or development. For example, the Economic Commission for Asia and the Far East handles separately its programs for mineral resources, water resources, energy and industrial utilization of natural resources. Likewise the Economic Commission for Latin America has distinctive programs for water resources, energy and petroleum. Even the comprehensive program of the Food and Agriculture Organization (FAO) is organized for single objective appraisal and development (e.g., soil, water, land, forest, wildlife, industry). We suggest that development should proceed from the philosophy of using land as a system, with the ultimate objective of land use being the preservation or improvement of man's environment.

The following report describes an ecological approach to land management and presents an analysis of selected land use problems. The report concludes with a case study of recent ecologically-based policy changes within the U.S. Forest Service.

5.C. ECOLOGICAL PRINCIPLES AND LAND MANAGEMENT PROGRAMS

Any successful plan for the integrated management of a land area should be preceded by a characterization of the ecosystem involved, a study of all the possible management alternatives and an analysis of the plan's probable impact on the environment.

Ecosystem Characterization

An ecologically sound land management plan must begin with a comprehensive ecosystem analysis. A resource survey which merely characterizes soils, minerals, terrain, demography, plants or animals is inadequate. Instead, these surveys must be comprehensive: an understanding of energy flow, nutrient cycling, population dynamics and other species relationships is crucial to successful land management (2, 3). For example, it is often necessary to know the reproductive cycle of key plants for successful range management (5, 6, 7). If certain range plants are heavily grazed before they reproduce, regeneration will be unsuccessful; and the desired species may be succeeded by ones with lower palatability (8) (see Chapter 4). Essentially, the ultimate objective of an ecosystem survey should be to predict system response, not merely to describe the system. A worthwhile survey procedure might be to:

1) Define and delimit the physical and biological resources which are found in the area being considered for rehabilitation or development.

2) Analyze and understand the factors which control the ecosystem distribution.

3) Arrange the information collected so that system response to both natural and man-made changes can be assessed. Because of physical and biological factors involved in these systems and their extremely complex interactions, ecologists are now relying heavily on mathematical systems analysis and computer techniques to do this job (9, 2).

Alternative Management Possibilities

The second step in integrated land management planning is to consider alternative proposals for land use. These alternatives may depend on historical and cultural factors of the region as well as on its natural resources and climatic features.

One primary consideration is the major management objective (i.e., preservation, grazing, irrigation) of each of the various regions of the land area studied.

The second is to consider alternative products and alternative uses for products that could be harvested from the land, depending on how it was managed.

Environmental Impact Analysis

To understand a land area well enough to make an environmental impact analysis, ecologists need specific information on how the system functions. Consequently, physical and biological parameters must be analyzed before any change in the system is made. Changes should then be made gradually and with adequate monitoring of system responses. Factors which must be measured include:

1) Indirect measurements such as the physical factors associated with biological change.

2) Direct measurements such as organism growth rates, changes in population densities and seasonality of life history events (e.g., reproduction, hibernation, growth period). These are accurate indicators of environmental conditions in an ecosystem. Because of year to year climatic variations, all monitoring should be designed to insure that the system response measured and the management procedures are related (8).

A detailed assessment of ecological costs and benefits of proposed activities should also precede any change in land use. An interdisciplinary team should conduct this assessment and then prepare an environmental impact evaluation. A procedure which might prove useful has been proposed to help administer the United States Environmental Policy Act of 1969 (10). Such assessments should greatly increase the success of our land management programs.

An excellent analysis of land management and of some factors which must be considered in managing natural ecosystems was provided by R. M. Moore (8). His recommendation that National Trusts staffed with trained ecologists be set up and made responsible for the preservation of grazing, recreational and aesthetic land values in grasslands should apply to all ecosystems and seems deserving of support by all countries.

5.D. SELECTED CASE STUDIES OF LAND USE

The following sections consider some ecological aspects of land use in four of the earth's major ecosystems. Together, these ecosystem types make up over one-third of the land surface of the globe (1).

The discussions here are neither comprehensive nor original, but they do review selected aspects of land use in diverse environments and are intended to clarify the relationship between ecological theory and practical land management.

For those who would like to pursue the topic of ecological input into land management planning, we recommend a textbook by Kenneth Watt (2) and a book edited by George Van Dyne (3).

D.1. Tropical Lowland Forests

In the lowland tropical regions of the world, where precipitation and soil are not limiting factors, we find a great variety of tree communities ranging from thorn tropical forests, less than 10 m in heigh to evergreen rain forests which grow to more than 40 m in height.

Man has been established in this wide variety of tropical ecosystems since ancient times and has played an important role in their evolution. Many well-known ancient civilizations lived in these ecosystems, and many primitive groups still live in these communities. The ecological impact of earlier cultures and these primitive groups was relatively small, but man's impact on tropical ecosystems has become greater in recent times.

As populations of the more temperate highlands have grown and the amount of available agricultural land has declined, the tropical forests have become important settlement areas in many countries. Increasing population in the lowland forest has created a whole new set of land management problems. Typical of the problems faced by tropical forest settlers is the constant threat of disease.

Carefully laid agricultural development plans can flounder if a prior evaluation of health hazards has not been made. For example, in 1954-55, Okinawan colonists pioneered a new settlement in the lowland rain forests of eastern Bolivia. This carefully planned settlement was supported by the Bolivian Government, the United Nations and the United States' foreign aid program. Shortly after the colonists arrived, the community began to experience an epidemic of a prolonged, severe illness and several deaths resulted. This outbreak of "jungle fever" was so severe that the settlement attempt was abandoned (11, 12).

The Demand for New Land

Over much of the Andean Region and in many areas of the Central American highlands, hundreds of thousands of people are moving downslope into the wetter and less populated areas of the "tierra caliente." One of the more conspicuous modern migrations, this movement is converting dense forests into fields and pastures at an unparalleled rate.

The extent of the settlement process in a few countries and the requirements for new land to accommodate present needs give some idea of the magnitude of the problem (see Table 5.1).

Altogether, about 200,000 new settlement farmers are striving to gain a livelihood in the tropical lowlands of these countries. Including their families, over a million people are involved in the tropical land settlement process; and there is no doubt it will continue. Right now, a tremendous number of settlement farms are needed to guarantee employment and income to rural people in almost every country in Latin America.

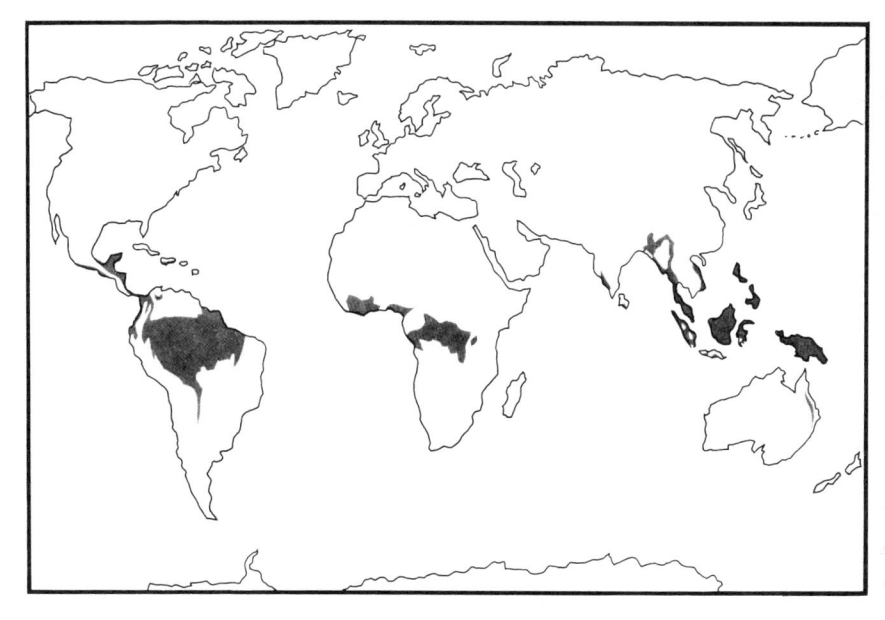

Figure 5.1. Distribution of tropical lowland forest.

Source: Redrawn from Richards, P.W., 1966.

	Colombia(13)	Ecuador(14)	Peru(15)	Bolivia(16)	Costa Rica(17)
Present settlement farmers*	80,000–100,000	20,000	25,000–30,000	40,000	30,000
Settlement farms needed*	250,000	100,000	225,000	110,000	Not available

*Exclusive of colonial and subsistence settlements.

Table 5.1. Land settlement trends in tropical lowlands in some Latin American countries. Numbers in parentheses indicate references from which figures were derived.

Objectives of Settlement

In Latin America huge sums have been spent on studies of proposed colonization projects, but very little has been spent on appraisals of what has been lost or gained as a result. The Inter-American Development Bank (IDB) recently evaluated the social and economic consequences of selected colonization projects. These included projects fully and partially directed by the government, various spontaneous settlement areas and some private land developments. The purpose of the evaluation was to set operational guidelines for member countries requesting loans for land settlement projects.

The IDB review uncovered several broad objectives which, in a logical combination, could serve as the basis for government programs aimed at settling and developing virgin lands in humid tropical areas: creating employment opportunities that foster social or political stability; generating new, viable economic activities to raise per capita incomes; conserving resources through planned and orderly development; and stimulating a dynamic national renewal process by opening up new lands for settlement and development or implementing agrarian reform of old lands.

In view of the magnitude and ecological impact of migration to the humid tropics, it is clear that land settlement should be made an applied science. With integrated surveys which take into account resources, capital investment, agricultural technology and legal control, it is possible to put man and land together in a more productive and harmonious relationship. There is a great need throughout the world for economically sound and ecologically-based land settlement programs, which would certainly be expedited by international cooperation.

Latin American Tropical Land Resources

In Latin America, the humid, tropical lowlands and foothills and the less humid chaco cover about 1,200 million hectares (18). In general these lands lie within the tropical latitudes (see Figure 5.1) below 500 meters elevation and have an annual rainfall in excess of 1,000 millimeters. The land resources include extensive forests, savannas, wildlife and water supplies.

On the basis of available soil maps and miscellaneous observations, the Food and Agriculture Organization (FAO) of the United Nations has made an estimate of the land capability in the humid tropics of Latin America. No satisfactory data is available on the areas of each soil type currently being used by man, nor on the extent to which man's use is incompatible with the land's suitability. The FAO estimated, however, that for six of the principal tropical countries of South America (Brazil, Bolivia, Columbia, Ecuador, Peru and Venezuela) there are about 340 million hectares of unused arable land, or five times the land area now being exploited in these countries (19). Nearly all of this land is in the humid tropics.

Types of Land Use

The economic uses of the rain forests can be divided into two main groups--those that involve a radical destruction of the natural system and those that do not (see Figure 5.2).

Nondestructive uses have been practiced mainly in areas in which the people are hunters and gatherers. But, even in advanced societies, nondestructive use continues with the selective harvest of valued trees or their products. Balata, which produces a latex, and rubber are exploited under natural conditions (20). Rhizomes of Barbasco (Dioscorea composita) are collected from the wild for the steroidal hormone production, and a few crops such as vanilla and coffee are raised in some areas with no apparent degradation of the ecosystem. Mahogany, red cedar primavera, and palo de rosa are a few of the trees selectively cut for lumber. These nondestructive practices are applied in the tropical rain forests of America, Asia and Africa and allow for natural regeneration following limited timber harvest (21, 22).

On the other hand, land uses which tend to destroy the natural ecosystems are agriculture, forestry, grazing and urban development. The first two are probably the most important land uses in tropical forests.

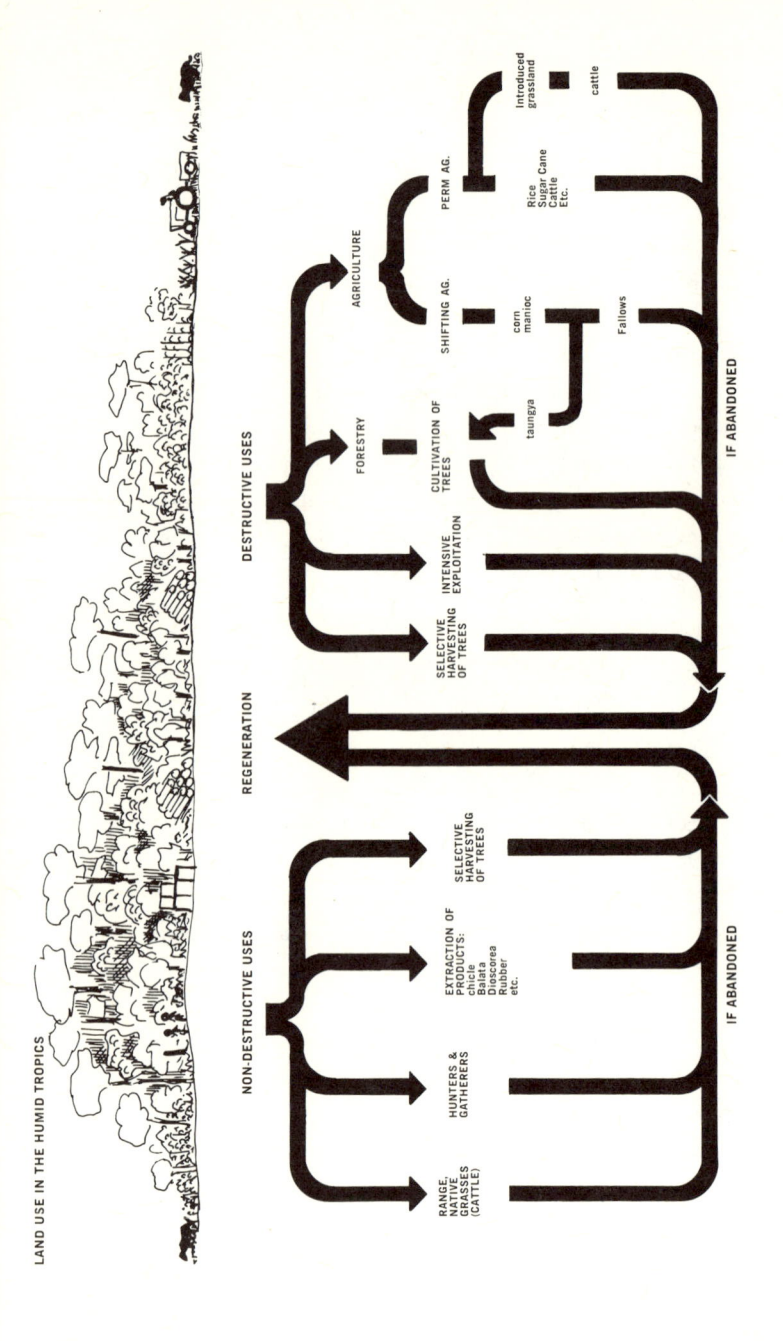

Figure 5.2. Land use practices in the tropical forests of Latin America.

Most of the tropical rain forest areas of the world are subject to a shifting or slash-burn agriculture (23, 24, 25, 26). This system consists of cutting trees and shrubs at the end of the dry season, letting them dry for ten days or more and then burning them. After burning, there is a significant increase in soil nutrients, particularly phosphorus, potassium, calcium and magnesium (23). The enriched soil is then prepared for planting corn, beans, cassava and other crops which give very high yields the first season (26). With the harvest of the first crop the soil is "cleaned" and a new crop is planted. According to Beirnaert, during the first year or two after the forest is cleared, about a ton of humus and five tons of old roots are oxidized per hectare per month (23). After a period of about three to four years, the land is abandoned because of poor yields, weed increases and soil nutrient depletions.

The abandoned land is allowed to recover; and during this period of rest, regeneration of the forest begins. Soils return to their original condition (27), and vegetation follows a definite pattern of succession (28, 29) that eventually leads to a new forest.

Though shifting agriculture has been the major type of land use in the tropical lowlands, there are other systems which are more permanent types of agriculture. These systems are found on the best tropical soils, such as the alluvial soils and several "Ando" soils of volcanic origin. For example, certain tree crops like cacao, coffee, rubber, cinchona, tea and many tropical fruits are permanent ones, not suited to shifting agriculture. Unfortunately, these are not major food crops, and demand for them is limited.

The permanent agricultural crops of major importance are sugar cane and rice. Tropical grasslands are also permanent and are important cattle raising areas, originally formed by clearcutting the forest and later maintained by grazing.

Another use of tropical lands is in forestry, though this varies greatly on the different continents. There are no general methods available for reforestation of rain forests in the tropical countries, and in most cases no efforts are made in this direction. Presently, the most sophisticated technique in tropical forestry is to grow a limited number of tree types like teak, pine or spanish cedar as a single crop and harvest them.

Another practice is to clearcut the forest, use the harvested trees and shrubs to produce a special type of compressed wood and then leave the area to return to a natural state.

A special type of forest culture known as "Taungya" has now been adopted by several tropical countries. This method mixes the normal food crops of shifting agriculture with a forest plantation. When the land is abandoned for crops, the forest takes over and a tree plantation is established.

The most common form of tropical forest exploitation has been to remove trees of special value (30), while leaving the forest with enough reserves to regenerate species taken from it.

Tropical Land Use Problems and Some Recommendations for Action

1) Maintaining a balance of land uses in tropical regions. There is a great need for ecologically-oriented land use planning in the tropics. The heterogeneity of most tropical regions has been demonstrated (31, 32, 33, 34), and it is obvious that not all soils are equally suited to the same use. Agricultural and pasture lands are generally planned with concern for local needs, marketing, costs of transportation, demand, etc. But to achieve a long-term, stable economy, factors like resource conservation and land area stability should also be considered. A balance of land use for each ecological region, including the preservation of some natural areas, will ensure both the optimum use and the preservation of resources.

2) Managing the regeneration of rain forests.
There is evidence that succession in tropical areas can be directed along certain pathways that will increase its regeneration rate and diversity (28, 35). But intensive research on the factors affecting

speed and mechanics of tropical forest regeneration is needed (36)
in order to understand the general patterns of succession that have
evolved through hundreds of years of shifting agriculture.

Information on the rate of recovery of various soils groups in
different climates is also needed in order to improve the efficiency of
successional systems. Most tropical soils depend upon a delicate balance
with the forest plants, which are the primary reservoir of nutrient
elements (37). Through decomposition of dead leaves and branches,
these elements are continuously released to the soil as part of the
cyclic process. If the forest is cleared, however, the natural cycle
is disrupted. Vegetation is destroyed and plant litter, which decomposes under high temperature and moisture, is not replaced. As a
result, released nutrients are rapidly leached from the soil and soil
fertility decreases.

3) Optimizing shifting agriculture under population pressure.
Shifting agriculture deserves special attention in the near future. It
is a system that has been in existence since ancient times and has been
effective in the conservation of soil and other resources. The
agricultural capacity of regions using this system is apparently not
destroyed, even over long periods of time. It is a highly advanced
system from the point of view of empirical ecology and according to
some experts is the best that could have been devised (28).

We suggest that research be focused on the response of soils to
intensive shifting agricultural practices because of the high risk of
long-term soil damage with frequent reclearing of only partially recovered land (38). This is happening now in many tropical areas of
the world where the time normally allowed for forest succession and recovery has been shortened by population demands on the land.

4) Preserving areas of tropical forest ecosystems.
Under land settlement pressures, the destruction of tropical forests
has accelerated rapidly. In contrast, the accumulation of knowledge
about this natural ecosystem has been very slow. The tropical lowland
evergreen rain forest is the most productive terrestrial ecosystem (39),
and there is a great need to understand how this system functions. But,

the opportunity to study global tropical forest ecosystems is rapidly disappearing. Not only are few scientists studying these forests, but also there are increasingly fewer forests to study. For these reasons, tropical countries should preserve part of their natural forest ecosystems.

5) Making use of the highly productive tropical ecosystem. Recent demands for greater food production have meant increased land cultivation and a subsequent disruption of many natural ecosystems. However, forcing the environment into a monospecific ecosytem for agriculture leads to a loss of diversity and general deterioration of the system (see previous chapter). In light of technological advances, it is time to consider some new, less traditional methods of utilizing the tremendously productive tropical forests.

Efforts should be made to use the products of the tropical forests more completely. Several attempts have already been made to use temperate forests in this way: wood residues have been used for livestock feed (40) and have also been converted into proteins through the use of yeasts (41).

One of the most interesting approaches has been the saccharification of wood, a process by which all kinds of plant material are converted into sugars and other derivatives (42, 43). Since cellulose is the most abundant of all photosynthetic products, the conversion of this plant material to digestible sugars could prove a valuable human food source. Tropical forest ecosystems offer lumber, pulp, resins, soil amendments and mulches among other things. As Hesse (44) said:

> One solution to the exploitation of mixed evergreen forests is multiple usage. With a wide variety of wood properties represented among the species, the manufacture of a variety of products would make most efficient use of the forest.

The tropical forests with their valuable species scattered through a diverse flora seem particularly suited to a multi-use approach from both economic and biological points of view.

Another "untraditional" alternative is a hydroponic system which emphasizes intensive food production in a closed system in a limited area rather than the conventional open system in an extensive area. Although under certain conditions this method may increase stream enrichment from a given acre or have other drawbacks, it does concentrate agricultural production on better land which is less subject to erosion. Intensive closed system farming methods might also release marginal lands from crop production and make them available for forestry and recreation.

Conclusion

We have inherited our land use practices from ancestors far in the past; and despite technological advances that have increased productivity, we have not appreciably changed these practices. The consequences of maintaining these traditional methods of land use in the face of increasing population pressures are reflected in the degradation of our environment.

D.2. Tropical Savanna

Savannas are tropical or subtropical grasslands populated sparsely with trees and drought-resistant shrubs. They occur widely in Mexico, Central and South America, Africa and Australia (see Figure 5.3).

Rainfall rather than temperature dictates the seasons in these tropical regions. Depending on the area, these precipitation patterns may range anywhere from a dry 30 cm per year to an annual total of 250 cm per year with few dry periods (45). Although some high rainfall areas are used for growing agricultural crops, the essential resource of the savanna is its suitability for grazing by large herbivores (46, 47). Several African countries have developed

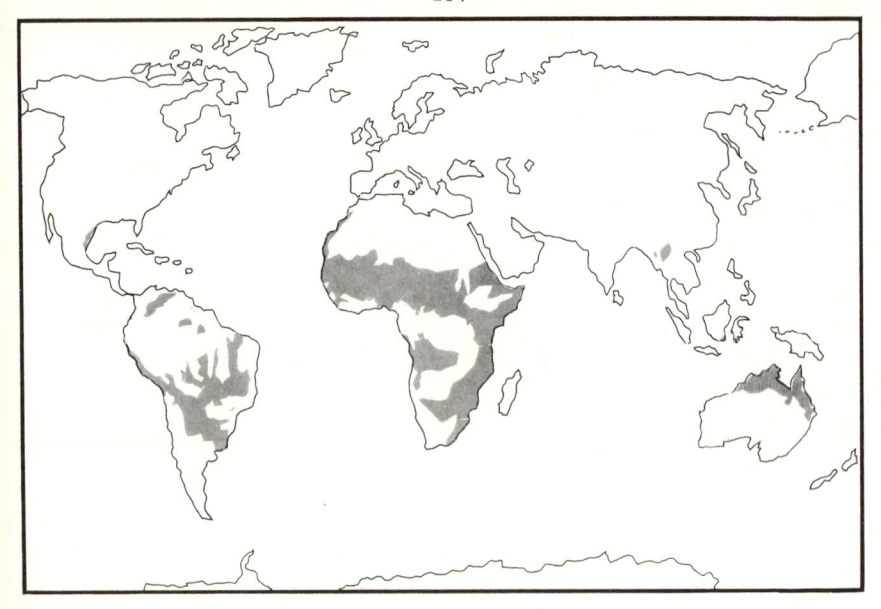

Figure 5.3. Distribution of tropical savanna.

Source: Redrawn from Kuchler, A.W., 1960.

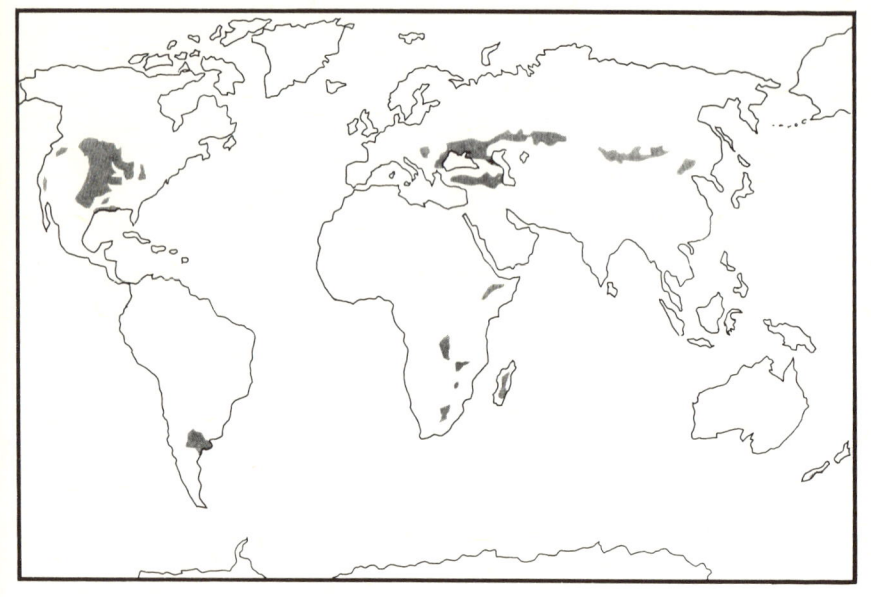

Figure 5.4. Distribution of temperate grasslands.

Source: Redrawn from Kuchler, A.W., 1960.

highly profitable tourism industries based upon the diverse array of native animals found on the savanna. Tourism in Kenya alone brought in about 42 million dollars in 1966 (48).

Ranching with these large native animals is an attractive potentia savanna-based industry which could provide protein supplements to native peoples (49, 50, 51, 52). Another great value of the savanna wildlife resource is its wealth of physiological variability. For example, there are savanna animals that never need to drink water (53), others that have remarkable forage gathering and digesting capabilities (54) and still others which are almost completely resistant to most local diseases. This diversity is not only important to ecosystem stability but is also of potential value to animal breeding and domestication programs. Judging by the success of Russian and Rhodesian eland domestications, the breeding of these native herbivores is a promising field (55).

Besides supporting large and diverse wildlife populations, the savanna is a unique land area which offers new insights into fundamental ecological theory.

Land Management Problems in the Savanna

The lack of water in the savanna is a major limitation on land use and has probably influenced both man and the animals that have evolved there (56). Without question, it greatly affects the distribution of people currently living in savanna regions. However, an even more serious threat to the sustained productivity of these systems is the development of local water sources without considering the underlying ecological, social and economic systems (50). Some of the most serious habitat degradation is occurring around newly established livestock watering points (57, 58, 59). Although there is little quantitative data on the rate and extent of habitat degradation, it is clear that the range productivity has been substantially **decreased** in many areas (59, 60, 61, 62, 63). In some cases, the range may be up to 12 times overstocked (64); and serious problems are expected to result from this intensive use (65).

The greatest single management problem in the savanna, then, is overgrazing. While human and livestock populations are increasing--the world's cattle population has been growing at a rate of 2.7% per year (66)--the ability of the land to meet the subsequent demands is decreasing.

A second limitation on man's use of tropical savanna ecosystems is the climate. The ratio between potential evaporation and actual precipitation is substantially greater in these regions than it is in the humid or temperate forests (67). As a consequence, rainfall quickly evaporates, and growing seasons are short. This means that a great deal of animal feed must be stored for use during the dry season. These storage facilities require capital investments which can seldom be made by individuals grazing small herds on tribal or national lands (68).

This shortened growing season also affects the savanna vegetation. Savanna grasses mature more rapidly than similar temperate species and are usually higher in fiber content and lower in digestibility (69).

The savanna climate also has a significant influence on cattle productivity. More productive stock varieties of the temperate regions frequently do not do well under tropical conditions because they require high grade ranges, ample water supplies, adequate feed storage and extensive veterinary care. While the tropical Zebu cattle (Bos indicus) are better adapted to the region than their temperate counterparts, their growth, milk production rates and meat quality are all very low (70).

Another obstacle to achieving highly productive beef industries in many savanna regions is disease (70). Although means of controlling all major diseases and parasites are available, economic considerations often work against their effective use.

These circumstances have led many scientists to espouse the direct domestication and ranching of wild herbivores like the eland, one of the African antelopes (71). It is unlikely, however, that these animals will ever replace cattle to any significant degree in the meat production industry, though they may eventually assist in the optimum utilization of marginal range lands (71).

Cultural Aspects of Savanna Management

Land use problems in tropical savanna regions are compounded by increasing population pressure (65) and shifts in population distribution (72). Many former tribal and family lands have been fragmented for political or administrative expediency (72, 73), resulting in the concentration of many cattle in a small area. To make the situation worse, technological advances have been introduced into these areas without thought for the ecological, economic or social systems of the savanna lands (74). Tanzania and Kenya are specific examples of countries where clashes between old and new land use methods have caused problems.

In these countries there is a rather severe annual dry season from June to October. Since early times, the people of East Africa have followed their herds from pasture to pasture, depending on them as "famine insurance." In these dry areas, a living animal--no matter how poor its quality--is a more reliable source of food than crops which depend on the rainfall.

Unfortunately, this nomadic way of life and its reverence for livestock are not often considered when medical and technological advances are brought to the region. Even such well-intentioned projects as the construction of an artificial dam or the drilling of a well can initiate a cycle of environmental deterioration. For example, if cattle movements are politically restricted, even though veterinary services and localized water sources are also introduced, range degradation is sure to follow. The cattle population grows,

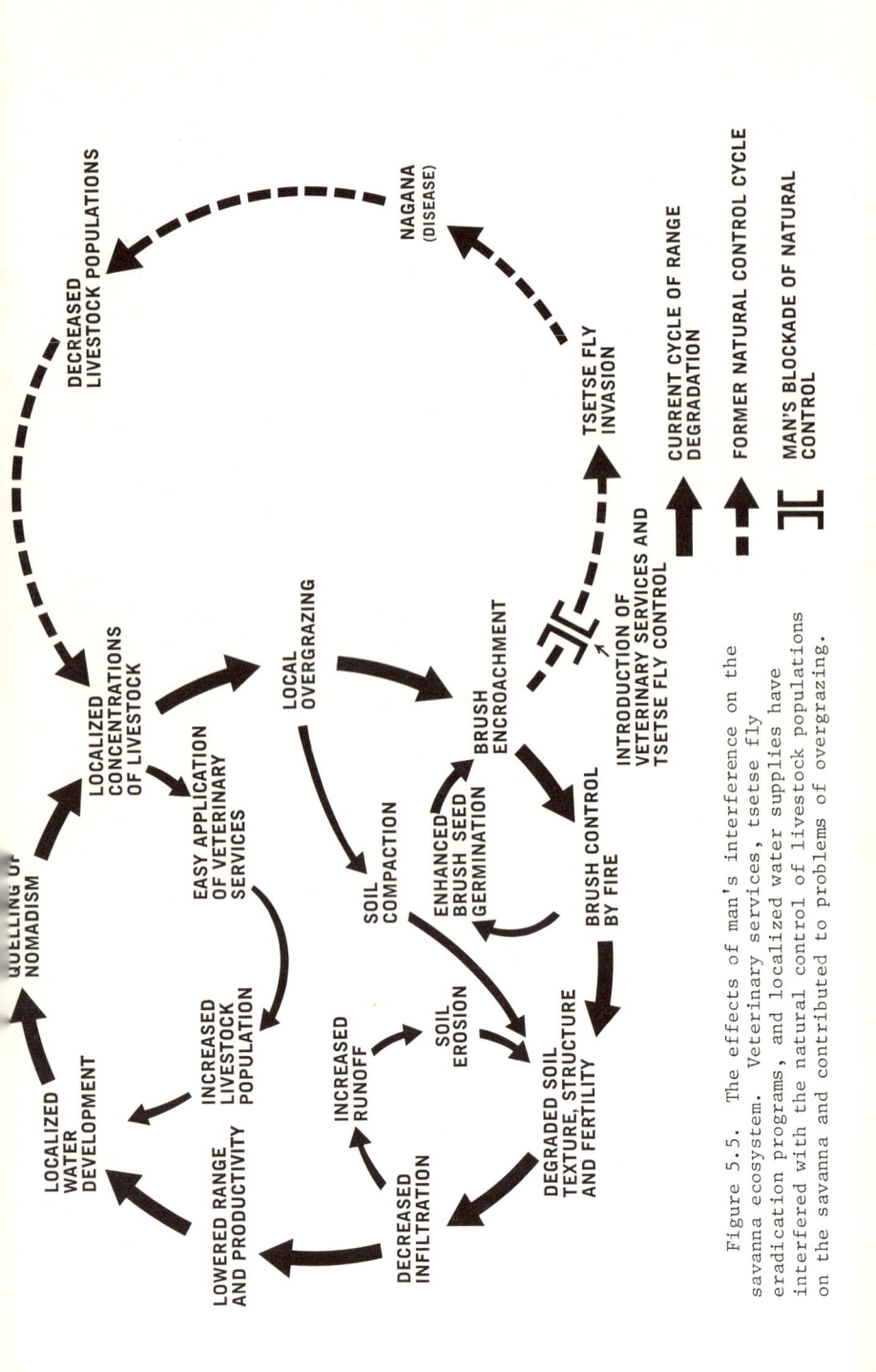

Figure 5.5. The effects of man's interference on the savanna ecosystem. Veterinary services, tsetse fly eradication programs, and localized water supplies have interfered with the natural control of livestock populations on the savanna and contributed to problems of overgrazing.

but it is confined to a small area. The nutritious and palatable
perennial grasses succumb to overgrazing, and shrubs and brush move
into the range (75). The trampled and deteriorated range becomes less
effective in holding what little rainfall it gets (8), and productivity
declines further (see Figure 5.5).

At this point the herdsman has two alternatives. He may seek
new range and move the cycle elsewhere, or he may attempt to reclaim
the range with fire. This is one of the most economical brush control
methods (76) and stimulates a green, lush regrowth which is highly
desirable forage. Unfortunately, however, it also reduces plant vigor
and productivity in the following year (77, 78), enhances germination
of brush species seeds (79) and exposes the range soil to further
dessication and erosion.

In early times there was a natural control in the system. As
the brush become sufficiently dense, tsetse flies (Glossina spp.) en-
croached and kept cattle densities down by transmitting the disease
"nagana" (80, 81). But veterinary services in the range have eliminated
this control and completed the cycle of degradation.

Conclusion

If future management of tropical savanna is to be successful,
a complete understanding of ecological limitation and potentials of
the land is needed as well as an appreciation of the cultural traditions of the savanna people.

D.3. Temperate Grasslands

From the standpoint of food production, the world's temperate
zone grasslands are perhaps more important than any other single land
form. There are about nine million square kilometers of temperate
grasslands on earth (1) and an additional 21 million square kilometers of agricultural land or woodland-brushland, which has largely
been derived from former grasslands.

These ecosystems are found primarily in the northern hemisphere (Figure 5.4). Typical of them are the Great Plains, Colorado Plateau and Palouse regions of North America; and the steppes of Eurasia. Other significant grassland areas are in southern Europe, northern Africa, southern Africa (the veld), Australia and South America (the pampa). Most if not all of these regions have suffered extensive degradation as the result of man's misuse (82).

Prior to the development of modern agriculture, men living in the extensive grassland ecosystems were either nomadic herdsmen or hunters and gatherers. Nomadism, in fact, is still well established in many parts of the world's grasslands but is rapidly dying out with modern advances in range management and farming. It is significant that primitive man's agricultural developments in the grassland were minor. The grassland ecosystem under its natural climatic and biological controls was stable, and immense amounts of energy were needed to convert it from a perennial, low production ecosystem to an annual, high production ecosystem.

Attributes of the Grassland Ecosystem

The major grassland ecosystems of the world occur in temperate latitudes and are maintained by climatic conditions. There are additional smaller grassland areas which result from atypical soils or special regional climatic conditions. This discussion will apply primarily to temperate grasslands that are currently being cultivated, managed as grazing and pasture lands or held as unmanaged range land.

Temperate grasslands are found primarily in regions with 25 to 75 cm precipitation per year (83). Climatic extremes, seasonality, unimpeded airflow over frequently monotonous topography and, in some cases, soils with low water-holding capacity, combine to produce evaporation-precipitation ratios which favor the maintenance of grassland vegetation.

Although highly variable from place to place, primary productivity in the grasslands is generally limited by annual rainfall (84). This limits the degree to which the grassland can be utilized without disrupting soil stabilizing properties (8).

Under these climatic conditions, the interaction of plants and animals with the underlying bedrock has produced a class of soils peculiar to grassland ecosystems (85, 86). The primary characteristic of these soils is an abundance of minerals and a scarcity of organic matter, especially in the more arid grasslands. By contrast, soils of wet and humid temperate regions are low in minerals, due to the flushing of loosely bound nutrient ions.

The extent to which the integrated forces of the ecosystem have influenced the development of the grassland biota, particularly the plants, is reflected in adaptations to drought stress. The amount of plant material found underground in organs like roots, bulbs, and corms is two to five times that found above ground in leafy photosynthetic and reproductive structures (84). This disproportionately large amount of underground biomass not only contributes to soil stability, but also supplies the plant with reserve food and water during short-term droughts.

Survival during long-term climatic fluctuations is assured by the genetic diversity of the plant population. This was demonstrated by the reversible changes in the composition of mid-American grasslands during the drought of the 1930's (85). Such changes provide a degree of rapid adaptability without effectively changing the nature of the ecosystem.

Animal diversity, on the other hand, tends to be low in grassland ecosystems (1) because grasslands tend to be relatively uniform over large areas. As a result, predator-prey relationships, which are important in regulating herbivore populations, tend to be more susceptible to disruption by human settlement.

Uses of Temperate Grasslands

Recent uses of the world's temperate grasslands appear to have generated two major types of environmental degradation—one resulting from overgrazing and the other associated with converting large areas of grassland to either dry or irrigated crop land.

The more arid grasslands are used primarily for grazing. Although minor areas are now under irrigation in some regions, most of this grazing land depends upon natural water sources. Land users are primarily the nomadic herdsmen of Europe, Asia and northern Africa (88, 89) and the sedentary, centralized landowners in the South African veld, portions of Australia and the Americas (87).

Although major problems of grassland degradation are common to all these regions (91, 92), the most acute problems appear near permanent water sources where the land is permanently occupied and intensely used. This has consistently lead to a decrease in the more palatable forage species and a decline in range productivity (88).

The same type of ecosystem damage is caused by overstocking (88, 92). This occurs primarily when nomadic herdsmen or sedentary land managers fail to lower their stocking levels during dry years, and especially during extended droughts.

Range degradation sets biological and physical changes in the ecosystem in motion which can be reversed only through reduced land use (93). Reclaiming severely degraded grasslands is extremely difficult and requires long periods of time. Reducing grazing intensity is probably the most feasible means of improving grassland production. Other alternatives like manipulating soil moisture levels and nutrient content are expensive (94) and have generally been out of the question for lesser developed nations.

Reduced grassland productivity has sometimes been the result of an imbalance between native, grazing or seed-eating animals and their predators. Predator control or extermination has been a contributor to many small animal population explosions. Large populations of rodents and rabbits, for example, not only compete with domestic animals for food, but may contribute to a change in plant composition, thereby reducing grassland potential (95).

Not all predator-prey imbalances involve mammals, however. Widespread devastation has occurred in the veld of South Africa as the result of the spread of harvester termites. The problem, which developed to acute proportions within a period of 50 years, devastated over a quarter of the grasslands of Zululand (87). In this case the outbreaks were the result of reductions in the numbers of ant bears, plovers and bustards, all of which fed upon the termite. This case illustrates the necessity for careful study before measures are taken to control any predator. This is especially true for grasslands where predator-prey systems tend to be relatively simple.

Another cause of reductions in range yields has been the ill-advised introductions of alien species, though, in some cases, this has proven a valuable tool in range reclamation. Both plant and animal alien species are involved. In the absence of co-evolved predators and parasites, the European rabbit and the prickly pear cactus (68) became serious problems in Australia and South Africa, spreading over vast areas and eliminating native species.

These two general problems, predator control and introduction of alien species, illustrate the inherent dangers in unenlightened manipulation of ecosystems.

Although the use of fire in maintaining grassland ecosystems has been questioned (96), evidence from North American grasslands suggests that fire has been important in impeding the encroachment of shrubs and trees (97, 98). Where range fires have been discontinued for up to 30 years, woody growth often becomes abundant and the productivity of forage species is reduced. Moreover, as the grass cover is reduced and broken up, it becomes less capable of feeding a fire. Mechanical or chemical means can be used to eliminate the woody plants, but such methods are expensive, especially when compared to the cost of prescribed burning. Although this problem of woody overgrowth is not a universal one, it has reduced the grassland areas in some regions (99).

Agriculture in Grassland Ecosystems

Dryland farming is potentially the most destructive agricultural method in the semi-arid grassland areas. Once man has disrupted the stabilizing properties of the natural system, the highly mineralized and nonaggregated soils, typical of semi-arid grasslands, are progressively eroded away by wind and water (100, 101). The problem becomes especially acute during drought years. This was illustrated by the wide scale degradation of the North American Great Plains during the "Dust Bowl" drought years of the 1930's (82). The fact that 23 major droughts occurred in the Russian Plain during the 19th and early 20th centuries (88) suggests the magnitude of risks involved in developing arid and semi-arid grassland and brushland.

Because the ecological nature of the problems which result from intensive dryland farming is not well known, this is a fruitful area for investigation. Presently, the danger of degrading soils in humid and semi-arid temperate grasslands is overridden by rapidly developing agricultural techniques. So far, improved methods of farming and soil treatments, like mulching, have reduced the risk of severe erosion (93); and most losses that do occur in the system are compensated for by fertilization, chemical control and plant breeding. But, how long these trends can continue without repercussion is unknown.

An additional problem associated with the agricultural development in grasslands is the tendency to develop very large areas so that the native plant and animal species are practically eliminated. This phenomenon has not been well documented, nor has its ecological significance been examined in detail. However, the natural biotic array in many large areas, like the North American humid grasslands, has been replaced by a mixture of species introduced from all parts of the world. The natural ecosystems and native species, especially plants, are now so reduced that they are difficult to find. This reduction of floral diversity and shrinkage of the native gene pool could have serious effects on ecosystem stability (see Chapter 4).

Conclusions

Management methods should be designed to prevent further environmental degradation in temperate grasslands and to ensure their continued use. In view of the destructive nature of placing temperate grasslands into crop production, integrated land use planning should precede all future land management action in this biome. To prevent range deterioration, nomadic grazing practices and rotational grazing (8) should be employed. Predator control and the introduction of alien species should be carried out only after detailed environmental impact analyses.

D.4. Arid and Semi-Arid Regions

In this analysis we will consider arid and semi-arid regions as defined by Meigs (102, 103) and shown in Figure 5.6. Accordingly, high latitude, cold, arid areas are not included. Approximately nine percent of the earth's total surface is made up of arid and semi-arid lands (46).

The arid regions of the world are diverse in distribution, soils and the history of their use; but they share climatic features of low, infrequent, generally unpredictable rainfall and generally high evaporation-precipitation ratios. High temperatures are a prevalent characteristic, but cool arid regions also exist.

In comparison to the great biological diversity and complex species interrelationship of the humid tropics and many temperate areas, the ecosystems of arid and semi-arid environments are relatively simple. In general, they have far fewer plants per land area, resulting in vegetation canopies which are much more open than those in temperate or tropical regions (104, 105, 106). Although arid zone soils often contain adequate amounts of the essential elements, they are relatively low in organic matter and are inclined to be sandy, rocky and high in salt content (107).

On a global basis many species of organisms have adapted in different ways to arid conditions. All of them, however, share the

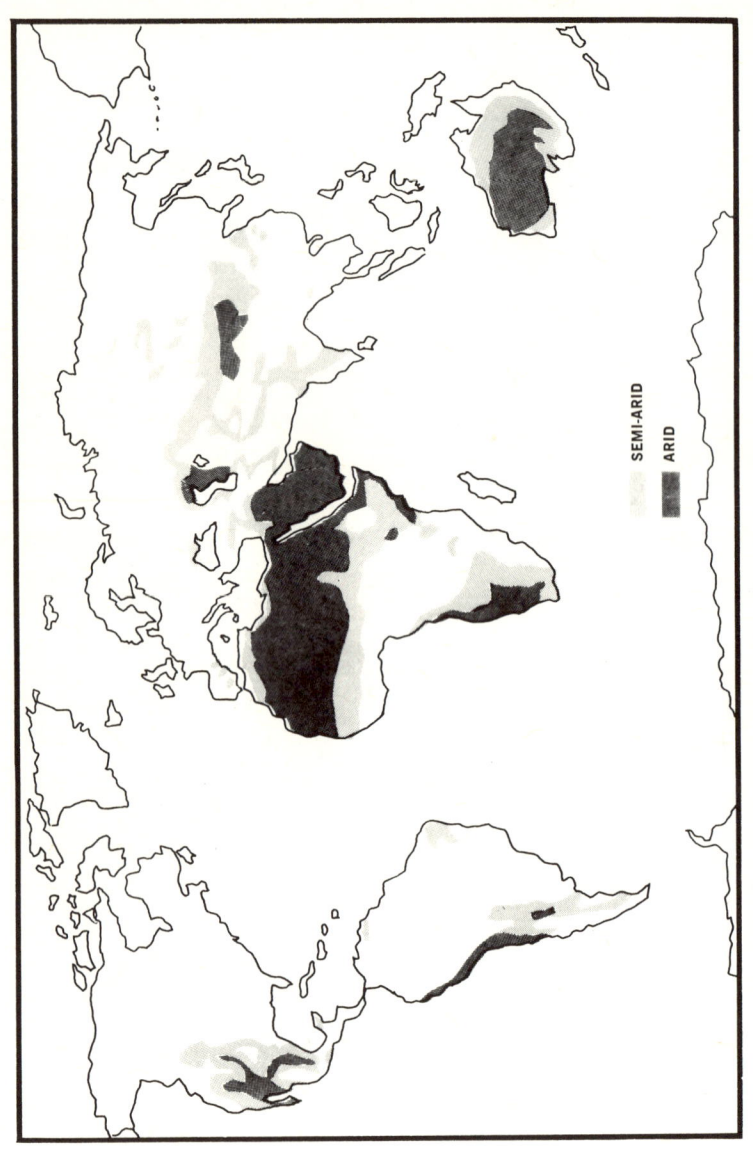

Figure 5.6. Distribution of arid and semi-arid lands.

Source: Redrawn from L.D. Stamp (ed.) A history of land use in arid regions. UNESCO, 1961.

ability to either tolerate or avoid drought (108). Nevertheless, fluctuations in the amount and occurrence of annual rainfall generates large oscillations in population densities (109). Consequently, arid zone ecosystems, in general, share the common features of high population fluctuations and instability (see Chapter 4).

Our environmental concerns in arid ecosystems are related to the question of whether intensifying their use will enable them to support increases in human and domesticated animal populations. Recurrent serious droughts in areas heavily grazed could cause excessive removal of vegetation (8). In terms of agriculture, intensive perennial irrigation would pose a problem. Such a system requires large amounts of water low in salts to prevent salinity buildup (107). Excessive leaching to remove base salts from the soil unavoidably removes other essential elements. This, in turn, necessitates intensive application of fertilizers, which results in the accumulation of salts and minerals and the eventual degradation of water and drainage basins below the irrigated fields (110).

Objectives of Settlement in Arid Lands

The objectives of those settling new lands will, of course, influence the nature of the land use. A major objective of land settlement in semi-arid and arid zones has been to practice subsistence level agriculture to accommodate an increasing human population. This is a particularly hazardous operation in arid zones because of their unpredictable environment and system instability.

Another primary objective of arid land use is to improve the economy and well-being of the region's inhabitants. Minimal modifications to the system coupled with a better understanding of local conditions and of the basic instability of desert systems should improve yield.

If, however, the settlement objective is to compete with other regions for economic gain, intensive system management including irrigation, soil treatment and mechanized agricultural techniques will be required.

Land Resources in Arid Zones

Where sufficient ground or surface water can be obtained to allow perennial irrigation, areas can be farmed using modern agricultural techniques. Elsewhere, semi-arid lands, devoid of irrigation water, provide a substantial grazing resource; and in these areas, there are possibilities for managing native or introduced species. Much of the arid area of the earth, however, is unusable for existing methods of agricultural production.

Ecological Constraints on Arid and Semi-Arid Land Use

The lack of sufficient quantities of water, low in salts, to support people and domesticated animals is perhaps the most overriding constraint on man's intensive use of dry lands. The low mean annual precipitation, the unpredictability of storm intensity and frequent and recurrent extreme droughts are central features of the arid environment (111). A high concentration of dissolved salts is often found in surface water from outside the system or groundwater taken from wells (112), and this creates problems when they are used for irrigation (113).

Another limiting factor is temperature. The short length of the growing season limits plant growth and causes relatively low productivity in the cold arid regions of North America and Asia (114). Perhaps the most important effect of high temperatures in arid zones is the high potential evaporation associated with high temperatures.

The soils of arid zones range from weathered surface materials lacking any organic matter to fertile alluvial deposits like those found in the Nile Basin. Soil fertility studies indicate that in intensive crop management, nitrogen is the limiting element (107).

Disturbance of the delicate surface crusts (desert pavement) as a result of grazing and other activities increases the loss of soil and decreases productivity (107). Low erratic rainfall and low organic content slows soil formation, and the exposed silt and sand then become very susceptible to wind and water erosion. An example is in the Iakla-Makan Desert where sand encroachment has destroyed many productive oases (107).

In natural ecosystems overuse or misuse of resources tends to cease when the resources become limiting (68). Many of the animals either migrate out of the system or perish. Man's solution, however, is to provide subsidies for resources which become limiting. These increase production, which increases the rate of use of other essential materials; and this, in turn, creates the need for additional subsidies. System management thus increases in overall complexity, and the unpredictability of climatic events compounds the problem (68).

In the developed countries there has been an increasing use of arid regions for industry. Logan predicts that if solar energy were developed as a cheap power source we could expect to see a tremendous industrial development in arid North America (115). In this light, however, Pettersen (116) cautions that because of global atmospheric circulation patterns arid portions of the earth are likely to be affected by increasing atmospheric pollution (see Figure 5.7).

It has been shown (see Table 5.2) that some desert plants are extremely sensitive to ozone as an air pollutant. One study found that desert plants are even more sensitive than the garden variety bean, known to be extremely sensitive to ozone (117, 118). This indicates that we can expect serious effects on desert ecosystems if toxic air pollutants begin to accumulate over desert regions as they are doing now in the San Bernardino Mountains of California, where more than 60,000 acres of ponderosa pine trees have been seriously damaged or killed (119). Of course, atmospheric pollution is not a problem unique to arid regions (see Figure 5.7). It is the kind of ecological consideration, however, which should go into comprehensive land management planning.

Species	Relative sensitivity index
Franseria dumosa Gray	7.0
Cercidium floridum Benth.	5.6
Chilopsis linearis (Cav.) Sweet	3.8
Phaseolus vulgaris L. (Black valentine variety bean)	2.3
Hyptis emoryi Torr.	1.9
Acacia Greggii Gray	1.8
Bebbia juncea (Benth.) Greene	1.4
Simmondsia chinensis (Link.) C.K.Schneid	0

Table 5.2. Relative ozone sensitivity of two-week old seedlings of selected desert plants and Black Valentine bean.

Source: Strain, B.R. and J.F. Buriel (1971).

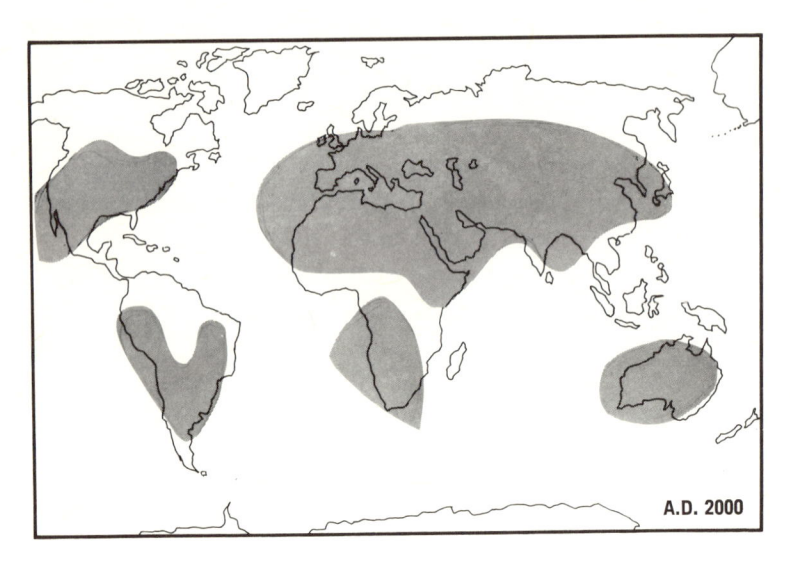

Figure 5.7. Regions within which severe pollution may develop by the year 2000.

Source: Redrawn from Pettersen, S. (1966).

Conclusion

Existing agricultural techniques are difficult to apply successfully in arid and semi-arid areas. Dry farming over much of the arid and semi-arid lands is hazardous because of climatic uncertainties. With good management, grazing natural vegetation is possible, but overgrazing must be avoided to assure continued production (8). Irrigation in arid regions is difficult because of water deficiency and salt accumulation. In addition the excessive water needed to drain salts off the fields also removes soil nutrients (107) and interferes with their natural cycling as discussed in Chapter 3. The salts, mineral and toxic chemicals washed through the system accumulate in inland basins or flow into drainage waters and become water pollutants.

5.E. INTEGRATED LAND USE PLANNING--A CASE STUDY

It is not enough to recognize and understand the capabilities and limitations of each vegetation type and land use situation. Ways must be found within the political and economic structure of each country to put this knowledge into planning and action programs. A primary responsibility for accomplishing this task rests with land management authorities.

The following is a case example of a government agency effort to take a fresh look at its policies and programs from the standpoint of the degree to which they serve the public purpose. The United States Forest Service had been accused of a strong product bias at the expense of other land values, and the following discussion describes the agency's response to this public criticism.

National Forests in the Western United States

There are 109 million acres of U.S. national forest land west of the Great Plains (exclusive of Alaska and Hawaii). Sixty-five percent, or 71 million acres, of this forest has been classified as suitable and available for timber production (120). This land is playing an increasingly important role in supplying the nation's wood needs.

Official U.S. Forest Service records (unpublished) were used to derive the following figures on use trends. In 1920, the timber cut in the western national forests amounted to something over 700 million board feet. A half century later in 1970, the cut was 9,504 million board feet--or 13 times as much. Mounting timber output has been accompanied by other changes in these forests. In the same half century, for example, recreational use of the western national forests has increased 50-fold. In this period, greater values have been placed on wildlife production, scenic beauty, watershed stability and water quality and quantity. These values coupled with demands for more timber products are resulting in a critical conflict of user interests. This conflict has resulted in direct confrontations between wilderness advocates and the timber industry over land allocation (121). On a broader scale there is a disagreement over the priorities of forest uses and concern about the impact of timber production and mining upon the quality of the forest lands and their utility for other purposes.

Internal Review of Management

Several analyses of land management practices have been made within the agency. One such review of the Bitterroot National Forest in Montana made the following observations (121):

1) "There is an implicit attitude among many people on the staff of the Bitterroot National Forest that resource production goals come first and that land management considerations take second place."

2) "Communications with the public and other interested agencies have been seriously inadequate."

3) "Multiple use planning on the Bitterroot National Forest has not advanced far enough to provide the firm management direction necessary to insure quality land management and, at the same time, to provide all segments of the public with a clear picture of long-range objectives."

4) "In several instances the land management has been substandard because of slips or lapses in quality control."
5) "The Bitterroot National Forest has a substantial timber producing capacity that can and should be utilized to help meet the nation's growing need for wood and to help support a stable economy in western Montana."
6) "The Forest Service has been remiss in not determining how much it would cost to do a balanced job of resource management and aggressively seeking the necessary finances for the total job."
7) "Increased funds alone will not solve present problems."
8) "The public should not expect that new management direction will appear instantly and completely in all activities."
9) "The information base for decision making should be enlarged."

Another land classification study on 6 western national forests found that some land previously classified for timber harvesting was so unstable that it should not be logged at all (122). They also found some forest areas so low in productivity that the economic gains from logging them would be more than offset by the dollar costs and land management problems encountered in their use. Also, some areas with high aesthetic and recreational values that would be damaged by timber production had been classified as "commercial." By eliminating all of these areas from commercial classification, the commercial forest area was reduced 22 percent (122).

These shortcomings in management can be attributed to two factors. First, there has been a continuous demand for heavy timber cutting to supply the nation's wood needs. Secondly, there has not been an adequate understanding of the physical limitations of forest ecosystems and the long-term effects of management operations. As a result, some foresters have failed to see the urgent need for total system considerations in land management actions.

The problem has been aggravated by the Forest Service's failure to obtain the necessary funds for balanced management. Table 5.3 shows fund requests and amounts received by the U.S. National Forest System during the period 1963-1970. Such imbalances in funding make the successful administration of integrated land plans impossible. Partly because it has been poorly financed and understaffed, and because of the great demand for forest products, overcutting of timber occurs. For example, for three out of four years, the actual timber removal exceeded the allowable cut in the Bitterroot National Forest (see Table 5.4). Although much of the overcut was unregulated, even the regulated cut was excessive during the first four years of the planned period. Such management deficiencies may cause lasting damage to the land.

Agency Reorganization

The significance of the situation described above is that a governmental agency in response to outside criticisms and its own internal concerns has made sweeping reviews of its operations and is moving rapidly to make changes (123). A major effort is being made to improve the planning process and to provide practical, multi-use management plans. Although the Forest Service employs people in more than 80 different professions, it is now expanding its expertise by hiring more soil scientists, plant physiologists, fish and wildlife biologists, landscape architects and other experts in resource related fields (123).

Efforts are being made to increase the environmental awareness of agency personnel and to improve quality control. Priorities are being redefined, and land use plans are being reviewed and tightened. Studies are underway to determine if the Forest Service can be reconstructured in a way that will enable it to fulfill its responsibilities more effectively.

Alternatives are being considered for questionable management procedures. A policy has been established that when environmental

Activity	Fiscal Years 1963-1970 8-year total		
	Planned level of financing	Actual financing	Percent financed
	----------Millions of dollars----------		
Timber sale administration and management	285	271	95
Reforestation and timber stand improvement	342	137	40
Recreation	572	260	45
Wildlife habitat management	54	34	63
Range management, revegetation and improvements	120	97	81
Soil and water management	94	49	52
Minerals and special uses	38	32	84
Land classification, adjustments, and surveys	68	41	60
Forest fire protection	283	203	72
Construction and maintenance of improvements for fire and general purposes	142	100	70
Insect and disease control	99	93	94
Acquisition of lands	52	14	27
Roads and trails	1,138	842	74

Table 5.3. Comparison of planned level financing for the National Forest System and the actual expenditures for the period fiscal years 1963-1970.

Source: Worf, et al., 1970.

		Actual Cut			
		Unregulated[1]			
Fiscal Year	Total	Under 11 inches	Intermediate and salvage	Regulated	Allowable Cut
	----------Million board feet----------				
1966	69.4	7.6	0.5	61.3	63.0
1967	58.3	6.4	1.2	50.7	63.0
1968	64.5	7.1	.5	56.9	50.3
1969	71.6	7.9	.6	63.1	50.3
Total	263.8	29.0	2.8	232.0	226.6

[1]Material not included in the allowable cut.

Table 5.4. Actual and allowable cut on Montana portion of the Bitterroot National Forest, fiscal years 1966-1969.

Source: Worf, et al., 1970.

impact studies show that a present management procedure is harmful to the environment and no alternative to the procedure is known, it will be dropped (123). For example, the agency is taking steps to phase out logging on steep slopes that require a network of closely spaced temporary roads. Plans also call for tightening the standards and supervision on the location, design and construction of roads.

Finally, the agency's own research program is moving toward a multidisciplinary approach to problems with greater emphasis on an understanding of ecosystems.

Conclusion

Whether these actions and revisions will be effective remains to be proven. Nevertheless, the necessity of integrated planning for land management has been demonstrated in this dramatic example of institutional response to changing management needs and to increasing knowledge of the ecological basis of land resources.

5.F. SUMMARY

This section analyzed some global land use problems and interpreted them in an ecological context.

A review and comparison of general land use trends in the tropical lowland forests, tropical savanna, temperate grasslands and deserts produced the following generalities:

1) Environmental quality has no meaning outside the human experience. Consequently, environmental destruction or degradation is considered a regressive change in land quality which makes it less capable of supplying man's needs. In the same way environmental improvement is described as a progressive change in land quality which makes it more suitable to man's needs. Modern man's needs involve more than nutritional and shelter requirements. Cultural, educational and recreational experiences are also human needs which are supplied by the environment.

2) Many cases of environmental degradation are due to poor land management practices, particularly single objective management practices. Many management institutions now realize this shortcoming and are initiating new land use planning procedures. These procedures (variously called multiple use, integrated or comprehensive land use planning programs) involve input by interdisciplinary teams of biologists, physical scientists, sociologists, economists, etc. Although it is difficult to overcome tradition, some agencies have already successfully adopted the integrated approach to land management.

3) Ways should be sought within the political and economic structure of each nation to implement an integrated land use plan that is based on ecological principles. The primary responsibility for accomplishing this rests with land management authorities in each nation. The facilities of the United Nations, however, should be used to encourage these goals.

4) Although this task group did not specifically consider the effect of human population size on environmental quality or land management, it is clear that global environmental degradation, as defined above, is inevitable unless the explosive human population increase is brought under control.

REFERENCES

1. Whittaker, R. H. 1970. Communities and ecosystems. Current Concepts in Biology Series. Macmillan Co. 162 p.

2. Watt, K. E. F. 1968. Ecology and resource management--a quantitative approach. McGraw-Hill, New York. 450 p.

3. Van Dyne, G. M. (ed.). 1969. The ecosystem concept in natural resource management. Academia Press, New York. 323 p.

4. United Nations. 1970. Natural resources of developing countries: investigation, development, and rational utilization. United Nations, Department of Economic and Social Affairs. United Nations publication, Sales No. E.70.II.B.2. 174 p.

5. Boykso, H. 1945. On pasture problems in Palestine. Palest. J. Bot. Rehovot. 5:52-58.

6. Khan, M. 1952. Improvement and management of the range lands of West Pakistan, p. 491-498. In Sixth Internat. Grassland Congress, Proc. Vol. I.

7. Canfield, R. A. 1957. Reproduction and life span of some perennial grasses of southern Arizona. Jour. Range Management 10:199-203.

8. Moore, R. M. 1960. The management of native vegetation in arid and semi-arid regions, p. 173-190. In Plant-water relationships in arid and semi-arid condition. UNESCO, Paris. Arid Zone Research 15:225 p.

9. Van Dyne, G. M. 1966. Ecosystems, systems ecology, and systems ecologists. U.S. Atomic Energy Comm. Oak Ridge Natl. Lab Report, ORNL 3957. 31 p.

10. Leopold, L. B., F. E. Clarke, B. B. Henshaw, and J. R. Balsley. 1971. A procedure for evaluating environmental impact. United States Geological Survey Circular 645. Wash., D.C. 13 p.

11. Schaeffer, M., D. C. Gajdusek, A. Brocen, and H. Eichenwald. 1959. Epidemic jungle fevers among Okinawan colonists in the Bolivian rain forests. I. Epidemiology. Am. J. Trop. Med. Hyg. 8:372-396.

12. Schmidt, J. R., D. C. Gajdusek, H. Schaeffer, and R. H. Gorrie. 1959. Epidemic jungle fevers among Okinawan colonists in the Bolivian rain forests. II. Isolation and characterization of Uruma virus, a newly recognized human pathogen. Am. J. Trop. Med. Hyg. 8:479-487.

13. Smith, T. L. 1967. Colombia: social structure and the process of development. Univ. of Florida. 389 p.

14. National Planning Board of Ecuador. 1963. Plan general de desarrollo economico y social, colonizacion. Vol. 6.

15. Estimations compiled from:
Present settlement farms: Compiled from La Carretera Marginal de la Selva. Tippetts-Abbett-McCarthy-Shatton, Lima and New York, 1965; Evaluacion del Potencial Economica y Social de la Zona Tingo-Maria-Tocache, Huallaga Central. Servicio Cooperativo Inter-Americano de Fomento, Lima, 1962; and Wolfram U. Drewes. 1958. The economic development of the western montana of central Peru as related to transportation. Peruvian Times.

Settlement farms needed: A rough approximation of the additional family farms needed in Peru, if a reasonably equitable distribution of land resources could be effected through an agrarian grant reform, is on the order of 550,000. This is arrived at by assuming that if the 694,000 sub-family farms could be reconstituted into viable small farms, about half or 350,000 families would need to be located elsewhere, and that farm opportunities are desirable for at least 1/3 or 100,000 of the 300,000 landless farm workers (data from Inter-America Committee on Agricultural Development reports). Crude estimation indicates that about half of these farm needs might be provided for if a fairly drastic redistribution of land resources on the 10,000 largest sized holdings were carried out, leaving the other half or 225,000 to be met through colonization.

16. Estimates compiled from:
    Wessel, K. L. 1968. An economic assessment of pioneer settlement in the Bolivia lowlands. Ph.D. Dissertation. Cornell University.

    Secretaria Nacional de Planificacion y Coordinacion. Plan general de desarrollo economico y social, 1962-1971. Republica de Bolivia.

17. Sander, G. 1961. Agrarkolonisation in Costa Rica, Siedlung, Wirtschaft and Sozialefuge an der Pioniergrenze. Schriften Geografisk Inst. der Univ. Kiel 19:(3).

18. Nelson, M. 1970. Public policy for new land development in the humid tropics of Latin America. Resources for the Future and the Latin American Institute for Economic and Social Planning. p. 1-9. (Unpublished).

19. FAO. 1969. Indicative world plans for agricultural development to 1957 and 1985. Regional Study No. 2. South America. Vol. 1. FAO, Rome. 286 p.

20. Williams, L. L. 1960. Little-known wealth of tropical forests, p. 2003-2006. In Fifth Forestry Congress, Proc. Vol. 3. Univ. of Washington, Seattle, Washington. 2066 p.

21. Srivastava, T. N. 1967. Forestry in India. "Indian Forester" (Pub.). 92 p.

22. MacGregor, W. D. 1934. Silviculture of the mixed deciduous forests of Nigeria. Oxford Forestry Memoirs 18:1-80.

23. Nye, P. H., and D. J. Greenland. 1960. The soil under shifting cultivation. Commonwealth Bureau of Soils, Harpenden. Tech. Commun. No. 51. 156 p.

24. Bartlett, H. H. 1957. Fire, primitive agriculture and grazing in the tropics, p. 692-720. In W. L. Thomas, Man's role in changing the face of the earth. Chicago. 1193 p.

25. Conklin, H. C. 1957. Hamunoo agriculture. FAO Forestry Department Paper No. 12. FAO, Rome. p. 109.

26. Martinez, M. A. 1970. Ecología human del ejido Benito Juarez, Oaxaca. Bol. Esp. Inst. Nac. Inv. For. México. 5.

27. Cuanalo, H. 1970. Los suelos de la región de Tuxtepec, Oax. Bol. Esp. Inst. Nac. Inv. For. México. 5.

28. Sarukhán, J. 1964. Estudio sucesional de un area talada en Tuxtepec, Oax. Bol. Esp. Inst. Nac. Inv. For. México 3:107-172.

29. Budowski, G. 1963. Forest succession in tropical lowlands. Turrialba 13:42-44.

30. Lamb, F. B. 1966. Mahogany of tropical America. The University of Michigan Press. 220 p.

31. Richards, P. W. 1966. The tropical rain forest: an ecological study. Cambridge University Press. 450 p.

32. Schulz, J. P. 1960. Ecological studies on rain forest in northern Surinam. Noord-Hollandsche Uitg. Mij., Amsterdam. 267 p.

33. Ashton, P. W. 1964. Ecological studies in the mixed dipterocarp forests of Brunei State. Oxford University Memoirs 25:62-65.

34. Gomez-Pompa, A. 1967. Some problems in tropical plant ecology. Jour. Arnold Arboretum 49:225-232.

35. Champion, H. G., and A. L. Griffith. 1960. Manual of general silviculture for India. Oxford University Press. 329 p.

36. INIF. 1968. Tercer informe de la comisión de estudios sobre ecología de Dioscoreas. Publicación del Instituto Nacional de Investigaciones Forestales, México.

37. Golley, F. (ed.). 1971. Mineral cycling in tropical forest ecosystems. University of Georgia. (In press).

38. Cook, O. F. 1921. Milpa agriculture, a primitive tropical system; Smithsonian Inst. annual report 1919. Wash., D.C. p. 307-326.

39. Westlake, D. F. 1963. Comparisons of plant productivity. Biol. Rev. 38:385-425.

40. Scott, R. W., M. A. Millett, and G. J. Hajny. 1969. Wood wastes for animal feeding. For. Prod. Journal 19:14-18.

41. Harris, E. E., J. F. Saeman, R. R. Marquardt, M. L. Hannan, and S. C. Rogers. 1948. Fodder yeast from wood hydrolyzates and still residues. Ind. Eng. Chem. 40:1220-1223.

42. Hall, J. A., J. F. Saemon, and J. F. Harris. 1956. Wood saccarification. UNASYVA 10:7-16.

43. Korolkov, I. I. 1968. Percolation hydrolysis of plant raw material. Moscow. 288 p. (In Russian).

44. Hesse, R. W. 1952. Pulpwood from tropical forests. In Symposium on tropical woods and agricultural residues as sources of pulp.

45. Beard, J. S. 1963. Savanna, p. 98-103. In The ecology of man in the tropical environment. IUCN New Series no. 4. Morges.

46. Shantz, H. L. 1954. The place of grasslands in the earth's cover of vegetation. Ecology 35:143-145.

47. Wahlen, F. T. 1952. Grassland resources and potentials of the world, p. 103-113. In Sixth Internat. Grassland Congr., Proc.

48. Ayodo, S. O. 1968. Address of welcome. Symposium on Wildlife Management and Land Use, Proc. E. Afr. Agric. For. J. 33:2-3.

49. Dasmann, R. F. 1964. African game ranching. Pergamon Press, London. 72 p.

50. Riney, T. 1968. Criteria for land use planning. Symposium on Wildlife Management and Land Use, Proc. E. Afr. Agric. For J. 33:34-37.

51. Davis, R. K. 1968. Some economic aspects of range management in Kenya, p. 73-79. In W. M. Longhurst, and H. F. Heady (ed.), East African range problems. Report of symp. held at Villa Serbelloni, Lake Como, Italy. 119 p. (Multilith).

52. Talbot, L. M., W. J. A. Payne, H. P. Ledger, L. D. Verdcourt, and M. H. Talbot. 1965. The meat production potential of wild animals in Africa. Commonwealth Agric. Bur. Farnham Royal. Tech. Comm. 16. 42 p.

53. Taylor, C. R. 1968. The minimum water requirements of some East African bovids. Symp. Zool. Soc. Lond. 21:195-206.

54. Hofmann, R. R. 1968. Comparisons of the rumen and omasum structures in East African game ruminants in relation to their feeding habits. Symp. Zool. Soc. Lond. 21:179-194.

55. Jewell, P. A. 1969. Wild mammals and their potential for new domestication, p. 101-109. In P. J. Ucko, and G. W. Dimbleby (ed.), The domestication and exploitation of plants and animals. Aldine. 581 p.

56. Leakey, L. S. B. 1963. Prehistoric man in the tropical environment, p. 24-29. In The ecology of man in the tropical environment. IUCN New Series no. 4. Morges.

57. McCulloch, B. 1965. Overstocking in Sukumaland, Tanganyika. E. Afr. Agric. For. J. 30:219-226.

58. White, G. F. 1968. Notes on water development in relation to East African rangeland management, p. 118-119. In W. M. Longhurst, and H. F. Heady (ed.), East African range problems. Rept. of symp. held at Villa Serbelloni, Lake Como, Italy. 119 p. (Multilith).

59. Glover, P. E., and M. D. Gwynne. 1961. The destruction of Massailand. New Scientist 249:450-453.

60. Kumar, L. S. S. 1952. The problem of pressure of grazing on native pastures, p. 114-123. In Sixth Internat. Grassland Congr., Proc.

61. Jordon, S. M. 1957. Reclamation and pasture management in the semi-arid areas of Kitui District, Kenya. E. Afr. Agric. J. 23:84-88.

62. Pereira, H. C. 1959. Lessons gained from grazing trials at Makavete, Kenya. E. Afr. Agric. J. 25:59-62.

63. Longhurst, W. M., and H. F. Heady (ed.). 1968. East African range problems. Rept. of symp. held at Villa Serbelloni, Lake Como, Italy. 119 p. (Multilith).

64. Robinette, W. L., P. Hemingway, and A. Cormack. 1966. Appraisal of range condition on the Kalimawe controlled area, p. 7-9. In D. G. Anstey, Kalimawe in relation to Inkomazi Game Reserve. Rept. to Reg. Dev. Comm., Kilimanjaro Reg., Moshi. Ref. no. TA/G/GR/MR. (Mimeo).

65. Tanner, R. E. S. 1961. Population changes 1955-59 in Musoma District, Tanganyika, and their effect on land usage. E. Afr. Agric. For. J. 26:164-169.

66. Moule, G. R. 1968. World distribution of domestic animals, Chap. 2. In E. S. E. Hafez (ed.), Adaptation of domestic animals. Lea and Febiger, Philadelphia. 415 p.

67. Carter, D. B. 1954. Climates of Africa and India according to Thornthwaite's 1948 classification. In Climatology 7:453-479.

68. Talbot, W. J. 1961. Land utilization in the arid regions of southern Africa, p. 299-331. In L. D. Stamp (ed.), A history of land use in the arid region. UNESCO, Paris. Arid Zone Research 17:388 p.

69. French, M. H. 1957. Nutritional value of tropical grasses and fodders. Herb. Abstr. 27:1-9.

70. Williamson, G., and W. J. A. Payne (ed.). 1965. An introduction to animal husbandry in the tropics. Longmans, Green and Co., London. 447 p.

71. Posselt, J. 1963. The domestication of the eland. Rhod. J. Agric. Res. 1:81-87.

72. Taylor, R. F. 1969. Agricultural change in Kikuyuland, p. 463-493. In M. F. Thomas, and G. W. Whittington (ed.), Environment and land use in Africa. Methuen and Co., London. 554 p.

73. Kay, G. 1969. Agricultural progress in Zambia, p. 495-524. In M. F. Thomas and G. W. Whittington (ed.), Environment and land use in Africa. Methuen and Co., London. 554 p.

74. Riney, R. 1968. Discussions, p. 413-415. In M. A. Crawford (ed.), Comparative nutrition of wild animals. Symp. Zool. Soc. Lond., No. 21. 429 p.

75. Walter, H. 1963. Productivity of vegetation in arid countries, the savannah problem and bush encroachment after overgrazing, p. 221-229. In Ninth Tech. Meeting, Proc., The ecology of man in the tropical environment. IUCN New Series no. 4. Morges.

76. West, O. 1965. Fire in vegetation and its use in pasture management with special reference to tropical and subtropical Africa. Commonwealth Bur. Pastures and Field Crops, Publ. No. 1. 53 p. (Mimeo).

77. Voisin, A. 1959. Grass productivity. Philos. Libr. Inc., New York. 355 p.

78. Daubenmire, R. 1968. Ecology of fire in grasslands, p. 209-266. In J. B. Cragg (ed.), Advances in ecological research 5. Academic Press, New York. 283 p.

79. Lamprey, H. F. 1967. Notes on the dispersal and germination of some tree seeds through the agency of mammals and birds. E. Afr. Wildl. J. 5:179-180.

80. Ford, J. 1970. Interactions between human societies and various trypanosome-tsetse-wild fauna complexes, p. 81-97. In J. P. Garlick, and R. W. J. Keay (ed.), Human ecology in the tropics. Symp. of Soc. for Study of Human Biology 9.

81. Uganda annual reports of veterinary services and animal industry. (Various dates, 1939-1949.) Kampala, Uganda.

82. Sauer, Carl. 1938. Destructive exploitation in modern colonial expansion. Comptes Rendues du Congrès International de Geographie 2:494-499. Amsterdam, 1938.

83. Kuchler, A. W. 1960. World natural vegetation, p. 16-17. In E. B. Espenshade, Jr. (ed.), Goode's world atlas. 11th ed. Rand McNally. 288 p.

84. Coupland, R. T. 1950. Ecology of mixed prairie in Canada. Eco. Mono. 20:241-315.

85. Weaver, J. E., and F. W. Albertson. 1956. Grasslands of the Great Plains: their nature and use. Johnsen Publ. Co., Lincoln, Neb. 395 p.

86. Curtis, J. T. 1959. The vegetation of Wisconsin. University of Wis. Press, Madison. 657 p.

87. Coaton, W. G. H. 1958. The hodotermitid harvester termites of South Africa. Department of Agriculture, Union of South Africa. Science Bull. No. 375 (Ent. Series No. 43).

88. Kovda, V. A. 1961. Land use development in the arid regions of the Russian plain, the Caucasus and Central Asia. In A history of land use in arid regions. UNESCO, Paris. Arid Zone Research 17:388 p.

89. Despois, J. 1961. Development of land use in northern Africa. In A history of land use in arid regions. UNESCO, Paris. Arid Zone Research 17:388 p.

90. Williams, R. E., B. W. Allred, R. M. Denio, and H. A. Paulson, Jr. 1968. Conservation, development and use of the world's rangelands. J. Range Management 21:355-360.

91. Moore, R. M., and E. F. Biddiscombe. 1964. The effects of grazing on grasslands, p. 221-235. In C. Barnard (ed.), Grasses and grasslands. Macmillan. 269 p.

92. Shantz, H. L., and B. L. Turner. 1958. Vegetational changes in Africa. University of Ariz., College of Agriculture Report No. 169.

93. Lewis, J. K. 1969. Range management viewed in the ecosystem framework, p. 97-187. In G. Van Dyne (ed.), The ecosystem concept in natural resource management. Academic Press, New York. 323 p.

94. Dyksterhuis, E. J. 1958. Ecological principles in range evaluation. Bot. Rev. 24:253-272.

95. De Vos, A. 1969. Ecological conditions affecting the production of wild herbivorous mammals on grasslands, p. 137-183. In J. B. Cragg (ed.), Advances in ecological research 6. 236 p.

96. Wadham, Sir S. 1961. The problem of arid Australia. In A history of land use in arid regions. UNESCO, Paris. Arid Zone Research 17:388 p.

97. West, O. 1965. Fire in vegetation and its use in pasture management, with special reference to tropical and subtropical Africa. Commonwealth Agr. Bur. Publ. 1:1-53. (Mimeo).

98. Box, T. W., J. Powell, and D. L. Drawe. 1967. Influence of fire on south Texas chaparral communities. Ecology 48:955-961.

99. Humphrey, R. R. 1958. The desert grassland: a history of vegetational change and an analysis of causes. Botanical Rev. 24:193-252.

100. Logan, R. F. 1961. Post-Columbian development in the arid regions of the United States of America. In A history of land use in arid regions. UNESCO, Paris. Arid Zone Research 17:388 p.

101. Darling, F. F. 1963. The unity of ecology. The Advancement of Science 20:297-306.

102. Meigs, P. 1953. World distribution of arid and semi-arid homoclimates. In Reviews of research on arid zone hydrology. UNESCO, Paris. Arid Zone Program 1:203-209.

103. Meigs, P. 1957. Arid and semi-arid climates of the world, p. 135-138. In International Geophysical Union 17th Congress, Wash., D.C. 8th General Assembly, Proc.

104. Richard, W. H., and J. C. Beatley. 1965. Canopy-coverage of the desert shrub vegetation mosaic of the Nevada test site. Ecology 46:524-599.

105. Cottam, G. P. Leaf area index in white oak-black oak forest of southern Wisconsin. (Unpublished data).

106. Child, G. I. 1971. A structural description of tropical forests in eastern Panama and northwestern Colombia. In F. B. Golley (ed. Mineral cycling in tropical forest ecosystems. (In press).

107. Dregne, H. E. 1968. Surface material of desert environments, p. 285-377. In McGinnies, et al. (ed.), Deserts of the world. Univ. of Arizona Press, Tucson. 788 p.

108. Oppenheimer, H. R. 1960. Adaptation to drought: xerophytism, p. 105-138. In Plant-water relationships in arid and semi-arid conditions. UNESCO, Paris. Arid Zone Research 15:225 p.

109. Beatley, J. 1967. Survival of winter annuals in the northern Mojave Desert. Ecology 48:745-750.

110. Hamden, G. 1961. Evolution of irrigation agriculture in Egypt, p. 119-142. In L. D. Stamp (ed.), A history of land use in the arid region. UNESCO, Paris. Arid Zone Research 17:388 p.

111. Hare, F. K. 1961. The causation of the arid region. In A history of land use in arid regions. UNESCO, Paris. Arid Zone Research 17:388 p.

112. Abell, L. F., and W. J. Geldermann. 1964. Annotated bibliography on reclamation and improvement of saline and alkali soils (1957-1964). Inter. Instit. for Land Reclamation and Improvement, Wageningen, Netherlands. 59 p.

113. Lehman, W. F., S. J. Richards, D. C. Erwin, and A. W. Marsh. 1968. Effect of irrigation treatments on alfalfa (Medicagu satira L.): production, persistence, and soil salinity in Southern California. Hilgardia 39:277-295.

114. Lieth, H. Versuch einer Kartographisdien Darstellung der Productivität der Pfanzendecke auf der Erde, p. 72-80. In Geographischer Taschenbuch 1964/65. Wiesbaden: Franz Steiver.

115. Logan, R. F. 1961. Post-Columbian developments in the arid regions of the United States of America, p. 277-297. In A history of land use in arid regions. UNESCO, Paris. Arid Zone Research 17:388 p.

116. Pettersen, S. 1966. Recent demographic trends and future meteorological services. Amer. Meteorol. Soc. Bull. 47:950-963.

117. Strain, B. R., and J. F. Buriel. 1971. Effects of air pollution on vegetation in the United States. Symposium on Effects of Man on Vegetation, Proc. Internat. Soc. Pl. Sociology and Ecology. Rinteln, Germany. (In press).

118. Hill, A. C., et al. 1961. Plant injury induced by ozone. Phytopathology 51:356-363.

119. Miller, P. R., and J. R. Parmeter, Jr. 1965. Effect of sustained low concentration ozone fumigation on ponderosa pine. Phytopathology 55:1068.

120. Forest Service, U.S. Department of Agriculture. 1965. Timber trends in the United States. Forest Resources Report 17:235 p.

121. Worf, William A., et al. 1970. Management practices on the Bitterroot National Forest. Forest Service, U.S. Department of Agriculture. 100 p.

122. Wikstrom, J. H., and S. Blair Hutchison. 1971. Stratification of forest land for timber management planning on the western national forests. (An in-house report).

123. Forest Service, U.S. Department of Agriculture. 1971. National forest management in a quality environment. 61 p. (Processed).

Chapter

6

Management of Aquatic Resources

TASK GROUP:

Kenneth Mann, Chairman
Calvin Kaya, Reporter
Rezneat Darnell
Arthur Hasler
Joseph Leach
Robert Ragotzkie
John Teal

6.A. MAJOR FINDINGS

1) The world's seas and inland waters are a major source of high quality protein. In recent years about one-third of the increase in food production has been from fisheries. While the full potential of the oceans is as yet unknown, it is likely that fishing by conventional methods could increase current yields by 50%, or to a total of about 100 million tons per year.

Conclusion

It is extremely important to avoid large scale contamination of the ocean's valuable food supplies by harmful pollutants.

2) The coastal zone of the ocean currently supplies about half our fish products and accounts for over half of the money made from ocean produce. But because sea coasts tend to be densely populated, the fisheries there are particularly vulnerable to interference by industrial development and pollution.

RECOMMENDATION

We recommend that ways be found to protect the coastal zone on a worldwide basis.

3) Estuaries, intertidal marshes and seaweed zones are among the most productive areas on earth. Their productivity is threatened by alteration in river flow, structural changes and pollution.

Conclusion

As far as possible, commercial, residential and recreational construction along coasts should be kept to a minimum and carried out in such a way as to minimize the destruction of productive intertidal and shallow water areas.

Before any decisions are made on proposals to modify river flow by impoundment, the adverse effect of these proposals on the migration of fish and on the productivity of estuaries should be recognized and considered.

4) There are good possibilities for developing aquaculture (fish farming) on a large scale. Selective breeding should be carried out to develop species best suited to the purpose. Ways should be found to make good use of waste heat from power generation plants and to fertilize aquacultural schemes with sewage products.

RECOMMENDATIONS

We recommend establishing regional centers for the selective breeding of animals for aquaculture.

We recommend that a policy of harvesting and utilizing nuisance aquatic plants be established, rather than a policy of controlling their growth with poisons.

5) There is strong evidence that man's pressure on aquatic resources is leading to local and worldwide extinction of many species.

Conclusion

We consider that increasing fishing efforts to the point that man could remove three or four times the present harvest of marine products would lead to further loss of species and create major instabilities in the stocks of fish, birds and mammals.

RECOMMENDATION

We recommend worldwide investment in aquaculture rather than in massive increases in fishing fleets.

We recommend the establishment of an international authority which would oversee the protection and management of the fish and whale stocks of the high seas.

6) Evidence is accumulating rapidly that toxic substances, harmful to aquatic animals and to man, are becoming widespread and

may lead to a drop in productivity and cause a significant proportion of fish stocks to become unfit for human consumption.

Conclusion

It is imperative that ways be found to remove harmful industrial products from sewage and agricultural wastes so that they can be reused in industry and kept from contaminating the biosphere. The remaining material can then be recycled in the biosphere.

RECOMMENDATION

We recommend that international standards be established for the discharge of pollutants into the rivers and the sea and that ocean dumping be controlled.

6.B. INTRODUCTION

Until a few years ago, there was great optimism about the oceans as the source of almost unlimited food for the world's rapidly expanding populations. With two-thirds of the surface of the globe covered with water and largely unexploited, it was thought that the possibilities for increasing the fish catch and, later, for harvesting the microscopic plants and animals in the plankton were almost unlimited.

The recent current of awareness of the extent to which fish have become contaminated with mercury, DDT or PCB's, or have been driven from our estuaries by the outpourings of sewage, has led us to question whether we can even continue to harvest the stocks which we are currently fishing.

Much has been made of the comparisons between hunting and husbandry. It has been pointed out that fishing is the equivalent of hunting and that if we could breed aquatic animals for domestic purposes, keep them under control, feed them like cattle on a pasture and protect them from pests and enemies, we could expect greatly increased yields from the sea and inland waters.

This chapter attempts to analyze these questions from the point of view of ecologists. Fishery specialists have often tended to take a rather narrow view of one or a few species: they assess the size of their stocks and devise plans for maximizing the catch without paying too much attention to the interplay of physical, chemical and biological events which influence the species. Ecologists, on the other hand, try to look broadly at such matters, considering plant production and the whole food chain which leads to the growth of the fish stocks. Ecologists also consider which sets of conditions are most likely to favor the biological cycle of events, and they try to see how man's activities are influencing the process at each stage.

In this light, the questions which we shall set out to answer include: What is our best assessment of the food potential of the oceans? What are the prospects for "farming the sea?" How should

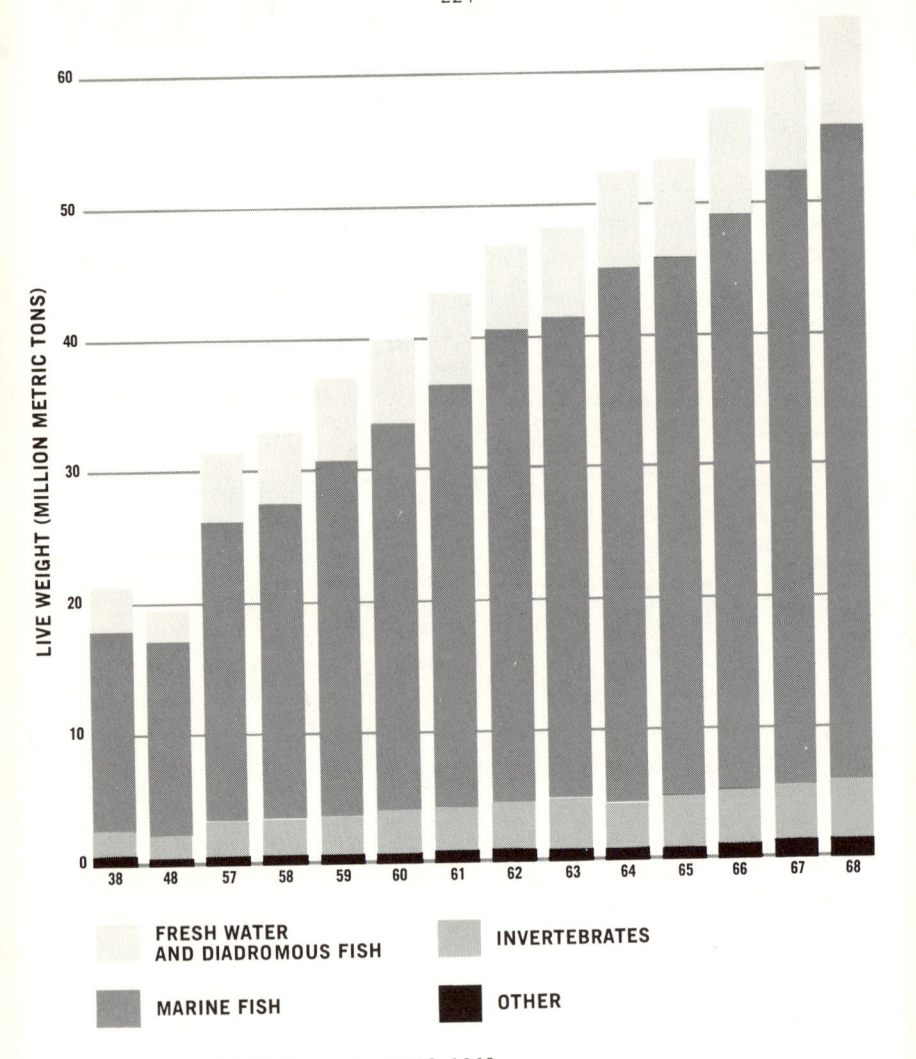

Fig. 6.1. World fish catch, 1938-1968

World catch of aquatic food animals has more than tripled since 1938, to an estimated 64 million metric tons in 1968. Only half of the catch is consumed directly by humans; the remainder is used as livestock feed.

Source: Redrawn from The Food Resources of the Ocean, S. J. Holt. © 1969 by Scientific American, Inc. All rights reserved.

we spend our resources, if there is a choice between expansion of fishing fleets or investment in aquaculture? What is the present state of marine pollution, and what should be done in the future?

Ecologists do not have all the answers to these questions, but they do have a distinctive point of view.

6.C THE FOOD POTENTIAL OF THE OCEANS AND INLAND WATERS

There are two main ways to assess the world's potential for providing fish food. The most direct method is to examine the statistics for world catches and estimate future trends (1, 2). The alternative is to consider the basic processes of biological production and estimate their capability for providing a yield to man (3, 4).

World fish catches increased steadily from 40 million tons in 1960 to 64 million tons in 1968 (see Figure 6.1)--although in 1969, catches were somewhat lower than in 1968. This amount represents about 18% of worldwide animal protein consumption (5). Fish is one of the few major foodstuffs which, on a global scale, has increased in supply over the past decade faster than the human population has increased. In recent years about one-third of the increase in production of food per person has been from fisheries (6). The cheapest and most accessible form of balanced protein food in many countries is fish, which is used as a protein supplement to cheap vegetable sources. Exports of shrimps and fish meal are also important sources of income to several developing countries.

About 86% of the world's fish catch comes from the sea, and of this, over 90% is fin fish. The rest is comprised of whales, crustaceans (e.g., crabs, lobsters, shrimps), mollusks (e.g., oysters, clams, mussels, squid) and a few other invertebrates. Seaweeds, though relatively unimportant in terms of nutritional value, are also harvested (nearly a million tons per year) and provide important industrial materials and food additives.

Estimating the future potential of the world's fisheries from present trends is difficult. On at least two occasions since World War II, predictions were made about the upper limits of what could be obtained from the oceans; and these were soon exceeded (1). The fisheries of the world's oceans may be grouped in about 30 major stocks, of which 14 are probably being fished near or beyond their limits (see Figure 6.2). There is a fair measure of agreement that by using present fishing techniques on stocks which are currently unexploited (around South America, off West Africa, in the Arabian Sea), fisheries could yield 100 million tons per year (1, 2).

There are also possibilities for further exploitation by using new fishing techniques and by using other kinds of creatures as food. There are many kinds of fish which at present are considered unsuitable for food because of their size, appearance or flavor. In many cases they could be converted into nutritious, highly palatable fish protein concentrate. There are others which, though palatable, are in relatively inaccessible places. These could be harvested, but at an increased cost per ton compared with present fisheries. Young fish are much more abundant and grow more rapidly than the adults. If the young fish were harvested, with suitable precautions to allow a percentage of the population to survive and breed, the yield to man would also be greatly increased. Finally, man could harvest the organisms in the plankton—the floating life on which the fish feed.

If several of these courses were followed, it is estimated that the oceans could yield two to four times the present catch, or 130 to 260 million tons (2). However, it is likely that the world's oceans would then show severe symptoms of over-exploitation (see Section 6.F).

The alternative approach to assessing the oceans' potential is based on considerations of their biological mechanisms. This has been attempted by many scientists (3), and they have arrived at very different conclusions. The first step in this process is to estimate the global marine plant production. Two recent estimates (4, 7)

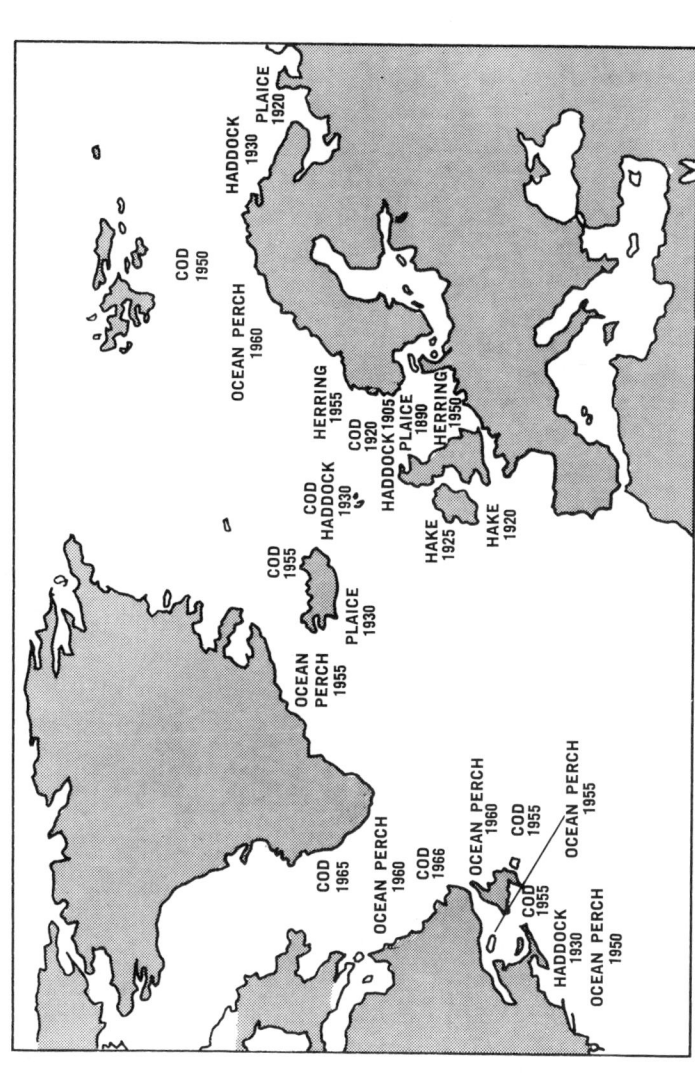

Fig. 6.2. Overfishing of North Atlantic Fish Stocks.
Locations of overfished stocks in the North Atlantic, with approximate times when overfishing began. Overfishing of a stock is indicated when increases in fishing effort do not produce an increase in harvest of that fish.
Source: Redrawn from The Food Resources of the Ocean, S. J. Holt. © 1969 by Scientific American, Inc. All rights reserved.

agree that, in terms of carbon content, this production amounts to about 20 thousand million tons of carbon per year. The next steps are to consider how this material is utilized by organisms in the water column and on the bottom, how many links are present in the food chain between the plants and the fish, and how efficiently each organism uses its food to grow and produce food for the next stage in the food chain. These calculations are difficult because food chains in the ocean are exceedingly complex and variable from place to place. Moiseev (7) calculated that the upper limit of the world fish catch is about 90 million tons per year; and Ryther (4) concluded that the upper limit of total fish production is about 240 million tons per year, of which man might expect to harvest only about 100 million tons.

Zonation of the Fisheries

One of the most important aspects of Ryther's study (4) was its assessment of the relative importance of the open ocean, the coastal zone and the regions of upwelling (where water rich in plant food wells up from the deep ocean to form areas of very high biological production). He showed that in the open ocean, which comprises 90% of the total area, primary production is low; and he estimated that there is an average of five steps in the food chain from plants to harvested fish, each step transferring organic matter to the next with an efficiency of only 10%. At the other extreme are the upwelling areas, which constitute only 0.1% of the total ocean area. These have high primary productivity and average only 1½ steps in the food chain, where material is transferred with a 20% efficiency (see Table 6.1).

Ryther concludes that half the world's fish production occurs in the coastal zone (depth less than 180 meters); that half occurs in the regions of upwelling (mainly off Peru, California, northwest and southwest Africa, Somalia and the Arabian coast); and that, in terms of fish production, the open oceans are virtually biological deserts.

Zone	Percentage of ocean area	Average plant production (grams of carbon/m^2/yr)	Average number of steps in the food chain	Efficiency of transfer at each step	Estimated total fish production (millions of tons)
Open ocean	90	50	5	10%	0.16
Coastal zone	9.9	100	3	15%	120
Upwelling areas	0.1	300	1.5	20%	120

Table 6.1. Steps used by Ryther (4) to calculate the potential fish production of the three major zones of the ocean.

With respect to man's impact on aquatic productivity, it is at once apparent that the coastal zone is both more important and more vulnerable than the open ocean. In the coastal zone, there are prospects for enhancing production by means of aquaculture. Hence, because of its present production, future potential and vulnerability to man's interference, the coastal zone deserves special attention.

The upwelling regions are also close to the coasts, but there water rises from the deep ocean and spreads away from the center of high productivity. Consequently, unless the deep waters of the ocean become seriously polluted, it is unlikely that pollution arising from the land will affect the food chains of the upwelling zones.

6.D. THE COASTAL ZONE

The world fish catch may be divided as follows (2). The most important group, accounting for 45% of the catch by weight, is comprised of herring, pilchards, anchovies and related forms that swim in open water. Next come the cod, haddock and hake group which lives mainly on the bottom and contributes 15% of the catch. Flatfishes, rosefishes, sea perches, mullets and jacks--a large proportion of them found in upwelling areas--account for 15%, and tunas and mackerel, 7%.

While tunas are open water fish, most of the remainder--probably more than 50% of the total catch--have spent some part of their life history in the coastal zone. They commonly spawn on the continental shelf; but, during their development as young fish, a very large proportion of them migrate into bays and estuaries, where biological productivity is particularly high. Factors contributing to this high productivity are: nutrient materials in fresh water running off the land, high plant productivity in coastal marshes and seaweed zones and the mixing of deep, nutrient-rich waters with the surface waters where rivers meet the sea. Another attraction of estuaries is a zone of low salinity. Fishes evolved in fresh water, and many species still have young stages which grow best in water low in salt content because their potential predators and disease-causing organisms cannot live there. Many commercially important species of clams, mussels, oysters, shrimps, prawns and crabs are highly adapted to life in estuaries.

At the same time, the estuaries offer a favorable climate for man's industrial development. The conjunction of river and sea provides fresh water for consumption and a large volume of salt water for effluent disposal. This, together with port facilities and the amenities of life by the seashore, has attracted large numbers of people and industries to the estuaries of the developed countries. There are strong indications that this situation is leading to the deterioration of the environment on which a large proportion of present and future aquatic production depends.

6.E. POSSIBILITIES FOR INCREASING AQUATIC FOOD PRODUCTION

Man has long dreamed of farming the sea. During the last decade about three million tons of fish (about 5% of the total world catch) have been produced in intensively managed ponds. One approach is to fertilize the water with plant nutrients and to make use of the increased production which follows by growing plant-eating species of fish. With only one step in the food chain, high efficiency is obtained from this method. Examples are the milk-fish of the Philippines and Indonesia and the Chinese grass carp.

Another approach is to bring in food from outside the area in which the animals are confined. Examples would be passing food-laden natural water over sedentary organisms like oysters or giving solid food to fish like trout or yellowtail (1). Most of the feed currently used in the latter process consists of other fish which are low in economic value. These are converted into fish of higher value with an efficiency of 13 to 20% (1). In addition there are various combinations of these methods of fish farming.

According to projections made by the Food and Agriculture Organization of the United Nations in 1966 (8), about 30 million tons of fish (half what is now harvested) could be obtained from aquaculture alone by the year 2000 if present average yields were raised to match the best yields now obtained. Even further increases would be possible by putting more area into production and by developing new techniques. Among the areas most readily converted to intensive aquaculture are natural marshes and shallow protected waters. Techniques which might be developed in the future include selecting particular animals or groups of animals suited to aquaculture, using sewage to fertilize areas of aquaculture, using warm waters from industrial processes like electricity generation to increase productivity, and manipulating physical oceanic processes like upwelling.

Manipulating Species Composition

In agriculture, we work with species that have been bred for high yield and exclude unwanted species such as weeds and pests. Similarly, it is possible to manipulate the species composition of areas used for aquaculture. A simple example is the growing of oysters or mussels on ropes hanging from rafts. In nature these shellfish are eaten by snails and starfish; but when cultured they are held clear of the bottom, and their predators cannot get at them (8). The mixture of species present in the cultured area can also be controlled for maximum efficiency. For example, ponds can be stocked with three species of fish--one that eats bottom-living plants, one that eats phytoplankton and one that eats zooplankton (8).

There are also combinations of aquaculture and agriculture which make very efficient use of natural fertilizing substances. In India, sewage ponds are used alternately to obtain a rice crop and to grow fish (9). In other cases, rafts or piers are constructed over fish ponds, and the rich mud from the bottom is piled on them and used to grow vegetable crops.

Selective breeding of animals for aquaculture is not very far advanced, mainly because it is difficult to keep aquatic animals through their breeding cycles and still retain control of their offspring (10). However, pilot studies have been done in selecting oysters for disease resistance and rapid growth, and in controlling the breeding cycles of some pond fish. Experiments indicate that fish can be trained to congregate at a certain place in response to an underwater sound, and they can then be easily fed or captured. This allows for a combination of natural and artificial rearing, with the fish foraging for themselves part of the time in natural waters, thus reducing fish crowding, the incidence of disease and the cost of feeding.

Waste Heat

At first sight, using waste heat in cultured areas is an attractive proposition. The growth rates of many species increase with an increase of temperature, and many species in north temperate latitudes have their breeding activity triggered by a temperature rise in spring. Waste heat has been used in attempts to rear oysters in New York (11), shrimp and pompano in Florida (12), and clams (13) and fishes (14) in England; but so far success has been limited. For example, a rise in temperature while desirable at one time of year may cause the animals stress at another. Nevertheless, there seems to be no good reason why such difficulties could not eventually be overcome.

Thermal effluents are also known to attract some kinds of fish to power-plant outfalls (15). While not necessarily increasing the production of these fish, this attraction could reduce the effort involved in harvesting them. On the other hand, thermal effluents could also cause fish to congregate in areas which have too little food to support them.

Sewage For Fertilization

A theme running through this report is the desirability of returning waste substances, rich in organic matter and plant nutrients, to useful biological cycles of production. One way of using sewage is to spread it on the land, another is to use it in aquaculture.

Fertilization with sewage effluent has been used in freshwater pond cultures of fish throughout the world for the double purpose of producing fish and providing sewage treatment. Yields of up to 6.7 tons per hectare per year are reported for ponds in China (9). Rope culture of mussels from rafts in Spanish waters that are enriched partly by sewage effluent produces about 300 tons/hectare per year of meat (8).

Animals like shrimps and mud-feeding fish can be grown on a mixture of sewage and algal plants. Recent experiments (Ryther, personal communication) have been directed towards a system in which algae are grown in sewage and fed to oysters. The oysters, in turn, filter the water; and their droppings accumulate on the bottom. Ideally, worms would eat the droppings, fish would eat the worms and seaweed would use the nitrogen compounds excreted by the animals. If kept in balance, such a system would reuse almost all the components of sewage effluent. Another ingenious system utilizing waste materials took the carbon dioxide from a power station chimney to stimulate the growth of algae which were then fed to clams, held in the heated effluent of the power station (16).

A common result of the release of sewage into lakes is the growth of bottom-living plants to the point that they become a nuisance. The usual method of control is chemical poisoning (17, 18). When this is done, the plants rot in the lake and fertilize the growth of the next year's crop, which, in turn, needs poisoning. A more constructive approach is to introduce a species which feeds on the plants or to harvest the plants and use them for animal food, compost or fiber (19).

Manipulating Physical Processes

The oceanic areas of most intensive fish production are those in which the deep waters, rich in plant nutrients, well up to the surface and stimulate the growth of plankton. A pilot feasibility study is now in progress to see whether such conditions can be produced artificially (20). A 7.5 cm pipe extending to about 700 m depth off the Virgin Islands is drawing cool, nutrient-rich waters up to the oyster lagoons with sufficient success to warrant increasing the scale of the experiment (21).

On a much larger scale, some have proposed that the ice cover be removed from large areas of the Arctic Ocean so that its biological productivity can be vastly increased. Opinions differ (22, 23) about whether or not this is feasible. In principle, if the freshwater content of the surface layers could be reduced, ice would form less readily. To achieve this, it has been proposed that major Siberian rivers be diverted southwards and that the Bering Strait be dammed while surface waters are pumped from north to south across it.

Difficulties and Disadvantages

A general objection to large-scale development of aquaculture is that by utilizing large areas of the coastal zone, it would interfere with the natural production processes that occur there and would probably enhance industrial impact.

A major difficulty in using sewage to fertilize aquaculture is that almost all sewage effluents in industrialized countries contain chemical pollutants which are liable to contaminate the fish and shellfish. This problem is already gaining serious proportions in conventional fisheries operations.

Conclusion

There is a considerable potential for producing human food by aquaculture, or fish farming. Research and development in this important field should be encouraged.

RECOMMENDATIONS

We recommend establishing regional centers for selective breeding of animals for aquaculture.

We recommend that a policy of harvesting or utilizing nuisance aquatic plants be fostered, rather than a policy of controlling their growth with poisons.

6.F. ALTERNATIVE STRATEGIES FOR INCREASING FISH PRODUCTION

The fisheries of the world have been shown to be an important and relatively cheap source of animal protein. In the face of the present population explosion, we should consider very carefully the best way of obtaining maximum yields from the fisheries while avoiding any long-term deterioration. But, to bring about even a 50% increase in landings of fish from the sea might require three times the present investment of ships and gear because this increase will depend upon fishing more distant and more dispersed stocks. For a further 50% yield increase, a five or sixfold increase in present equipment would be necessary, provided such yields were feasible at all (1). Beyond this, additional investments in processing facilities would be needed since species presently considered less desirable would need more processing to make them palatable. A question then arises: Is this heavy investment in traditional "hunting" methods the best way to use limited economic resources, or are they better spent in developing aquaculture? The question is complex and difficult to answer; but before attempting to resolve the economic problems, man must consider the effect he is already having on stocks of fish, whales and other creatures of the ocean.

Overfishing and Mismanagement

A fish or whale stock is a mass of living tissue which produces new living tissue by growth and reproduction. When the amount removed from the stock (either by man or by natural causes) exceeds the rate of replacement, the size of the stock declines. As a result, the creatures become more sparsely distributed in the oceans and are more difficult to catch; so that catch per unit effort declines, and finally total catch size begins to decline. If the fishing effort is too small, the yield is low; if too great, the yield is also low and may decline rapidly (see Chapter 4). Between the two is a point at which the sustainable yield is at its maximum.

When a stock is in international waters, it is extremely difficult to ensure that the fishing fleets of several nations cooperate to reach this optimum yield. Rather, the interests of each separate nation dictate that it should take as much as possible for itself. This problem has been elegantly discussed by Garrett Hardin in "The Tragedy of the Commons" (24). One example of this tragedy is that of the whale fisheries. Technology (helicopters, sonar and factory ships) has made it possible for man to hunt whales wherever they occur, bringing several species close to extinction. In 1931 the League of Nations drew up a Convention for the Regulation of Whaling, but not until 1944 was an overall limit on the Antarctic catch agreed upon. It was decided to express it in "blue whale units" (1 blue = 2 fin = 2½ humpback = 6 sei), and the first limit was set at 16,000 units. By 1963 it was found necessary to lower the limit to 10,000 units. The authority now enforcing this limit is the International Whaling Commission, founded in 1946.

The history of the catches is summarized in Figure 6.4. Since the limit was set in "blue whale units," it became more economical for each country to seek preferentially the larger whales, i.e., the blue whales. As a result, the blue whale and the humpback are now virtually extinct, and catches of fin whales have decreased 80% in 10 years (25).*

---

*With the disappearance of the larger whales, the smaller sei and sperm whales have become subjected to greatly increased hunting pressure (Figure 6.4). Continual intensive hunting of these small species is likely to reduce them to dangerously low numbers also.

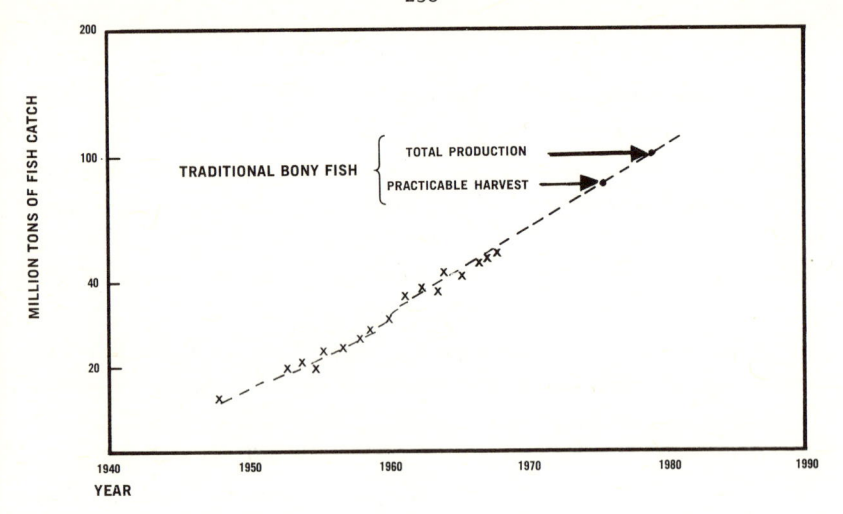

Fig. 6.3. Trend in total world marine fish catch.

Points (X) for total marine catch for each year since 1950, plotted on a logarithmic scale, fall closely on a straight line. Extrapolation of line gives indication of total potential harvest.

Source: Redrawn from Gulland, J.A. (ed.) 1970. The fish resources of the ocean. FAO Fisheries Technical Paper No. 97. FAO, Rome.

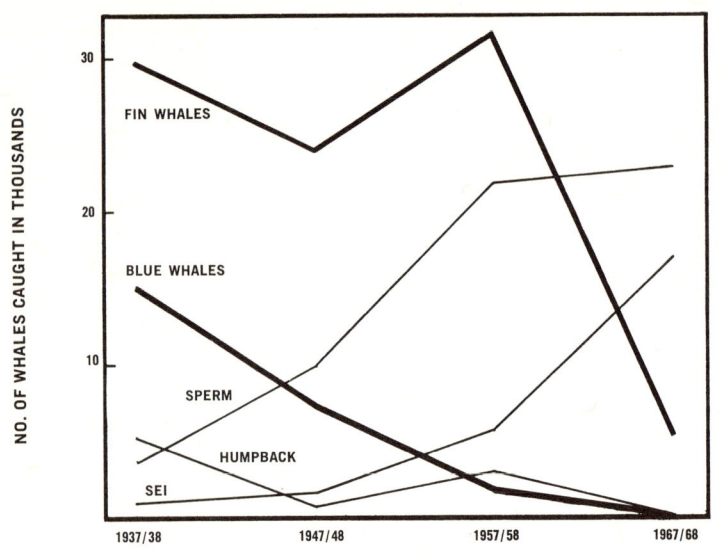

Fig. 6.4. Number of whales caught, by species.

Source: Data for figure from FAO Yearbook of Fishery Statistics, 1969.

An example of what might happen if better cooperation were obtained is illustrated in the case of the seal herds of the Pribilof Islands off Alaska. Early in the present century, Canada, Japan and the United States agreed by treaty to cease the competitive exploitation of these stocks and establish a single agency which would harvest the herd in the name of all three countries. From a harvest of 3,396 seals in 1912, this herd has increased to a point that 50 years later, it sustained an annual harvest of over 80,000 animals with no diminution of the breeding stock (26). This success story can be repeated in whaling, but the scientific management of the resource will have to be undertaken at once; and restoration of a harvestable population of whales will probably require a long period of time.

Fish stocks in various parts of the world are also being overfished. Over 80 years ago, it was found that increased fishing of the plaice stocks of the North Sea produced no increase in the catch. Species which have declined with no significant recovery include: East Asian sardine, California sardine, Northwest Pacific salmon, Atlanto-Scandinavian herring and Barents Sea cod. Stocks now showing signs of strain include the Newfoundland cod, North Sea herring, menhaden, British Columbia herring, Bering Sea flat fishes and yellow fin tuna in the eastern Pacific (1). For example, the landings of sockeye salmon by the U.S.A. and Canada in the northeast Pacific dropped from 31 million fish in 1913 to 1.7 million in 1921 and since then has only once exceeded 4 million fish (27).

Conclusion

The past record of international commissions for the regulation of whaling and fisheries is poor. We suggest they be encouraged to study the wider systems, of which the fisheries are a part, in order to deepen their understanding and predictive power.

RECOMMENDATION

We recommend the establishment of a world authority which would oversee the protection and management of the fish and whale stocks of the high seas.

Disappearance of Animal and Plant Species

When we consider the kinds of animals and plants that are found in the water or on the land, we are struck by their enormous diversity. Each distinct type is a species, and biologists characterize ecological systems according to their amount of species diversity. In Chapter 4 the importance of this diversity to the proper, stable operation of ecological systems was illustrated. Mankind has benefited greatly from species diversity, which has made available to him a great variety of wild plants and animals from which to choose those species best suited for development into useful and productive domesticated varieties. This has been the basis of terrestrial agriculture and will be the basis for the future development of aquaculture. Further, many of our valuable drugs, antibiotics and industrial products are derived from natural species. Penicillin is a spectacular example. Finally, the abundance of wildlife in nature is a source of profound aesthetic satisfaction to many people.

To reduce the number of species in man's environment, then, is to invite instability, to reduce man's freedom to choose new species for exploitation and to impoverish the quality of his life. Driving a species to extinction is a process which cannot be reversed. Unlike a mineral which, though exploited until it is scarce, will always be somewhere on the earth—in a scrap heap or in the depths of the ocean—a biological species is unique and, once lost, cannot be re-created. Over millions of years, evolution has experimented with countless biological types and has preserved those which are successful and well-adapted to their environment. They are the world's living museum and, as such, belong to humanity. No local group is justified in depriving future generations of species and their potential use by causing their extinction.

Apart from spectacular examples like the blue whale, there are many species that are being driven towards extinction. A U.S. government agency in 1966 listed six extinct and 38 rare and endangered fish species (28). Such a list could be repeated for many countries of the world. Among the U.S. examples are the Lake Sturgeon, the largest fish of the Great Lakes, and the Blue Pike, for which the yearly catch in Lake Erie, in times past, frequently exceeded 20 million pounds (9 million kg).

There are also a great number of species being locally exterminated. The Atlantic salmon, once abundant in most major rivers in northeastern North America and Western Europe, is now gone from all but eight U.S. rivers and from the Thames and the Rhine, to name only two rivers in Europe (29). Examples could be added to show how shellfish have disappeared from estuaries in which they were once abundant, how plants have been obliterated by filling in marshes and how whole communities of organisms have been obliterated by the dumping of dredge spoils and sewage solids. Many such local populations have characteristics which distinguish them from others of the same species. For example, the oysters of Chesapeake Bay (U.S.A.) are as different from the oysters of a Louisiana marsh as the human population of Sweden is from the human population of Biafra. Total loss of a species is a rather dramatic happening, but the insidious loss of local populations throughout the world may be just as important in terms of loss of diversity.

RECOMMENDATION

To offset both the local and worldwide extinction of species, we recommend that representative examples of different kinds of aquatic ecosystems be protected from human interference and preserved for humanity.

Consequences of Increased Fishing Pressure

There are strong arguments in favor of intensifying the world fishing effort to increase the yield from the world's oceans (see Section 6.C). At each step in a food chain, an organism consumes its prey but passes on to its predator only a fraction (5-25%) of what it consumes. The rest of the food is used for its own bodily functions. It follows, then, that from a given amount of plant production in the ocean, the greatest amount will be utilized if man keeps the food chain as short as possible. In general, smaller organisms are linked to the plants by fewer intermediate stages. So, it seems good strategy to harvest small or young fish or invertebrates like krill which are very abundant in the southern hemisphere and are the whales' source of food. There is little doubt that if fishing activity were increased to obtain these small forms, there would, at the same time, be intensified fishing pressure on conventional, more economic fish stocks.

Hence, the fish stocks of the world would be under pressure from two directions: from man's fishing activities and from man's exploitation of the smaller organisms that form their food sources. Unless extremely skillful management were achieved, it is probable that many fish stocks would show sharp declines as a result.

A further problem in increasing fishing pressures would arise with respect to the large animals (seals, porpoises, walruses) which compete with man for fish stocks. It has been estimated that the harp seals of the northwest Atlantic consume about one million tons of pelagic fish a year, mainly capelin (30). This amount exceeds man's entire catch of capelin in the whole north Atlantic and exceeds his 1968 catch of herring, capelin and mackerel in the northwest Atlantic.

Conclusion

If man should begin to fish the ocean's stocks to the limit of their sustainable yield, it seems inevitable that the world's population of large marine animals, including the larger fishes, would be seriously affected. Species would be driven to extinction, and the oceans' biological systems would become unstable with large, unexpected outbreaks of pest species and large fluctuations in fishing yields (see Chapter 4).

Aquaculture--the Alternative

Aside from the impoverishment of world marine faunas which might result from very intensive fishing for small organisms, the costliness of the operation in terms of energy and resources should be considered. Small organisms are widely dispersed in the ocean, and a vast quantity of water has to be filtered to harvest a ton of such material. Large fish, on the other hand, have already performed the filtering work in their normal process of feeding. They present us with a convenient package of concentrated material. So, if man attempts to harvest the small, abundant organisms, he has to do all the work nature normally does for him. This is sure to be a very costly process both in energy and economic resources. Although a quantitative comparison of the alternatives is not possible here, it seems likely that the resources required to double or treble the catch of fish from the oceans would be better spent in boosting controlled production through aquaculture. Coastal and inland waters are already enriched by sewage pollution and by fertilizers draining from the land. With intensive management and careful siting, man could obtain products of desirable size and quality from these waters at the time and place of his own choosing; and he could practice selective breeding for fish that grow rapidly and utilize food efficiently. He could also make use of the heated water emerging from his power generators and use sewage wastes to improve the fertility of the coastal waters. Predators and disease could be controlled there as they are in agricultural systems.

A prime requirement for any expansion of aquatic production is a halting of the present trend toward pollution of inland and coastal waters. In particular, it is essential to find a way of removing industrial pollutants from sewage waste, so that they can be recycled and kept out of the biosphere, while the remaining material can be used to promote biological productivity.

RECOMMENDATION

We recommend worldwide investment in aquaculture rather than in massive increase in fishing fleets.

6.G. POPULATION PRESSURE ON THE ESTUARIES AND COASTAL ZONE

About 70% of the earth's population lives within an easy day's travel of the coast, and many of the rest live on the lower reaches of rivers which empty into estuaries. Furthermore, coastal populations are increasing more rapidly than those of the continental interiors (31). Seventeen percent of the world's oil production now comes from offshore (continental shelf) fields, and that percentage is increasing yearly (32). Sedimentary rocks, like phosphorite, and placer deposits of tin and gold are most abundant along the continental margins. Mineralized crystalline rock, though covered with sediment, extends under the continental shelves (32). In view of dwindling reserves and increasing demand for oil, gas, heavy metals and phosphates, the coastal marine environment undoubtedly will be subject to rapidly increasing pressure from the exploitation of minerals.

Settlement and industrialization of the coastal zone has already led to extensive degradation of highly productive estuaries and marshlands. For example, in the period 1922-1954 over one-quarter of the salt marshes in the U.S.A. were destroyed by filling, diking, draining or by constructing walls along the seaward marsh edge (33). In the following 10 years a further 10% of the remaining salt marsh between Maine and Delaware was destroyed (33). On the west coast of the U.S.A. the rate of destruction is almost certainly much greater, for the marsh areas and the estuaries are much smaller.

Man's dredging of harbors and channels causes turbidity in the water which cuts down plankton production and smothers organisms in the bottom. Modification of river flow is often detrimental to the biological productivity of estuaries. According to Niering, 40% of the estuarine areas in the U.S.A. have been subjected to severe modification (34). To understand the significance of such changes for the productivity of the coastal zone, a knowledge of the ecology of estuaries and coastal areas is important.

Biological Productivity of Estuaries

Estuaries are noted for their high biological productivity. Probably the most important factor is the mixing of water which occurs there. In the open ocean, plant production is limited to the surface layer of waters where the light intensity is reasonably high. As plants and animals disperse downwards from this zone they liberate materials which are valuable plant fertilizers. These tend to accumulate in deeper waters and can only be used by the plants when the deep waters are brought to the lighted surface zone.

In estuaries, three mechanisms operate to mix the deep waters with the surface waters. One is the outflow of fresh water from the rivers (see Figure 6.5). This fresh water is less dense than seawater and moves out to sea in a distinct surface layer. As it flows, it tends to carry out to sea a considerable volume of the salt water below it. To compensate for this, there is an inshore flow of deep salt water, rich in nutrients. The second mechanism is tidal mixing. Estuaries are often shaped so that large volumes of water move in and out on every tide. This tidal movement may, in some circumstances, be the dominant force causing surface and deep waters to become mixed together. The third mechanism, common to all coastal inlets, is wind action. For example, large quantities of surface water are blown out to sea, whereupon they are replaced by an equal volume of deep, enriched water.

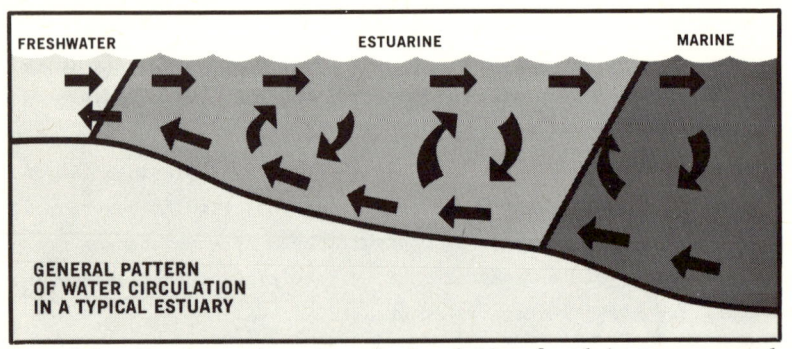

Fig. 6.5. Two-layered system of circulation found in many coastal plain estuaries.

The lighter fresh water from the river is found near the surface and undergoes a net downstream movement. The heavier salt water from the ocean is found near the bottom and undergoes a net upstream movement. The distinctive, stratified, estuarine pattern of circulation is created.

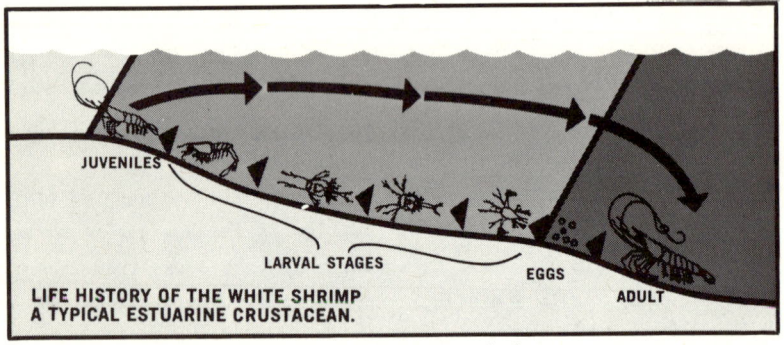

Fig. 6.6. Life history of an estuarine shrimp.

Source: Redrawn from Cronin L. and A. Mansueti. 1971. The biology of the estuary, p. 14-39, In A symposium on the biological significance of estuaries. Sport Fishing Institute, Washington, D.C.

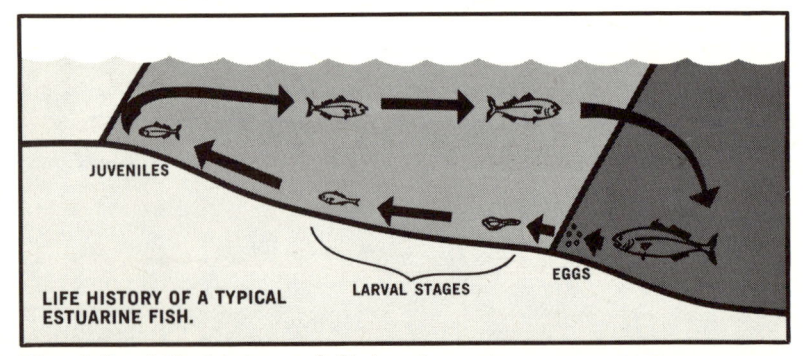

Fig. 6.7. Life history of fish using estuary as nursery.

Source: Redrawn from Cronin and Mansueti, 1971.

These three mechanisms combine in different proportions to produce areas of very high biological productivity, but the first is the one most characteristic of estuaries. Rivers emptying into estuaries tend to have distinct seasonal patterns of high flow and low flow. Over thousands of years the organisms in the estuaries have adapted to seasonal changes in the amount of mixing generated by rivers. For example, in the spring the melting of ice and snow in northern latitudes coincides with a time of high biological productivity in the estuaries.

When rivers are dammed for power generation or irrigation, this annual flow cycle is modified. In extreme cases, like that of the Nile River, runoff is virtually eliminated (35); and the result is that organisms which depend on this seasonal cycle are unable to flourish in the river's estuary. One such organism is the white shrimp found in Texas estuaries (36). Another example is the fall in the productivity of the Sea of Azov since the damming of the Don River (37).

Another characteristic feature of estuaries is the gradient in salinity from the river mouth to the open sea (see Figures 6.5, 6.6 and 6.7). Some animals, like oysters, are adapted to life in a zone of low salinity, and a great many others require low-salinity water during some phase of their life cycle. Reducing river flow tends to reduce the extent of these low-salinity zones and, consequently, the estuary's productivity.

In addition to the rich supply of nutrient substances brought up from the deep waters of the sea, there is normally a steady supply of nutrient substances running off the land and down the rivers. Dense human settlements provide additional supplies of nutrient materials in the form of sewage. In moderation, these sources can add to the productivity of the estuaries; but, in the majority of cases, their effect has been detrimental. Sewage waste requires large amounts of oxygen for its biological degradation; and when the amount of added sewage is excessive, the water's oxygen supply is depleted, and fish and shellfish cannot live there. As an example, for many years the estuary of the River Thames below London was devoid of oxygen, especially in warm weather, and no fish could live there (29). But, since the recent improvement of London's sewage treatment about 50 species of fish have returned to the estuary (38).

There is a second source of difficulty with sewage. In industrial areas it is frequently contaminated with chemicals which either poison the fish or make them unfit for human consumption (see Section 6.H).

Finally, the sediment load which the rivers bring to the estuaries must be considered. In areas in which fresh water meets the sea, nutrient-rich sediment, with its texture varying from clay and fine silt to coarse sand and shingle, is deposited according to the patterns of water movement. Marsh plants, eel grass, turtle grass and mangroves, growing in profusion between tidemarks and in shallow water, act as a further trap for the sediment. This creates an ideal environment for a wide variety of resident species and for the larvae and juvenile forms of deep-water species. The productivity of the estuaries is reduced, however, when rivers are dammed. Damming causes the sediment load to be deposited in an upstream impoundment where its potential for stimulating biological productivity is often wasted.

Some of our most prized fish, notably the salmon and related species, live and grow in the open sea but migrate through the estuaries and up the rivers to breed. Many of man's alterations--damming the rivers, polluting the streams and estuaries and changing the seasonal pattern of flow--make it increasingly difficult for these fish to reproduce or to complete their life cycles.

For example, salmon once spawned in the rivers of all countries surrounding the Baltic Sea area. But, industrial pollution--principally pulp mill effluent--has depleted oxygen in many streams; and hydroelectric power dams have thwarted the upstream immigration of spawning adults (39). It costs Sweden about one million dollars per year to rear young salmon in hatcheries for release into the Baltic

Sea. Society is now paying for a service previously rendered free by nature's salmon streams (40, 41).

Conclusion

Before any decisions are made on proposals to modify river flow by impoundment, the adverse effect of these proposals on the migrations of fish and on the productivity of estuaries should be recognized and taken into consideration.

Productivity of the Coastal Zone

After the estuaries, the coastal zones are the sea's most productive regions. This is partly because they are adjacent to the estuaries and partly because of their own special biological properties. In temperate coastal zones, the water becomes divided in summer into a warm, light, upper layer and a cool, lower layer which accumulates nutrient substances. When the surface temperature falls, late in the year, convection and wind action bring about the vertical mixing which is so essential to high biological productivity.

The coastal waters also owe their productivity to the large plants which grow along the water's shore. Marsh grass and mangrove swamp communities are known to be among the most productive plant associations on earth (33) (see Figure 6.8), and much of this productivity is released into coastal waters as suspended organic matter. It was recently discovered that seaweed beds may be equally productive (42, 43). Their ability to synthesize organic matter at a high rate depends in part on their special position at the edge of the sea, where they are attached to rocks and are constantly washed over by water which brings them nutrients and carries away their waste products.

Conclusion

The concentrations of population and industry around estuaries and along the coastline are threatening the highly productive coastal

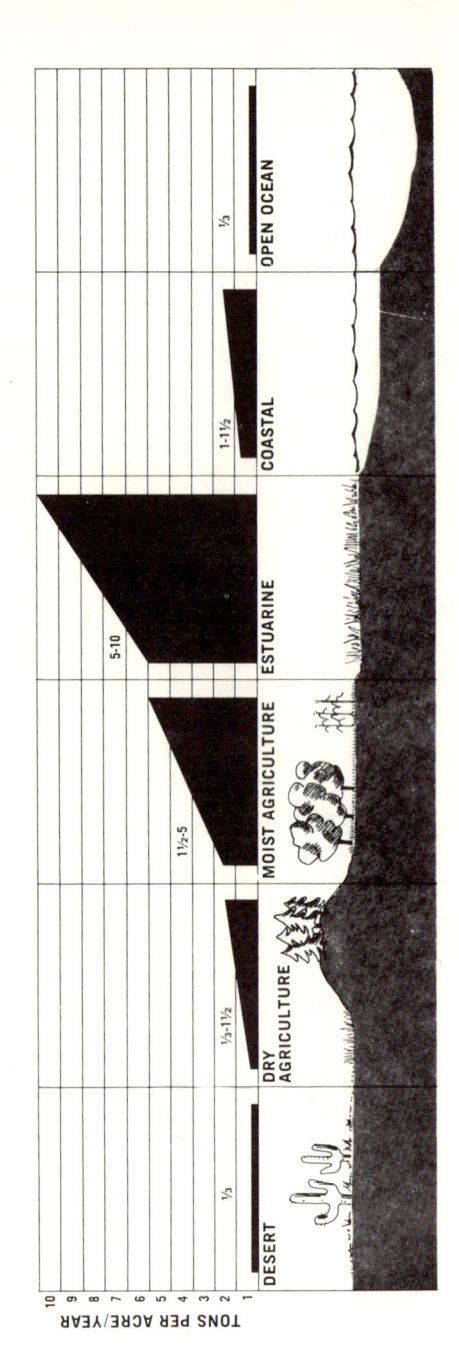

Fig. 6.8. Comparative production rates among terrestrial and aquatic systems.
Source: Redrawn from Teal and Teal, 1969.

zones which, at present, supply half the world's fish and which are looked to for increased yields through aquaculture.

RECOMMENDATIONS

We recommend that the amount of commercial, residential and recreational construction along coasts be kept to a minimum and that it be carried out in such a way as to minimize the destruction of productive intertidal and shallow water areas.

We recommend that ways be found to protect the coastal and estuarine environment on a worldwide scale.

6.H. THE EFFECTS OF POLLUTION

Pollution of inland and coastal waters has been amply documented (44, 45, 46, 47, 48), and the purpose of this section is to relate available information to the ecological analysis which has been made in preceding sections. A clear distinction must be made between pollution from organic materials like human fecal matter and nitrogenous fertilizers and pollution from industrial substances like heavy metals and pesticides, which are often poisonous to living organisms.

The effects of natural organic pollutants and inorganic nutrients may be summarized in a word--enrichment. If adequately diluted, these materials stimulate biological productivity at all levels of the system. This has not been proved in marine situations but has been documented in the fresh water of the Thames (49), in which sewage solids and nutrient salts support a food web leading to one of the densest fish populations on record, outside of artificial ponds.

In highly productive lakes, a large amount of waste material accumulates in the lake basin and decomposes there. This leads to loss of amenity value often accompanied by changes to less desirable species of fish. For example, in Lake Erie, sewage pollution has lead to a twentyfold increase in the biomass of phytoplankton in the last 50 years (50). In summer, this material decomposes in the deep part of the basin, using up all the oxygen. This situation has caused changes in the species of zooplankton, bottom fauna and fish. Though the total fish catch has remained approximately constant (around 2,300 tons per year) desirable species like cisco, blue pike, sauger and white fish have been replaced by sheepshead, carp, smelt and other less desirable species.

Extreme enrichment may lead to a loss of productivity, because the dense phytoplankton at the surface cuts down the penetration of light and hence the total amount of photosynthesis in the water column. In very confined spaces overenrichment may eventually lead to complete de-oxygenation of the water and a loss of fish and other animals as it did in the Thames estuary mentioned earlier (38).

The North Sea is a prime example of the effects of pollution on aquatic productivity. The North Sea probably has a larger concentration of population and industry along its coasts and along the rivers emptying into it than any other sea area of comparable size. The countries surrounding it all have estuaries which have been severely damaged and, in some cases, left fishless by pollution. Many rivers which formerly carried migratory fish no longer do because their lower sections are impassable. Nevertheless, one cannot demonstrate that the North Sea, as a whole, is less productive than it used to be. Landings of some species have declined (e.g., turbot), others show sharp fluctuations (herring, Norway pout, sandeels, sprats) and still others are being exploited more heavily than before (e.g., mackerel). Yet the total catch from all countries has increased steadily from about 1.5 million tons in 1950 to more than three million tons in 1967, 1968 and 1969 (52).

The most serious problems arise from pollution in industrial areas in which sewage is invariably mixed with industrial wastes. Evidence is accumulating that many of these materials either adversely affect aquatic production processes or contaminate fisheries products to the point that they constitute a human health hazard. Many industrial products have been introduced only recently, and their effects may become much worse before they can be brought under control.

Chlorinated Hydrocarbons

1) DDT

The global importance of DDT in the marine environment was given particular attention in the SCEP report (44). It had been suggested earlier (53, 54) that DDT could adversely affect photosynthesis in the oceans and that, in turn, it might reduce marine productivity or even reduce the world's oxygen supply. Not only has this been shown to be an unlikely large-scale phenomenon (44), but recent calculations indicate that, even in the event of a major inhibition of marine photosynthesis, we will not have to worry about our oxygen supply for millions of years (55, 56).

The aspects of DDT contamination which are of particular ecological concern, however, are its food-chain concentration and its contamination of human food. As energy and materials pass through the food chain from phytoplankton to invertebrates to fish to fish-eating birds, DDT is progressively concentrated. Birds may, in fact, have concentrations of DDT residues a million times greater than the water. This effect has been clearly demonstrated in lakes (57) and in the coastal environment (58). It has also been shown that DDT and its residues are widely distributed throughout the world's oceans, even to Antarctica (59). Of serious ecological concern are resultant declines in the numbers of fish-eating birds and in the productivity of marine food fish. It is probable that large amounts of DDT already released over land will enter the aquatic environment in years to come and that the effects of DDT would become worse even if its use were to be banned immediately on a worldwide scale.

The hazard to man of accumulating DDT residues as a result of eating food contaminated with DDT has not been fully assessed. A 1969 report of a U.S. Government Commission (60) lists DDT, aldrin, dieldrin and heptachlor as having been judged positive for tumor induction in laboratory animals and stated "with the evidence now in, DDT can be regarded neither as a proven danger as a carcinogen for man, nor as an assuredly safe pesticide; suspicion has been aroused and it should be confirmed or dispelled."

2) PCB's

Polychlorinated biphenyls, which have been available commercially since 1929, were not identified in the environment until 1966. These compounds, now considered to be as widespread as DDT, are being found all over the world (61). In addition to their many industrial applications, their use in domestic products like paints, adhesives and plastics has enhanced their distribution. They are not destroyed by the usual waste disposal methods and enter the aquatic environment through sewage effluents, land runoff from industrial wastes and condensation following incineration. High PCB residues have been found in fish and fish-eating birds (see Table 6.2). They have also been detected in human adipose tissue (62).

They have properties similar to those of DDT but are more persistent and stable. Compared with DDT, PCB's are more toxic for shellfish (69) but less so for fish and birds (67, 69). PCB's affect the reproductive system of birds in a manner similar to DDT and dieldrin and may have contributed to observed cases of reproductive failure (67). In man, these compounds can cause skin lesions and liver damage (69).

3) Polyvinyl Chloride By-products

A newly recognized pollutant (chlorinated aliphatic hydrocarbons or C-Cl), which is a by-product in vinyl chloride manufacturing, has been detected in the North Atlantic, the Norwegian Sea, the Barents Sea and the North Sea (70). Its distribution indicates that the compound originates from industries on both sides of the Atlantic Ocean. Unwanted industrial by-products are apparently disposed of by dumping at sea. Observations of dead plankton in the dumping areas and toxicity experiments indicate that these compounds present a new threat to pelagic and benthic organisms. Fish caught recently in areas of highest concentrations of C-Cl in the North Sea showed indications of liver damage (71).

Type	Organ	Location	Concentration (ppm)	Source
Herring	Fat	Baltic	0.5-23	63
Salmon	Eggs	Sweden	7.7-34	64
Pike	Muscle	Sweden	6.0-48	65
Eider duck	Liver	Holland	2.1-96	66
Heron	Liver	Britain	0-900	67
Heron	Fat	Stockholm	9,400	63
Dolphin	Fat	Sargasso	33	68
Seal	Fat	Baltic	16-44	63

Table 6.2. PCB residues in fish, birds and mammals.

Petroleum Hydrocarbons

Another environmental problem which was well documented in the SCEP report (44) is petroleum hydrocarbons. Since that report was published, one scientist has suggested the total hydrocarbon influx to the ocean may be as high as 10 million tons per year (72). These hydrocarbons comprise an extremely diverse range of compounds, and their observed effects in nature also vary. In some cases, for example, oil appears to be relatively inert biologically with most of the environmental damage being done by dispersants (73); while in others, oil has extinguished almost all life over a considerable area (74). In the Caspian Sea a marked reduction in productivity at all levels of the food chains has been noted in oil polluted areas, and fish catches there have been reduced by two-thirds (75).

Blumer (72) has stated categorically that "all crude oils and all oil fractions except highly purified and pure materials are poisonous to all marine organisms," while Simpson (76) claims that "there is no evidence that oils spilt round the British Isles have ever killed any of these shellfish (mussels, cockles, winkles, oysters, shrimps, lobsters, crabs)." Blumer (72) has rightly emphasized that concentrating on damage to adult fish or on reduced fish catches is not adequate when considering the effects of toxic oil fractions on total marine productivity. Rather, young fish and intermediate stages in the food chain are more likely to be affected.

It has been shown that when ingested by marine organisms, hydrocarbons pass through the gut wall and are stored in fat reserves (72). These substances may be concentrated in food chains in a manner analogous to DDT and could show up in potentially dangerous concentrations in human food. Carcinogens are known to exist in crude, fuel and waste oils and have been detected in oyster tissue and sediments (77). Although the consumption of carcinogen-containing seafood is not now known to be dangerous to man, the combination of sources could pose a potential hazard (78). The ability of oil dispersed at sea to concentrate chlorinated hydrocarbons is an additional undesirable consequence of oil pollution.

Heavy Metals

Since the production of the SCEP report, it has been suggested that the fallout of mercury from fossil fuel combustion is of the order of 3,000 tons per year (79), a quantity comparable to that emitted as waste from industrial processes. By contrast, it is estimated that only about 230 tons of mercury are released globally through natural weathering processes.

Mercury is concentrated by aquatic organisms and, in general, the highest levels are found at the end of long food chains in fish and fish-eating mammals (see Table 6.3). Mercury concentrations in fish may be up to 10,000 times those found in seawater (86). Industrial wastes are largely responsible for the high levels found in some Japanese, Swedish and Canadian waters.

Mercury in animal tissues consists almost entirely of methyl mercury, the form most easily absorbed and most slowly excreted (87). The toxicity of mercury to man has been well documented. In Minimata and Niigata, Japan, the ingestion of mercury-contaminated fish and shellfish caused 168 cases of mercury poisoning, resulting in 52 deaths (82). Poisoning can also occur prenatally and, as there is no effective means of treatment, permanent disabling may result. Organic compounds of mercury have also been shown experimentally to produce genetic mutations and chromosomal aberrations in some plants (87).

Because of its wide distribution and high toxicity, mercury has justifiably attracted attention as a major environmental pollutant. There is evidence, however, that other heavy metals such as arsenic, cadmium, copper, lead, nickel and zinc are also environmental hazards and may, therefore, also affect aquatic food resources (83, 88, 89).

Synergistic Effects

It is easy to understand that when organisms are exposed to a complex mixture of industrial pollutants, many of which concentrate in the food chain, their activities may be altered in a number of

Material	Location	Concentration ppm	Source
Typical surface sea water		0.0001–4	80
Sewage sludge	Wisconsin, U.S.A.	1.4–29	81
Sediments	Minimata Bay, Japan	133–2,010	82
Herbivorous zooplankton, snails	Canada	0.01–0.18	83
Carnivorous aquatic insects	Canada	0.14–1.16	83
Predatory aquatic insects, frogs	Canada	0.01–5.82	83
Perch	Sweden	1.4–4.1	84
Plaice	Sweden	0.07–3.1	84
Beluga Whale (liver)	Canada	8.87	83
Pilot Whale (liver)	California	7.4–25.9	85

Table 6.3. Concentrations of mercury in sea water, sediment and aquatic organisms.

ways which reinforce one another. Pollutants which, considered separately, are not toxic and might be considered relatively harmless can interact to produce serious disruption of the working of biological systems.

Such synergistic interactions are extremely difficult to document, but many ecologists have recorded their observations of insidious alterations of aquatic environments, especially estuaries (90).

Heated Effluents

The generation of electric power inevitably involves the production of waste heat which is dumped into cooling waters and passed out into the environment as heated effluent (91). It is a form of pollution which is invisible, odorless and often not lethal. In tropical and subtropical areas, organisms live near the limits of their thermal tolerance, and large-scale deaths can occur when water temperatures are raised higher (92). In other situations large numbers of microscopic organisms, passed through the cooling system, are subjected to thermal shocks which may change their physiology and behavior in ways that are difficult to demonstrate in nature. In experimental situations, for example, it has been shown that temperature changes affect hatching dates and the normal development and survival of fishes (92, 93). Physiological shocks in early life can affect growth and food conversion efficiencies even after sexual maturity (94).

It is therefore important to be aware of the possibility that the effects of heated effluents may extend far beyond the plumes of warm water and that delayed effects may disrupt biological events long after the organisms have come in contact with the effluent.

Conclusions

The discharge of sewage or fertilizers, uncontaminated by industrial pollutants, very seldom endangers the productivity of aquatic resources. From the point of view of conservation of nutrients (see Chapter 3), discharge of high concentrations of phosphorus-rich material into the oceans, from which they cannot be reclaimed, is a wasteful process. Recycling of nutrients by putting them back on the land is ecologically more desirable, but if the enrichment of water can be harnessed to aquaculture, the economy may be almost as great.

The problem which is becoming daily more acute is that of separating from the organic enrichment those materials of industrial origin which are long-lived, toxic and which accumulate in food chains. The danger that a large proportion of the high-protein food, which we obtain from the sea and the lakes, may become so contaminated as to constitute a health hazard should be viewed with the utmost concern.

RECOMMENDATION

We recommend that international standards be established for the discharge of pollutants into the rivers and the sea and that ocean dumping be controlled.

REFERENCES

1. Ricker, W. E. 1969. Food from the sea. In P. Cloud (Chairman), Resources and man. W. H. Freeman & Co., San Francisco. 259 p.

2. Dickie, L. M. 1971. Food chains and fish production in the northwest Atlantic. ICNAF Environmental Symp., Dartmouth, Nova Scotia. (Mimeo).

3. Holt, S. J. 1969. The food resources of the ocean. Scientific American 221(3):178-194.

4. Ryther, J. H. 1969. Photosynthesis and fish production in the sea. Science 166:72-77.

5. Global Ocean Research. 1969. Report of a joint working party of the Advisory Committee on Marine Research (FAO), the Scientific Committee on Ocean Research (ICSU) and the World Meteorological Organization (WMO). Ponza and Rome. Published at LaJolla, Calif.

6. Stewart, R. W., and L. M. Dickie. 1971. Ad Mare: Canada looks to the sea. Information Canada, Ottawa. 175 p.

7. Moiseev, P. A. 1969. (Living resources of the world's ocean.) Pishchevaya Promyshlennost', Moscow. (Fish. Res. Bd. Canada Translation Series No. 1369 of p. 216-230 and No. 1531 of p. 177-204).

8. Ryther, J. H., and J. E. Bardach. 1968. The status and potential of aquaculture. Vol. 1. Particularly invertebrate and algae culture. Springfield, Va. Clearinghouse for Federal Scientific and Technical Information. U.S. Dept. Commerce Doc. PB 177 767. 261 p.

9. Allen, G. H. 1970. The constructive use of sewage, with particular reference to fish culture. FAO Tech. Conf. Marine Pollution MP/70/R-13.

10. Simon, R. C. 1970. Genetic and marine aquaculture, p. 53-63. In W. J. McNeil (ed.), Marine aquaculture. Oregon State Univ. Press, Corvallis. 172 p.

11. Kovaly, K. A. 1968. Heat pollution or enrichment. Industrial Research, July 1968. p. 31.

12. Anonymous. 1968. Mass culture of pink shrimp and pompano studied by Miami University. Comm. Fish. Rev. 30:13.

13. Ansell, A. D. 1969. Thermal releases and shellfish culture: possibilities and limitations. Chesapeake Science 10:256-257.

14. Iles, R. B. 1963. Cultivating fish for food and sport in power station water. New Scientist 17:227-229.

15. De Sylva, D. P. 1969. Theoretical considerations on the effects of heated effluents on marine fishes, p. 229-293. In P. A. Krenkel, and F. L. Parker (ed.), Biological aspects of thermal pollution. Vanderbilt Univ. Press, Portland, Oregon. 407 p.

16. Ansell, A. D. 1962. An approach to sea farming. New Scientist 14:408-409.

17. Steenis, J. H., and V. D. Stotts. 1965. Tidal dispersal of herbicides to control Eurasian watermilfoil in the Chesapeake Bay. 18th annual meeting, Southern Weed Conf., Dallas, Texas.

18. Holm, L. G., L. W. Weldon, and R. D. Blackburn. 1969. Aquatic weeds. Science 166:699-709.

19. Livermore, D. F., and W. E. Wunderlich. 1969. Mechanical removal of organic production from waterways, p. 494-519. In Eutrophication. Nat. Acad. Sci., Washington, D.C. 661 p.

20. Gerard, R. D., and D. A. Roels. 1970. Deep ocean water as a resource. Marine Tech. Soc. J. 4(5):69-78.

21. (National Sea Grant Program, National Oceanic and Atmospheric Administration, personal communication.)

22. Budyko, M. L. 1962. Climatic change and climatic control. (Translated title; original paper in Akademiia Nauk, USSR, Vestnik, No. 7, 1962.) Amer. Met. Soc. translation under Contract AF 19 (628)-3880, Boston, Mass. 1964.

23. Badgley, F. I. 1961. Heat balance at the surface of the Arctic Ocean. 29th W. Snow Conf., Proc. Spokane, Wash., April 1961.

24. Hardin, G. 1968. The tragedy of the commons. Science 162:1243-1248.

25. Food and Agricultural Organization (FAO). 1969. Yearbook of fishery statistics, 1969. FAO, Rome.

26. Roppel, A. Y., and S. P. Davey. 1963. Evolution of fur seal management on the Pribilof Islands. Paper presented at the 14th Alaskan Science Conference, Aug. 29, 1963, Anchorage. 24 p. (Mimeo).

27. International Pacific Salmon Fishery Commission. 1969. Annual report.

28. U.S. Department of the Interior, Bureau of Sport Fisheries and Wildlife. 1966. Rare and endangered fish and wildlife of the United States. Washington, D.C.

29. Mann, K. H. 1971. The River Thames--a case history. *In* International Symp. on River Ecology and the Impact of Man. (In press).

30. (Sergeant, D. E., personal communication.)

31. Ginsberg, N. 1971. The lure of the tidewater: problems of the interface between land and sea. *In* Pacem in Maribus. University of Malta Press. (In press).

32. Cloud, Preston. 1969. Mineral resources from the sea, p. 135-155. *In* Preston Cloud (Chairman), Resources and man. W.H. Freeman and Co., San Francisco. 259 p.

33. Teal, J. M., and M. Teal. 1969. Life and death of a salt marsh. Atlantic, Little, Brown and Co., Boston.

34. Niering, W. H. 1970. The dilemma of the coastal wetlands; conflict of local, national, and world priorities. In H. W. Helfrich (ed.), The environmental crisis. Yale University Press, New Haven.

35. Hammerton, D. The Nile River--a case history. In International Symposium on River Ecology and the Impact of Man. (In press).

36. Copeland, B. J. 1966. Effects of decreased river flow on estuarine ecology. J. Water Poll. Cont. Fed. 38:1831-1839.

37. Moiseev, P. A. 1969. (Living resources of the world's ocean.) Pishchevaya Promyshlennost', Moscow. (Fish. Res. Bd. Canada Translation Series No. 1369 of p. 216-230 and No. 1531 of p. 177-204).

38. Wheeler, A. 1970. Fish return to the Thames. Sci. J. November: 28-32.

39. Netboy, A. 1968. The Atlantic salmon. Houghton Mifflin, Boston. 457 p.

40. Lindroth, A. 1963. Salmon conservation in Sweden. Trans. Amer. Fish. Soc. 92:286-291.

41. Carlin, B. 1968. Salmon conservation in Sweden, p. 4-7. In Atlantic Salmon Association Centennial Award Fund. The Atlantic Salmon Association, Montreal, Canada.

42. Leighton, D. C., C. G. Jones, and W. J. North. 1966. Ecological relationships between giant kelps and sea urchins in southern California, p. 141-153. In 51st Internat. Seaweed Symp., Proc. Permagon, New York.

43. Mann, K. H. Ecological energetics of the seaweed zone in a marine bay on the Atlantic coast of Canada. II. The productivity of the seaweeds. (In progress).

44. Study of Critical Environmental Problems (SCEP). 1970. Man's impact on the global environment. MIT Press, Cambridge, Mass. 319 p.

45. Hynes, H. B. N. 1960. The biology of polluted waters. University of Liverpool Press, Liverpool. 202 p.

46. National Academy of Sciences. 1969. Eutrophication: causes, consequences, correctives. Proc. of a symp. National Academy of Sciences, Washington, D.C.

47. Food and Agricultural Organization (FAO). 1970. FAO Technical Conference on Marine Pollution and Its Effects on Living Resources and Fishing. FAO, Rome.

48. Sinha, E. 1970. Coastal/estuarine pollution. An annotated bibliography. Ocean Eng. Inf. Ser., La Jolla, California.

49. Mann, K. H., R. H. Britton, A. Kowalczewski, T. J. Lack, C. P. Mathews, and I. McDonald. 1971. Productivity and energy flow at all trophic levels in the River Thames, England. UNESCO/IBP Symp. on Productivity Problems of Fresh Waters, Proc. Polish Academy of Sciences, Warsaw. (In press).

50. Hartman, W. L. Presented at Lake Erie Enforcement Conference, Detroit, Michigan, 1970.

51. Findenegg, I. 1964. Bestimmung des Trophiegrades von Seen nach der Radiocarbonmethode. Naturwiss 51:368-369.

52. Cole, H. A. 1970. North Sea pollution. FAO Technical Conference on Marine Pollution and Its Effects on Living Resources and Fishing. FAO, Rome.

53. Wurster, C. F. 1968. DDT reduces photosynthesis by marine phytoplankton. Science 159:1474-1475.

54. Menzel, D. W., J. Anderson, and A. Randtke. 1970. Marine phytoplankton vary in their response to chlorinated hydrocarbons. Science 167:1724-1726.

55. Broecker, W. S. 1970. Man's oxygen reserves. Science 168:1537-1538.

56. Ryther, J. H. 1970. Is the world's oxygen supply threatened? Nature 227:374-375.

57. Rudd, R. L. 1964. Pesticides and the living landscape. University of Wisconsin Press, Madison. 320 p.

58. Woodwell, G. M., C. F. Wurster, and P. A. Isaacson. 1967. DDT residues in an east coast estuary: a case of biological concentration of a persistent insecticide. Science 150:821-824.

59. Tatton, J., and J. Ruzicka. 1967. Organochlorine pesticides in Antarctica. Nature 215:346-348.

60. Secretary's Commission on Pesticides and their Relationship to Environmental Health. 1969 report. U.S. Dept. of Health, Education, and Welfare, Washington, D.C.

61. Jensen, S. 1970. PCB as contaminant of the environment--history. Ms. PCB Conference, Stockholm.

62. Biros, F. J., A. C. Walker, and A. Medbery. 1970. Polychlorinated biphenyls in human adipose tissue. Bull. Environ. Contam. Toxicol. 5:317-323.

63. Peakall, D. B., and J. L. Lincer. 1970. Polychlorinated biphenyls. Bioscience 20:958-964.

64. Johansson, N. 1970. PCB--indications of effects on fish. Ms. PCB Conference, Stockholm.

65. Johnels, A. G. 1970. PCB--occurrence in Swedish wildlife. Ms. PCB Conference, Stockholm.

66. Koeman, J. H., and G. Van Genderen. 1970. Tissue levels in and effects caused by chlorinated carbon insecticides, biphenyls and mercury in the marine environment along the Netherlands coast. FAO Technical Conference on Marine Pollution and Its Effects on Living Resources and Fishing. Rome. Ms. MP/70/E-21.

67. Prestt, I., D. J. Jefferies, and N. W. Moore. 1970. Polychlorinated biphenyls in wild birds in Britain and their avian toxicity. Environ. Pollut. 1:3-26.

68. (Harvey, personal communication.)

69. Gustafson, C. G. PCB's--prevalent and persistent. Environ. Sci. Technol. 4:814-819.

70. Jensen, S., R. Lange, A. Jernelov, and K. H. Palmork. 1970. Chlorinated by-products from vinyl chloride production: a new source of marine pollution. FAO Technical Conference on Marine Pollution and Its Effect on Living Resources and Fishing. Rome. Ms. MP/70/E-88.

71. (Lange, personal communication.)

72. Blumer, M. 1970. Oil contamination and the living resources of the sea. FAO Technical Conference on Marine Pollution and Its Effects on Living Resources and Fishing. Rome. Ms. MP/70/R-1.

73. Smith, E. J. (ed.). 1968. "Torrey Canyon" pollution and marine life. Cambridge University Press, Cambridge. 197 p.

74. Hampson, G. R., and H. C. Sanders. 1969. Local oil spill. Oceanus 15:8-10.

75. Kasymov, A. G. 1970. Industry and the productivity of the Caspian Sea. Marine Poll. Bull. 1:100-103.

76. Simpson, A. C. 1968. Oil, emulsifiers and commercial shellfish. Fld. Stud. 2(suppl.):91-98.

77. Murphy, T. A. 1970. Environmental effects of oil pollution. Ms. American Society of Civil Engineers, Session on Oil Pollution Control. Boston.

78. Suess, M. J. 1970. Polynuclear aromatic hydrocarbon pollution of the marine environment. FAO Technical Conference on Marine Pollution and Its Effects on Living Resources and Fishing. Rome. Ms. MP/70/E-42.

79. Joensuu, O. I. 1971. Fossil fuels as a source of mercury pollution. Science 172:1027-1028.

80. FAO Seminar on Methods of Detection, Measurement and Monitoring of Pollutants in the Marine Environment. 1970. Rome. TPME/70/6.

81. Konrad, J. G. 1971. Mercury content of various bottom sediments, sewage treatment plant effluents and water supplies in Wisconsin. Wisc. Dept. of Natural Resources, Research Report No. 74.

82. Takeuchi, T. 1970. Biological reactions and pathological changes of human beings and animals under the condition of organic mercury contamination. Ms. International Conference on Environmental Mercury Contamination. Ann Arbor, Michigan.

83. Bligh, E. G. 1971. Mercury levels in Canadian fish. Symposium on Mercury in Man's Environment, Ottawa. (In press).

84. Ackefors, H., G. Lofroth, and C. G. Rosen. 1970. A survey of mercury pollution problems in Sweden with special reference to fish. Oceanogr. Mar. Biol. Ann. Rev. 8:203-224.

85. Marine Pollution Bulletin. 1971. Mercury in whales. Mar. Poll. Bull. 2:68.

86. Klein, D. H., and E. D. Goldberg. 1970. Mercury in the marine environment. Environ. Sci. Technol. 4:765-768.

87. Nelson, N. 1971. Hazards of mercury. Special report to the Secretary's Pesticide Advisory Committee, Department of Health, Education and Welfare. N. Nelson (Chairman). Environ. Res. 4: 1-69.

88. Gardner, G. R., and P. P. Yevich. 1970. Histological and hematological responses of an estuarine telost to cadmium. J. Fish. Res. Bd., Canada. 27:2185-2196.

89. Nielson, E. S., and S. Wium-Andersen. 1970. Copper ions as poison in the sea and in fresh water. Marine Biology 6:93-97.

90. Odum, W. E. 1970. Insidious alteration of the estuarine environment. Am. Fish. Soc., Trans. 99:836-847.

91. Krenkel, P. A., and F. L. Parker (ed.). 1969. Biological aspects of thermal pollution. Vanderbilt University Press. 407 p.

92. Coutant, C. 1970. Biological aspects of thermal pollution. I. Entrainment and discharge canal effects. CRC Critical Reviews in Environmental Control. Nov. 1970:341-381.

93. Colby, P. J., and L. T. Brooke. 1970. Survival and development of lake herring (Coregonus artedii) eggs at various incubation temperatures, p. 417-428. In C. C. Lindsey, and C. S. Woods (ed.), Biology of coregionid fishes. University of Manitoba Press. 560 p.

94. Kinne, O. 1962. Irreversible nongenetic adaptation. Comp. Biochem. Physiol. 5:265-282.

Glossary

Alien species: species not native to a region; introduced species.

Aquaculture: a method of increasing productivity of selected marine organisms by enclosing them within their natural environment and providing them with predator control, increased nutrients, shortened food chains, etc.

Biogeochemical cycles: the circulation of chemical elements from physical environment to organisms and back to physical environment.

Biological control: the use of predatory, parasitic, or pathogenic organisms to control a pest species.

Biomass: the weight of living organisms, expressed as either wet or dry weight.

Biosphere: the portion of the earth in which ecosystems operate.

Chemical fallout: the natural movement of solid matter through the air as dust particles.

Chronic toxicity: long-term toxic effects.

Clear cutting: removing the entire timber stand from an area.

Co-adaptation: interrelations between species that vary from total dependence on one another to casual and temporary interaction.

Coastal zone: the narrow region where ocean and land meet and where estuaries, lagoons, marshes, beaches, cliffs, bays, harbors, spits, and peninsulas form the major physical resources.

Comprehensive land planning: a program for land use that includes ecological analysis and resource inventory of the land, consideration of alternative land uses, and analysis of the impact of proposed land use on the ecosystem.

Continental shelf: the nearly flat submerged border of a continent, generally less than 200 m. below the sea and averaging 60 km. in width.

Crop (or habitat) management: manipulation of an ecosystem in such a way that pest species are naturally controlled by physical or biological factors and ecosystem yield remains high.

Cross-resistance: a phenomenon which occurs when a species of insect acquiring resistance to one specific insecticide also acquires resistance to other insecticides.

Diadromous fish: fish capable of migrating between fresh and salt water.

Dryland farming: a kind of farming common in arid regions in the absence of irrigation; production relies on conservation of the natural soil moisture and the use of drought-resistant plants.

Ecosystem: a living community and its non-living environment functioning together.

Energy budget: successive fixation and transfer of solar energy through the ecosystem.

Environmental degradation: a regressive change in land or water quality that decreases the system's ability to meet the needs of the biological community.

Environmental impact analysis: the direct and indirect measures of real or potential biological change in a system resulting from change in land and water use practices.

Estuary: a shallow body of water of variable salinity, formed by the merging of a river with the ocean.

Eutrophication: the biological enrichment of an aquatic system resulting from high nutrient input. Characterized by excessive aquatic plant growth, it is a natural process that can be accelerated by man-made effluents such as fertilizer run-off or sewage.

Food chain: a series of organisms, generally beginning with green plants, through which energy is transferred as each organism is eaten by the next, usually higher, member of the series.

Food web: the interconnection of food chains.

Fossil fuels: the coal, oil, and natural gas deposits which contain solar energy trapped by organic synthesis millions of years ago.

Genetic diversity: genetic differences among individuals in a population or species.

Hydroponics: the science of growing plants in nutrient solutions rather than in soil.

Industrial agriculture (agro-industrial complex): a system of intensive farming that relies on industrially produced supplements such as fertilizer, pesticides, and fossil fuels for its high productivity.

Industrial pollutants: materials that occur as a direct result of industrialization, some of which are long-lived, toxic, and tend to accumulate in food chains.

Integrated pest control: the combining of two or more pest control strategies--habitat management, selective crop breeding, biological control, or chemical control with field monitoring--to limit pests with a minimal amount of damage to the ecosystem.

Intensive fishing: harvesting from a fish stock the maximum number of fish that can be removed without damaging the stock's ability to reproduce or sustain itself.

Mobilization: putting a relatively insoluble element into a chemical form (e.g., phosphate fertilizer) that is readily available to plants.

Nutrient flow: the movement of essential elements through an ecosystem.

Organic synthesis: the production of organic carbon compounds (carbohydrates) by green plants and the production of organic nitrogen and sulfur compounds (proteins) by green plants, fungi, and bacteria.

Overfishing: the exploitation of a fish stock to the point where it is a small fraction of its virgin size and the fish harvest accordingly declines.

Plankton: small floating organisms (both plant and animal) whose movements are chiefly dependent on water currents.

Primary productivity: the rate at which photosynthesizing organisms convert and store radiant energy in an organic form that can be used as food.

Selective breeding: the selection of individuals possessing some special attribute or desirable characteristic to become parents of future generations.

Spatial heterogeneity: variations in the physical structure of the environment caused by areas being temporally out of phase with each other or qualitatively different in biological composition.

Species diversity: the ratio between the number of species in a community and the number of individuals in each species (e.g., low diversity occurs when there are few species but many individuals per species).

Stability: a state of thermodynamic equilibrium based on self-regulating mechanisms which operate at steady rates and aid the efficient cycling of energy.

Succession: the orderly process of change in which biotic communities successively modify the habitat and replace one another in a given area, often leading the ecosystem to a relatively stable equilibrium.

Thermal effluent: waste heat picked up by waters of industrial cooling systems and passed into nearby aquatic systems as hot or warm water.

Index

Africa: selective timber cutting in rain forests, 177; tourism in, 183-184; domestication of wild herbivores, 187

Age: and population diversity, 115

Agricultural systems: shifting, 30, 179, 181; effects of culture on, 30, 183, 187; nomadism, 187-188, 190; industrially based (see Intensive agriculture)

Air pollution: from nitrogen oxides, 73; from ozone, 153; future areas of, 200 (fig.)

Alaska: salmon fishery, 134; seal herds in Pribilof Islands, 239

Alien species: effects on ecosystem stability, 113, 134-136, 135 (fig.), 193

Amazon rain forest: atmospheric chemistry of, 80

Americas: arid grasslands of, 192

Anchoveta fishery, 27-28, 104-107, 105 (fig.)

Andean Region: population shifts in, 174

"Ando" soils, 179

Antarctica: whale fishing in, 28; decline of fin whales in, 32-33; atmospheric chemistry of, 80; whale catch limit, 237

Appalachians, southern: dry fallout amounts for various elements, 84

Aquaculture, 34-35, 223, 231-236, 243-244; and recycling of sewage, 34-35, 112, 233-234, 260; and thermal effluents, 35, 233; methods of, 231-235; potential productivity of, 231-232; in marshes and estuaries, 232; and habitat manipulation, 232-233; and selective breeding, 232, 236; problems of, 235; and need for pollution control, 243-244

Aquatic ecosystems: recommendations for protection of, 220-222

Aquatic plants: utilization of, 234, 236; and eutrophication, 234, 251-252

Arabian coast: region of upwelling near, 228

Arabian Sea: unexploited fish stocks of, 226

Arid and semi-arid ecosystems: soil erosion in, 24, 198-199; effects of overgrazing on, 24, 201; characteristics of, 195; diversity of, 195; soils of, 195, 198; distribution of, 196 (fig.); stability of, 197; irrigation and soil salinity, 197, 201; economic uses of, 198;

natural limitations on intensive use, 198-201; industrial development in, 199; sensitivity to ozone, 199

Arsenic, 152

Asia: endangered species in, 32; selective timber cutting in rain forests, 177

Asian arid grasslands: land users nomadic herdsmen, 192

Asian cold arid regions: short growing season in, 198

Atlantic Ocean: capelin catch in, 242; consumption of fish by harp seals in, 242; distribution of polyvinyl chloride in, 254

Atlanto-Scandinavian herring, 32-33, 239

Australia: Opuntia (prickly pear) in, 117, 124, 193; the pampa, 190; sedentary landowners in arid grasslands of, 192; European rabbit in, 193

Baltic Sea: salmon spawning in rivers surrounding, 248; young salmon released in, 248-249

Barents Sea: cod, 32-33, 239; polyvinyl chloride in, 254

Beirnaert, A. D. F., 179

Belgium: nutrient cycle in forest of, 101

Beryllium, 153

Biological control: and species diversity, 94, 112-114, 137; methods of, 124-125; success of, 125, 129-130; effects of pesticides on, 129, 142

BHC (benzene hexachloride): effectiveness against cotton pests in United States, 118

Biafra, 241

Biogeochemical cycles: and eutrophication, 42; monitoring of, 44, 83; interrelationships of, 45, 48, 69-74; man's impact on, 45-48, 72-73; phosphorus, 48-58; sulfur, 59-62, 77-83; nitrogen, 62-69; problems of analyses, 75-77, 80-85, 76 (fig.)

Bitterroot National Forest: review of management practices, 201-207; timber harvest of, 206 (fig.)

Blumer, M., 256

Bolivia: population shifts in, 30; Okinawa colonists pioneer in rain forests of, 174; FAO estimates of unused arable land in, 177

Bos indicus (Zebu cattle): adaptability of, 186

Brazil: FAO estimate of unused arable land in, 177

British Isles: effects of oil spills around, 256

Bulgaria: changes in malaria morbidity, 141 (fig.)

Cactoblastis: control of prickly pear in Australia by, 124

Cadle, R. D., 80

Cadmium, 96, 150-151

Cain, Stanley, 5

California: mussel population, 115; scale control in citrus orchards, 124; Great Central Valley of, 126; vineyards, 129-130; citrus scale insects in, 130; toxic air pollutants in San Bernardino Mountains of, 199; regions of upwelling near, 228

California sardine, 32-33, 239

Canada, eastern: spruce budworms in forests of, 114, 115; exploitation of seal stocks, 237; sockeye salmon, 237; mercury concentration in waters of, 257

Canete valley, Peru, 123

Carbon dioxide, 74

Carcinogens, 153, 253, 256

Carriacou: changes in malaria morbidity, 141 (fig.)

Central America: population shifts, 174

Chemical fallout: of sulfur, 61, 79, 84-85; of nitrogen dioxide, 68-69; of lead, 146; of nickel, 153

China: grass carp of, 231; sewage effluent used for fish in ponds of, 234

Clear cutting, 22, 101, 103 (fig.), 180

Closed system agriculture, 33-34, 183

Coadaption: among species, 100, 113

Coastal zone, 35-37, 230-231, 244, 249; productivity of, 27-28, 104-107, 228-230, 229 (fig.), 249; potentials for aquaculture, 35, 230, 232; man's impact on, 35-36, 244, 249-252; need for protection of, 37, 249-251; pollution of, 37, 252; and continental shelf, 249

Colorado Plateau, 190

Columbia: population shifts in, 30; cotton crops, 127; FAO estimates of unused arable land in, 177

Continental shelf (see Coastal zone)

Cooper, Charles, 5

Cross-resistance: of insects to pesticides, 92-93, 120 (fig.), 121-122, 122 (fig.)

Costa Rica, 30

Cotton: problems of pest control, 118-119

Coweeta site, southern Appalachians: dry fallout amounts, 84

Cuba: changes in malaria morbidity, 141 (fig.)

DDT: malarial control with, 140, 141 (fig.); concentration in food chains, 142, 253; effects on birds, 142-143, 253; monitoring use of, 144; in aquatic ecosystems, 253; human health hazard of, 253

Deever, Edward, 5

Delaware: salt marshes, 244

Denaeyer-De Smet, S., 84

Dentrification, 64

Desulphovibrio type bacteria, 79

Dominica: changes in malaria morbidity in, 141 (fig.)

Dominican Republic: changes in malaria morbidity in, 141 (fig.)

Don River, 247

Douglas fir ecosystem: second growth, 101; annual transfer of N, P, K, and Ca, 103

Doutt, R. L., 124

Drought: biological adaptations to, 191, 194, 195-197; and soil erosion, 194

Dryland farming: and soil erosion in temperate grasslands, 194; and damage to arid ecosystems, 198-199, 201

"Dust Bowl," 194

Duvigneaud, P., 84

Eadie, J., 132

East Asian sardine, 32-33, 239

Ecology: definition of, 13

Ecosystem analysis: for land management programs, 171

Ecosystem preservation: and species diversity, 31-32, 95, 167, 240-

241; for selective breeding, 32, 94, 240; dependence of managed systems on, 95, 137, 169; establishing criteria for, 138

Ecuador: population shifts in, 30; FAO estimates of unused arable land in, 177

Energy transfer: in a salt marsh, 105 (fig.); in aquatic ecosystems, 105 (fig.), 226-228; in intensively managed ecosystems, 107-109, 108 (fig.), 111 (fig.); in a rainforest, 110 (fig.); in moderately managed ecosystems, 110 (fig.), 111 (fig.)

England: waste heat used for fisheries, 233

Environmental degradation: in the coastal zone, 35-36, 244-245, 248, 249-252; as a result of population growth, 167-168, 181, 187, 208, 244; definition of, 169, 207; and ecological land management, 169-170, 208

Environmental impact analysis: for land management, 172-173

Erosion (see Soils, erosion of)

Erythroneura elegantula, 113

Eskimo curlew, 32

Estuaries, 36; effects of sewage and industrial pollution on, 20, 231, 241, 247-249, 251-252; productivity of, 230, 245-249; salinity of, 230-231, 247; nutrient flow in, 230, 245, 247; as fish nurseries, 230-231, 246 (fig.), 248; and aquaculture, 232; water movement in, 245-247, 246 (fig.); effects of river dams on, 245, 247, 248, 249; river sediments in, 248

Ettinger, M. C., 67

Eurasian steppes, 190

European arid grasslands, 192

European rivers: sulfur in runoff, 80

Eutrophication: caused by fertilizers, 25, 42, 51-52, 65, 73; caused by sewage, 37-38, 73-74, 234, 251; of terrestrial systems by chemical fallout, 74; effects on productivity, 247, 251-252

FAO (Food and Agriculture Organization [of the United Nations]): data on levels of farm production, 15, 16; data on disproportional ratio between fertilizer increase and farm yield, 107; programs of, organized for single objective appraisal, 170; projections of fish obtainable from aquaculture, 231-232

Fertilizers: diminishing returns of, 15-17, 16 (fig.), 33, 53; and intensive agriculture, 25, 99, 107, 108 (fig.); and eutrophication, 25, 42, 51-52, 65, 73; phosphate, 51, 53-55, 54 (fig.), 57-58; nitrate, 57, 65

Fire: for brush control, 189, 193

Fisheries (see World fisheries)

Florida: phosphorus removal from land-pebble fields, 56; waste heat used for aquaculture, 233

Food chains: productivity of trophic levels, 105 (fig.), 228, 242; concentration of pesticides in, 142, 253; lead in, 146; cadmium in, 150-151; PCB's in, 152, 254; petroleum hydrocarbons in, 252; mercury in, 257

Food webs: and ecosystem stability, 106 (fig.), 113-114

Forestry practices: clear cutting, 22, 101, 103 (fig.), 180; in western U.S. national forests, 201-207, 206 (fig.); and use of pesticides, 140; in tropical forests, 179-180

Forestry products: new uses of, 30, 182-183

Genetic diversity: for selective breeding, 94, 137; and population stability, 115-117, 191

Georgia: phosphorite deposits off coast, 58; energy budget for salt marsh of, 104; food web in salt marsh, 106

Golley, Frank, 5

Great Central Valley of California: alfalfa management in, 126

Great Lakes: man's impact on fisheries of, 134-136, 135 (fig.); PCB's detected in fish from, 152; Lake sturgeon in, 241

Great Plains, North American, 190, 194

Grenada: changes in malaria morbidity in, 141 (fig.)

Groundwater: nitrates in, 65, 67, 72; PCB's in, 152; salinity in arid regions, 197, 198

Habitat manipulation: for pest control, 125-126; of grasslands with fire, 189, 193; for aquaculture, 231-235

Hardin, Garrett, 29, 237

Hasler, Dr. Arthur, 9

Heavy metals, 144-153, 257

Herbicides, 128, 140

Hesse, R. W., 182

Hitchcock, D., 84

Hubbard Brook Experimental Forest: watershed ecosystem in, 101; dissolved solids in runoff in, 103

Huffaker, C. B., 124, 126

Human Environment, United Nations Conference on (1972), 5, 6, 8

Hydrogen sulfide, 72; and the sulfur cycle, 59, 77, 79, 81 (fig.), 84-85

Hydroponics (see Closed system agriculture)

Iakla-Makan Desert, 199

India: endangered species in, 32; monsoon agriculture, 109; energy transfer in monsoon agriculture, 111; changes in malaria morbidity, 141 (fig.)

Industrial pollution, 37, 38, 95-97; and contamination of sewage, 37-38, 235, 252, 259-260; toxic effects of, 38; international control of, 39; effects on productivity, 252

Integrated Natural Resources Research: UNESCO program for, 130

Integrated pest control, 123-124; in the tropics, 31, 128-129; with biological agents, 124-125; by habitat manipulation, 125-126; and field monitoring of pests, 127

Intensive agricultural systems: diminishing returns of, 15-17, 16 (fig.), 33, 107; dependence on technological support, 20-22, 25, 26, 92, 98-99, 107-109, 108 (fig.), 199; nutrient loss in, 22, 25, 92; and selective breeding, 25, 126-127; dependability of, 92, 93, 99, 118; productivity of, 99, 107, 111 (fig.); and energy transfer, 107-109, 111 (fig.)

Intensive fishing, 226, 242; and competition with natural predators, 28-29, 242; ecological cost of, 34, 242-243; economic cost of, 236 (see also Overfishing)

Inter-American Development Bank, 176

International Pollution Control Commission, 39

International Union for the Conservation of Nature, 32

International Whaling Commission, 237

Italy: changes in malaria morbidity in, 141 (fig.)

Jamaica: changes in malaria morbidity in, 141 (fig.)

Japan: removal of forests of, 22; mercury contaminated fish, 138; maximum allowable of cadmium, 150-151; agreement on exploitation of seals, 237; mercury concentration in water of, 257

Johnson, W. K., 67

Junge, C. E., 85

Kadlec, John, 5

Kaskaskia River, 65

Kenya: tourism in, 185; land use problems, 187

Lake Erie: blue pike in, 241; increase of phytoplankton in, 251

Lake Mendota, 52

Lake Michigan, 134

Lake trout, 134-135

Land development: and population growth, 24, 29-30, 31, 167; and comprehensive land planning, 24, 176; in tropical lowland forest, 174-176, 175 (fig.); in arid ecosystems, 197

Land management programs: training for, 94, 131; based on ecological knowledge, 166, 169-170; and integrated land use planning, 166, 195, 201-208; of the U.N., 170; need for in tropics, 176; and cultural traditions, 187, 189

Latin America: settlement farms needed, 174; proposed colonization projects, 176; savanna in, 176; FAO estimate of land capability in, 177

Lead: toxicity of, 95, 146-147; need for restrictions on use of, 96, 147; emissions from gasoline, 144, 146; uses of, 145 (fig.)

League of Nations: Convention for the Regulation of Whaling, 237

Lickens, G. F., 84

Livingstone, D. A., 79

Logan, R. F., 199

Ludzak, F. J., 67

Lygus, 126

McCabe, Dr. Robert, 9

Maine salt marshes, 244

Malaya: cockchafer beetles in, 127

Managed ecosystems, 25-32, 98-100; stability and diversity of, 26, 99, 100; dependence on natural systems, 98, 99-100, 107; energy transfer in, 107-109, 108 (fig.), 110 (fig.), 111 (fig.); maintenance costs of, 136

"Man's Impact on the Global Environment"(see SCEP report)

Marine plants, 28, 225, 226-228, 245, 249

Mauritius: changes in malaria morbidity, 141 (fig.)

Meigs, P., 195

Mercury: restrictions on use, 96, 149; toxicity of, 138, 257; uses of, 148 (fig.), 149; sources of pollution, 149, 257; concentration in aquatic food chains, 257, 258 (fig.)

Mid-American grasslands, 191

Minimata Bay, Japan: poisoning from mercury in fish, 138, 257

Moiseev, P. A., 228

Monitoring: global standards for, 39; nitrate in groundwater, 43, 67; of biogeochemical cycles, 44, 83; nitrogen dioxide, 69; cadmium, 96; pesticides, 144; lead, 147

Monitoring Commission: recommended, 44, 83

Moore, R. M., 173

Mudflats, 84-85; as sources of atmospheric sulfur, 59, 72

National Trusts, 173

Nelson, Craig, 5

New Hampshire: Hubbard Brook watershed ecosystem, 101

New York: waste heat used for oyster cultivation, 233

Niagara Falls, 134

Nickel, 153

Niering, W. H., 245

Niigata, Japan: poisoning from fish in, 134, 257

Nile Basin, 198

Nile River, 247

Nitrates: contamination of groundwater, 42-43, 65-67, 72; monitoring of, 43, 67; release from fertilizer, 65, 72; and eutrophication, 65, 66 (fig.), 73; effects on sulfur cycle, 67

Nitrification, 64

Nitrogen: industrial production of, 46, 47 (fig.); natural cycle of, 62-70, 63 (fig.), 66 (fig.), 71 (fig.), 76 (fig.); and nitrates, 65-67; and nitrogen oxides, 67-69

Nitrogen dioxide: as an atmospheric pollutant, 67-69

Nitrogen fixation, 62-64, 63 (fig.); man's impact on rates of, 64-65

Nitrogen oxide: release from fossil fuel, 43, 46-48, 47 (fig.), 67-68; in soils, 69

Nomadism, 187-188, 190

North Africa: phosphorus mining, 56; grassland area of, 190, 192

Northwest Africa: regions of upwelling near, 228

North America: early levels of population, 14; Great Plains, 190; humid grasslands, 194; cold arid regions, 198; solar energy as heat source for, 199; Atlantic salmon in northeastern rivers, 241; polyvinyl chloride in, 254

North Sea: plaice stocks in, 239; pollution effects on aquatic productivity in, 252; polyvinyl chloride in, 254

Northwest Pacific salmon: decline of, 32-33, 239

Norwegian Sea: polyvinyl chloride in, 254

Nutrient cycling, 20, 23 (fig.), 101; in the urban-agricultural complex, 20-22, 21 (fig.), 38, 92, 107, 112; in forest systems, 22-24, 101, 103 (fig.); in closed system agriculture, 33-34; in coastal zones, 104-107, 230, 245, 247, 249; in aquaculture, 34-35, 112, 233-234, 260

Oil spills, 256

Okinawa: settlement in Bolivia by colonists of, 174

Open oceans: productivity of, 228

Opuntia (prickly pear), 117, 124, 193

Organic synthesis: and carbon-nitrogen ratios, 69-70, 71 (fig.)

Overfishing: and world-wide decline of species, 28-29, 32-33, 237, 239; of whales, 29, 237, 238 (fig.); and diminishing returns, 134, 135 (fig.), 236-239; in the North Atlantic, 227 (fig.); successful international control of, 239

Overgrazing, 24, 133 (fig.); in tropical savannas, 185-186, 187-189, 188 (fig.); in temperate grasslands, 191-192; control of, 195; in arid regions, 201

Oxygen, 45; alternate sources of, 70-72; effects of DDT on, 253

Ozone: in smog, 153; health hazards of, 153; sensitivity of desert plants to, 199, 200 (fig.)

Pacific Northwest: ecosystem of second-growth Douglas fir of, 101

Palouse region, 190

Panama: atmospheric chemistry of, 80

PCB's: restriction on use, 96-97, 152; similarities to DDT, 143, 151, 254; sources of pollution, 151, 152, 254; in groundwater, 152; toxicity of, 152, 254; in aquatic ecosystems, 254, 255 (fig.)

Peru: anchoveta fisheries of, 27; population shifts in, 30; salt marsh ecosystem, 104; control of cotton pests in, 123; FAO estimate of unused arable land in, 177; regions of upwelling near, 228

Pesticides: insect resistance to, 26-27, 118-122, 120 (fig.), 127; alternatives to, 27, 93, 123-131; persistence of, 27, 140, 253; in the tropics, 31, 128-129; cross resistance to, 92-93, 121-122, 122 (fig.); and intensive agriculture, 93, 130; toxicity of, 93, 138, 142-143, 253; international control of, 95, 143-144; effects on species diversity, 128, 129; effects on bio control, 129, 142; kinds of, 139; benefits of, 139-140; effects on soil fauna, 142; concentration in food chains, 142, 253

Petroleum products: and pollution, 256

Pettersen, S., 199

Phosphorus, 48-58; population demands on and potential shortage of, 17, 25-26, 42, 53, 54 (fig.); conservation of, 26, 42, 56-58; problems of recycling, 42, 53; industrial production of, 46, 47 (fig.), 51; natural cycle of, 48-50, 49 (fig.), 52 (fig.), 54 (fig.); immobilization in soil and sediments, 50, 51, 53; and eutrophication, 50, 51, 52 (fig.), 73-74; mobilization in fertilizer, 51; reserves of, 53, 54 (fig.), 55, 58

Pollutants: nitrates, 65-67, 72; DDT, 142-143, 253; lead, 144-147, 145 (fig.); cadmium, 150-151; arsenic, 152; PCB's, 152, 254; polyvinyl chlorides, 254; beryllium, 153; nickel, 153; ozone, 153

Pollution (see Air pollution, Industrial pollution, Water pollution, and Pollutants)

Polyvinyl chlorides: and aquatic pollution, 254

Population growth: and population density, 14-15; and standard of living, 14-15, 19; rate of, 17-19, 18 (fig.); recommendations for control of, 19, 208; effects on ecosystems, 19-20, 21 (fig.), 24, 31-32, 167-168, 170, 181, 187, 208, 244; and land development, 24, 29-30, 31, 167, 174-176; and future fertilizer demands, 53-55

Predator control, 192-193

Predator-prey relationships: and species diversity, 113-114; in temperate grasslands, 191, 192-193

President's Science Advisory Committee, 119

Preston, Steve, 5

Pribilof Islands: seal herds in, 237

Prickly pear cactus (Opuntia): in Australia, 117, 124, 193

Proceedings of Tall Timbers Conference, 126

Productivity: and diminishing returns under intensive use, 15-17, 16 (fig.), 33, 107, 132-136, 133 (fig.), 236-237; of aquatic ecosystems, 27-28, 104-107, 228-230, 229 (fig.), 245-249; of intensive agriculture, 99, 107, 111 (fig.); and species diversity, 131-132; maximizing, 182; and trophic levels, 242; of terrestrial vs. aquatic systems, 250 (fig.)

Protein: synthesis of, 69-70, 71 (fig.); from world fisheries, 225

Range degradation, 192-193 (see also Overgrazing)

Rimberg, Felix, 9

Rhodalia (lady-bug), 124

Romania: changes in malaria morbidity in, 141 (fig.)

Russian Plain, 194

Ryther, J. H., 228, 234

Saccharification of wood, 182

Salmon: overfishing of, 134; damage to spawning grounds, 248-249

Salt marshes: productivity of, 36, 104; energy transfer in, 105 (fig.); food web of, 106 (fig.); as sites for aquaculture, 232; destruction of, 244-245

San Bernadino Mountains, 199

Savannas, tropical, 183-189

SCEP, 96, 144, 147, 149

SCEP report ("Man's Impact on the Global Environment"), 5, 15, 39, 45, 139, 253, 256, 257

Schoepfer, G. J., 67

Schroeder, H. A., 150

Sea of Azov, 247

Sediments: immobilization of phosphorus in, 50, 51, 53; mercury in, 149; and estuarine productivity, 248

Selective breeding: and intensive agriculture, 25, 127; based on ecosystem preservation, 32, 94, 240; for pest control, 94, 118,

126-127; and genetic diversity, 94, 137; of wild herbivores, 185; for aquaculture, 232, 236

Sewage: nutrient loss in, 20-22, 38; as cause of eutrophication, 22, 37-38, 73-74, 234, 251; as fertilizer for aquaculture, 34-35, 112, 233-234, 235, 260; contamination by industrial pollutants, 37-38, 235, 252, 259-260

Shifting agriculture: and nutrient cycling, 30; in tropical forests, 179; and forest succession, 179, 180-181; optimization of, 181

Simpson, A. C., 256

Skillet Fork River: nitrate concentration in, 65

Smith, Frederick, 5, 84, 124

Smog: and nitrogen oxide, 73; and ozone, 153; in arid regions, 199, 200 (fig.)

Soils: tropical, 22-24, 30, 181; leaching of, 22-24, 181, 191, 197, 201; and recycling of nutrients, 22, 179, 181; effects of overgrazing on, 24; erosion of, 24, 194, 198-199; of temperate grasslands, 191; of arid regions, 195, 198

Somalia: region of upwelling near, 228

South African veld, 190, 192, 193

South America: FAO estimates of unused arable land in, 177; the pampa, 190; unexploited fish stocks of, 226

South Carolina, 58

Southern Europe, grasslands area, 190

South Pacific: current patterns, 27

Southwest Africa: region of upwelling near, 228

Spain: mussel culture, 35, 234; changes in malaria morbidity, 141 (fig.)

Spatial heterogeneity: in modern agriculture, 93, 129-130, 131; and ecosystem stability, 113, 114-115; and species diversity, 116 (fig.); aesthetic values of, 138

Species diversity: and ecosystem preservation, 31-32, 94, 240-241; aesthetic values of, 32, 95, 138; and selective breeding, 94, 185, 240; and biological control, 94, 113-114, 136, 137; and ecosystem stability, 112-114, 117, 197, 240; and food webs, 113-114; and spatial heterogeneity, 114-115, 116 (fig.), 117; intraspecific, 115-117, 191; and ecosystem productivity, 131-132; and stability of grasslands, 191, 194; of arid regions, 195

Species preservation: and declining species, 31-33; and ecosystem stability, 136; and selective breeding, 137

Spruce budworm, 112, 114-115

Stability: effects of species diversity on, 26, 29, 100, 112-114, 117; and ecosystem preservation, 32, 95, 136; of managed systems, 100, 118-119; of a salt marsh, 104; within a population, 115-117, 191; and spatial heterogeneity, 113, 114-115, 116 (fig.), 117; and alien species, 113, 134-136, 135 (fig.), 193; of man-managed grasslands, 194; of arid systems, 195-197

Stern, V. M., 126

Succession: and shifting agriculture, 167, 179, 180-181

Sulfur: as a pollutant, 43-44, 61-62; industrial production of, 46, 47 (fig.); natural cycles of, 59-61, 60 (fig.), 77-80, 81 (fig.); in the atmosphere, 59-62, 77-80; chemical fallout as sulfate, 61, 62, 79-80, 81 (fig.), 84-85; reserves, 62, 78 (fig.)

Swank, Wayne, 84

Sweden: suspension of methyl mercury seed treatment in, 149; maximum allowable concentration of cadmium, 150-151; salmon rearing in, 248; mercury concentrates in water, 257; mentioned, 241

Synergism: of industrial pollutants, 38, 257-259

Taiwan: changes in malaria morbidity, 141 (fig.); land use problems in, 187

Task Groups, 7, 8

Taungya, 180

Teal, J. M., 104

Temperate grasslands, 189-195; distribution of, 184 (fig.), 189; characteristics of, 190; productivity of, 190; and range degradation, 191-193; soils of, 191; economic use of, 192; effects of alien species on, 193; dryland farming in, 194; need for integrated land planning, 195

Tennessee: phosphorus removal in, 56

Texas, 247

Thames River: Atlantic salmon in, 241; estuary below London, 248; food web in, 251

Thermal effluents: in aquaculture, 35, 233; and pollution of aquatic systems, 259

Tobago: changes in malaria morbidity in, 141 (fig.)

Toxic substances: released by urban-agricultural complex, 38, 100, 138-139; international control of, 154

Trace elements, 80, 82 (fig.)

Trinidad: changes in malaria morbidity in, 141 (fig.)

Tropical forests: leaching of soils in, 22-24, 181; maximizing productivity of, 30, 182-183; pesticides in, 31, 128-129; characteristics of, 173, 175 (fig.), 176-177; land development in, 174-176, 175 (fig.); land use in, 177-181, 178 (fig.); forestry practices, 177, 179-180; shifting agriculture in, 179, 181; problems of management, 180-183; preservation of, 181-182; and closed system agriculture, 183

Tropical savanna: characteristics of, 183; economic uses of, 183-185; distribution of, 184 (fig.); overgrazing and range degradation, 185-186, 187-189, 188 (fig.); factors limiting land use, 185-187; effects of local water supplies, 185, 187

Turkey: changes in malaria morbidity in, 141 (fig.)

Uganda, 110

United Nations Conference on the Human Environment (1972), 5, 6, 8

United Nations: recommendation for institutions of higher learning, 94, 131; UNESCO program for Integrated Natural Resources research, 130; pollution control central commission recommended to, 97, 154; Economic Commission: for Asia and Far East, 170, for Latin America, 170; programs for development and conservation of natural resources, 170; support of Okinawan settlement in Bolivia by, 174

United States: endangered species in, 32; coastal marshes, 37; western high-grade phosphorus ores, 56; phosphate supplies, use of, 57; phosphorite deposits off coast of, 58; nitrate in drinking water, 67; sulfur in river runoff, 80; analysis of precipitation, 85; energy transfer in industrial agriculture, 111; cotton pests in, 118; rust disease in, 127; annual food crop losses: from plant diseases, 139, from insects, 139-140, from weeds, 140; lead pollution, 144; cadmium contamination, 150; supports Okinawan settlement in Bolivia, 174; national forest land west of Great Plains, 201; agreement on seal exploitation, 239; salmon, 239; extinct and endangered fish species, 241; destruction of salt marshes, 244; river estuaries in, 245

United States Bureau of Mines, 56

United States Department of Health, Education and Welfare: Secretary's report on pesticides, 143

United States Environmental Policy Act of 1969, 172

United States Food and Drug Administration: cadmium levels allowed by, 151

United States National Forest System: general management practices, 201-202; management of Bitterroot National Forest, 202-207; budget of, 205 (fig.)

Upwellings, oceanic: and fishery productivity, 27-28, 104-107, 228-230, 229 (fig.)

Uranium: in phosphate rock, 57

Venezuela: changes in malaria morbidity in, 141 (fig.); FAO estimate of unused arable land in, 177

Virgin Islands, 235

Water pollution, 251-260; mixing of sewage with industrial pollutants, 37-38, 235, 252, 259-260; by industrial pollutants, 248, 253-260; effects on productivity, 252; health hazards of, 252; by heated effluents, 259

Welland Canal, 134

West Africa: unexploited fish stocks, 226

Western Europe: Atlantic salmon in rivers of, 241

Whales: overfishing of, 28, 32-33, 237; trends in annual catch, 238 (fig.)

WHO (World Health Organization), cadmium levels allowed by, 151

World fisheries: overfishing of, 28-29, 32-33, 227 (fig.), 237, 239; potential productivity of, 105 (fig.), 225-228; estimating population of, 132-134; management alternatives, 223-225; as sources of protein, 225; zones of productivity, 228-230, 229 (fig.); important species of, 230; international management of, 239-240

Workshop on Global Ecological Problems: goals, 5-8; task group members, 41, 91, 165, 219

World War II: removal of forests in Japan, 22; predictions of fishery potential since, 226

Wuhrman, K., 67

Yugoslavia: changes in malaria morbidity in, 141 (fig.)

Zebu cattle (Bos indicus): adaptability of, 186

Zinke, Paul, 5

Zululand, 193